W9-AOY-172

Queen of the Negro Leagues

Effa Manley and the Newark Eagles

James Overmyer

The Scarecrow Press, Inc.
Lanham, Md., & London
1998

SCARECROW PRESS, INC.
Published in the United States of America
by Scarecrow Press, Inc.
4720 Boston Way
Lanham, Maryland 20706

4 Pleydell Gardens
Kent CT20 2DN, England

Queen of the Negro Leagues originally appeared in hard cover as *Effa Manley and the Newark Eagles*, published in 1993 by Scarecrow Press, Inc.

British Library Cataloguing in Publication Information Available

Library of Congress Cataloging-in-Publication Data
Overmyer, James
Queen of the Negro leagues : Effa Manley and the Newark Eagles / James Overmyer.
p. cm.
Rev. ed. of: Effa Manley and the Newark Eagles. 1993.
Includes bibliographical references and index.
ISBN 1-57886-001-6 (pbk. : alk. paper)
1. Manley, Effa, 1900– . 2. Baseball team owners—United States—Biography. 3. Newark Eagles (Baseball team)—History. 4. Afro-American business enterprises. I. Overmyer, James. Effa Manley and the Newark Eagles. II. Title.
GV865.M325094 1998
338.7′61796357′092—dc21
[B] 97-49909

ISBN 1-57886-001-6 (alk. paper)

The paper used in this publication meets the minimum requirements of American National Standard for Information Sciences—Permanence of Paper for Printed Library Materials, ANSI Z39.48–1984.
Manufactured in the United States of America.

To
Matthew Overmyer
and
Peter Weiden

Contents

Introduction

I'd like to be able to say I got my inspiration to write about Negro league baseball by having seen the great black players and teams play before professional ball was integrated. That's what originally piqued the interest of some of the best writers on this subject.

Unfortunately, by the time I was old enough to be a baseball fan, the Negro leagues had nearly faded away into history. I knew about Satchel Paige, but mostly just as an extraordinary player who had somehow broken into the (white) big leagues at a very late age, as baseball years go. I never gave a thought as to where he had been before that.

I was dimly cognizant that my favorite player, Ernie Banks of the Chicago Cubs, had started his career with a Negro league team called the Kansas City Monarchs. However, I think I regarded the Monarchs as some sort of semiprofessional club, maybe not even of minor league caliber.

I was, to a nearly perfect extent, ignorant of the Negro leagues until one day when my wife Ellen and I took a drive to Cooperstown, New York, home of the National Baseball Hall of Fame. I had a Society for American Baseball Research (SABR) meeting to attend; she would enjoy herself more by touring the Hall's museum.

On the way out of the village, out of the blue, she asked, "Who was Effa Manley?" I, being infinitely knowledgeable about the National Pastime, answered "Who?"

"Well," she said, "her picture's in the museum. She did all sorts of progressive things to make Negro league baseball better, but the caption on her picture just calls her the 'glamor girl of the Negro leagues'." Being sensitive both to women whose accomplishments aren't properly recognized and to those described as sex objects, she was naturally concerned and had thought of a way to make things right: "You ought to write an article about her."

But some topics have a way of setting their own agendas, and it soon became clear that Effa Manley deserved more than a magazine article. The more I researched, the more I found evidence of a remarkable woman who unstintingly bucked both racial and gender prejudice to make her mark in the 1930s and 1940s.

And I found out that the baseball played in the Negro leagues was something special, too. The secondary theme of this book, after telling Effa's story, is to tell the story of her much-admired Newark Eagles and the league they played in. I'm pleased to see that so much attention is coming to black baseball these days after many years of neglect, and I'm proud to make my own contribution.

Perhaps farthest from my original expectations, I found myself telling about Newark, New Jersey, before and during World War II. As it turned out, the story of the Eagles was inseparable from Newark and its rapidly growing black population, which had made for itself a thriving life paralleling that of the city's majority white community—a community which was often closed to blacks.

Since this book's original publication in its hardcover edition of 1993, there have been some changes in the circumstances of figures mentioned in it. Some just have to do with the passage of time. For example, the section about the many natives of New Jersey who became major league baseball players describes Bobby Brown as president of the American League—he has since retired. Also, Jeff Torberg, described as a big league manager, is now a baseball broadcaster. One should read *Queen of the Negro Leagues* with this slight time warp in mind.

Of more importance, in several places I described Eagle pitcher Leon Day and shortstop Willie Wells as players whose induction into the Baseball Hall of Fame was overdue. I am happy to report that both have now been voted into the Hall, Day in 1995 and Wells in 1997. The Hall of Fame museum has also done greater justice to Effa, and to the history of black baseball. A greatly expanded Negro leagues exhibit, "Pride and Passion," opened in June 1997. The photo of Effa with its offending "glamor girl" caption has been replaced by a segment of a computerized interactive photo exhibit which gives both her and the Eagles much more appropriate credit. Some Eagle historical artifacts, primarily the enormous Baccardi trophy the team won in the Puerto Rican winter league in 1936, which is mentioned in the book, are also on display.

A book is an enormous undertaking, and before it is finished the writer owes many debts of gratitude. One of my largest is to my editor, David Biesel, who successfully campaigned for the selection of the manuscript as the first choice in Scarecrow Press's American Sports History Series, then oversaw the project to successful publication not just once, but twice with this edition.

But it is not an understatement to say there never would have been a book in the first place without the aid of Dr. Lawrence Hogan of Union County College near Newark. Before I even met him, Larry had been instrumental in having the Eagle's business files (abandoned in the mid-1950s when Effa Manley moved from Newark, but discovered by the new owner of her former residence) donated to the Newark Public Library. The files open a door directly into the Eagles' office during those years—and those of us who do research into black baseball would be much poorer without them.

In the process of my work, Larry made most of the photographs in this book available from his large collection, and granted me access to transcripts of interviews he and Thomas C. Guy, Jr., had videotaped for their Negro league documentary, "Before You Can Say Jackie Robinson."

Reading through the 11 years of voluminous Eagles team files took some doing, and I am indebted to the patience and assistance of the folks who oversaw the New Jersey Room of the Newark Public Library when I was doing my research, in particular George Hawley and James Osborne. Thanks also go to Robert Browning, who made Effa Manley's scrapbook, another rare original resource, available while he was on the staff of the National Baseball Hall of Fame Library in Cooperstown.

I conducted a number of personal interviews, and everyone to whom I spoke was helpful. But some subjects stand out, particularly two former Eagle players, Monte Irvin and Maxwell Manning, whose reminiscences went beyond recounting their playing experiences and included thoughtful commentary on what it was like to be a Negro leaguer and to live in Newark in those days. I also interviewed four journalists—Jerry Izenberg, who writes for the Newark *Star-Ledger*; two former reporters, John T. Cunningham and Connie Woodruff; and Jocko Maxwell, a retired sportscaster—all of whom were most helpful in imparting to me the social and cultural fabric of Newark and its baseball tradition. The extra insight that newspeople acquire about their beats was of great help to me.

Although Effa herself was unavailable (she died in 1981), two persons who had interviewed her, William Marshall of the University of Kentucky and Donn Rogosin, author of a general history of the Negro leagues, made copies of their tapes available to me.

My general research would have been much more difficult without the help of Dick Clark, who on behalf of SABR's Negro Leagues Committee runs an information clearinghouse out of his home in Ypsilanti, Michigan. Dick's files filled a multitude of gaps.

Closer to home, I owe thanks to David Pietrusza, Richard Puff, and David Walsh, all SABR members who offered the right mix of constructive criticism and encouragement when it appeared this project might never get off the ground, and to William Howard and William Reichert, who handled the technical chores of copying and printing most of the book's illustrations.

Finally, thanks to Ellen, who saw her simple suggestion evolve into a role for herself as a critic and one-person emotional and logistical support group.

Chapter 1
Introducing Effa

Invest your best years in baseball, and your profits will include some good stories to tell. Perhaps a single story will sum up all those years. This is Effa Manley's.

She had traveled all the way from Newark, New Jersey, down to Washington, D.C., where the country's capital was preoccupied by the end of World War II and crowded full of the sort of people who would change the world. Washington happened to be a good location for her mission, because a big change was her goal, too.

Effa had come to try to help draw back an Iron Curtain, but not the one about to drop between Western and Eastern Europe. She wanted to lift the one that had fallen across baseball fifty years before, segregating the national pastime's white and Negro teams.

She was a self-appointed emissary for the black side, her qualifications for the role being that she and her husband, Abe, ran the Newark Eagles in the Negro National League. They had a partnership, but everyone knew she was the one to see about business off the ball field. This was so even though at that time women baseball executives were nearly as nonexistent as, say, a black baseball player in the white baseball organization called the "major leagues."

The only times Effa told this story for the historical record was when she was in her seventies. Some of the details, although none of the essence, of her baseball career had eluded her, and she could not supply the specific date of the trip more than thirty years before, but it could have been August, 1945, when Jackie Robinson was still just a former college football star, a war veteran, and an up-and-coming Negro leaguer.

Robinson had yet to become the first black man in white professional baseball since the race's total exclusion from established "organized baseball" in 1896. However, the willingness of Robinson and other American blacks to go into uniform for their country and support the war effort in other ways was hurrying change along. Effa was certainly alert to this.

"I could see that this interest was building up by leaps and bounds, and common sense just made me feel that they were going to some day do something [to integrate baseball]," she said. When "they" did it, she was determined that the Negro leagues, black America's best professional baseball, would be included, ideally as part of organized baseball's minor league system.

Without telling her fellow black baseball owners of her mission, the glamorous Mrs. Manley, undoubtedly as well dressed as always and looking every inch the society matron she had a claim on being, appeared at the front desk of a downtown Washington hotel and asked for George Trautman.

In the summer of 1945, Trautman was one of the most influential people in baseball. He was president of the American Association, one of the highest-ranking minor leagues, and in a year and a half would become head of all the minors. In August, 1945, the likely date for Effa's mission, he was in Washington for a meeting of baseball's Post-War Planning Committee. The eighteen members of the committee were a perfect cross section of contemporary baseball management: They were all middle-aged white men.

"I went right to the hotel and introduced myself," she recalled, leaving word that she wanted to see Trautman.Then, she waited. And waited some more. Finally, the executive sent his wife down to see her. He executed a neat maneuver, the double brush-off, since Effa came from not one, but two, of baseball's "outsider" groups—blacks and women. "It was," she figured, "his way of saying, 'I don't give a darn'."

Although the meeting eventually took place, it accomplished nothing, and so was an exceptional failure for Mrs. Manley, who rarely came away from a venture empty-handed. She had, by her own account, had a scandalous birth, and had grown up lower class, but beautiful. She married a man who had his own somewhat nefarious background, but who also had money, and she had risen into the fringes of black high society in the metropolis of New York City, and then to a more substantial spot in the smaller black Newark community.

But she was also a woman before her time, both a civil rights advocate who would take her turn on the picket line and one of the most unusual and compelling baseball personalities of her day. She was both aggressive and progressive, and did not allow the male power structure that ran black (and white) baseball to go unchallenged when she thought it wrong, as she often did.

There being no organized feminist movement in her day, Effa Manley simply made her point about women's abilities by being what she was. Her socialite demeanor barely concealed a hard-headed businessperson who never shrank from mixing it up with anyone's Old Boy Network.

While the episode in Washington was not the only time a figurative door had been shut in her face, it was also true that she rarely shrank from controversy, and most often tried to open those doors with a figurative sharp kick. This was a woman, after all, who shocked a white businessman by injecting the subject of prostitution into the midst of fair hiring negotiations, chastised a ballpark spectator who dared denigrate her beloved black baseball, castigated her fellow Negro league owners in private meetings, and challenged the famous Branch Rickey, president of the Brooklyn Dodgers, in the aisles of Yankee Stadium.

Max Manning, one of her former Eagle star players, describes her struggle for acceptance among the men who ran black baseball teams in the lonelier terms of integration. He envisions her as being "like a black male in the '60s, going into a board room, and he's the lone black in there."

But while none of the baseball executives, a patriarchal bunch in either race, would ever have thought to have invented Effa, the Negro leagues profited from her presence in their midst. The rest of baseball might have, too, if one of their chief executives had come down to see her in Washington that day.

Women, either black or white, are still rare in baseball's executive suites. Black players are not, because in the summer of 1945, the sports world was on the verge of a revolution it did not precisely know was coming. Branch Rickey had already made his decision to integrate the Dodgers, but it was a closely held secret not to be disclosed for a few more months, until Robinson signed a contract.

While Trautman was by no means one of the determined group of segregationists in baseball at that time, his behavior gives us a clue as to why almost fifty years later the sport still has a deplorable minority hiring record in its management ranks. Beginning with Robinson, the major leagues skimmed the cream of the player crop from the Negro leagues, and the clubs that integrated most boldly, particularly the Dodgers, improved their teams as a result. However, for a variety of reasons that included status, money, and, of course, uneasiness with the other race, the white lords of baseball kept the Negro league owners out, eliminating the natural progression through the executive ranks that would have given blacks numerous opportunities to eventually run teams.

But to say that Effa Manley's involvement with baseball never got her to the big time is not at all to imply that it was either dull or unimportant. A casual follower of the sport until she met her future husband, Abe, an absolute fanatic about it, she shortly was living in a vital part of baseball that now is only a dim memory. Because they died out completely after integration focused the attention of all fans on the major leagues, the separate Negro leagues were nearly lost to time. Their history was really only saved when the booming interest in baseball during the last ten or fifteen years drew writers and researchers to go interview the players and management officials still living. Although the success of Robinson and the others in the majors made the Negro leagues an anachronistic remnant of segregation, while the leagues thrived, they were as real as Babe Ruth, Bob Feller, Yankee Stadium, and Wrigley Field.

And the teams in the black leagues meant as much, sometimes more, to their fans than did the major league clubs. To think of baseball as just a game played in a stadium is to miss a great deal of its meaning. It also takes place in the communities in which those ballparks are located, news of each game fanning out across town, the players being recognized celebrities on the streets, and the home team becoming a prized local institution.

This process was especially true of the black teams, playing for fans who, even in the Northern cities, were denied anything approaching equal rights. They needed heroes, and it was in this greater sphere of baseball that Effa Manley contributed the most to the game and to Newark, her adopted city. There, the Eagles were a summertime institution in Newark's crowded black section. The team was used as a fund-raising attraction for the NAACP and a host of local black charities. It staged ceremonies to honor black achievers and, since the Eagles also happened to be a winning team, it gave blacks in Northern New Jersey something to cheer about.

That controversy was attracted to Effa Manley (and she to it) should not have been surprising, since, by her own account, her very entry into the world shook up a small part of Philadelphia society. Late in her life, when she was called upon for interviews by those who were discovering the nearly lost legacy of the Negro leagues, Effa claimed she was the illegitimate offspring of a liaison between her mother, a seamstress named Bertha Ford Brooks, and a man at whose house she worked, financier John M. Bishop. And since both of them were Caucasian, Effa in fact was a genetically white person who nevertheless spent her entire life living, without regret, in a black world.

In 1977 she said, "My mother was a white woman. Her first husband was a Negro by whom she had four children.

In the course of her sewing she met my father, who was a wealthy white man (he had a seat on the New York stock exchange) and I was born as a result." Because of her birth on March 27, 1900, her mother's husband, Benjamin Brooks, sued the white financier for alienation of Mrs. Brooks' affection and won a $10,000 settlement.

Mr. and Mrs. Brooks parted company over the affair, and Effa's mother married another black, B. A. Cole. The family eventually included seven children, six whose black fathers made them definitely regarded as Negroes, plus Effa, about whom questions were frequently raised. "I was always this little blond, hazel-eyed, white girl, always with Negro children," she recalled.

She was happy with those children, several of whom were her half-sisters and brothers. Her mother, for whom she held a great deal of regard, did not tell her she was white until she was nearly grown. Then, the attentions of a young white man who worked across the street from the family home, who seemed to have a crush on Effa, served to bring out the truth. It also served to finally illuminate some of Bertha's earlier behavior that had struck her daughter as odd. "When I was very young, in the first grade, the principal sent for me. At that time Negroes and whites weren't supposed to mix, and she asked me why I was always with these colored children." Effa went home and told her mother, and thought Mrs. Cole's response, "You go back and tell her you're just as white as she is," to be undiplomatic and strange.

It also represented an attitude young Effa was uninterested in adopting, then or later. She could never offer a real reason for choosing to live as a black, even when the truth told to her in her teens might have caused her to abandon a life that would clearly subject her to bias, no matter how subtle. But there was no question she was content to have stayed the way she was. In her old age she related her unusual genesis matter-of-factly, and idly mused: "I've often wondered what it would be like to associate with white people."

Aided by an olive complexion, she represented herself to the black community as a Negro, but seemed to enjoy the confusion her light skin could create. She recalled her engagement to Abe Manley in New York City in 1933: "Abe and I went right to Tiffany's for the ring, and I picked out a five-carat stone. When we went back to pick it up, every salesgirl in the store was there to take a peep at us. They had heard this old Negro man (Abe was fifteen years older than Effa) had bought a five-carat ring for this pretty young white woman. I got a kick out of that."[1]

She was also not averse to taking advantage of her Caucasian appearance for better reasons than shocking shopgirls. Before her marriage she "never worked as a Negro" in her adopted New York City, and so took jobs more likely to go to whites than blacks, with the financial advantages that came with that choice. When she traveled alone, she often would stay at first-class hotels, where black people might work in menial jobs but could not sign in as guests.

In the 1930s, though, marriage to a black man made her an unquestioned member of the black world. Several people interviewed for this book admitted they had heard secondhand that she was white, or perhaps had suspected it themselves. "I can never remember, was she black or white? She was very fair," said Harriette Everett, one of many black teenage girls living in Newark in the 1930s who admired Effa's looks, clothes, and style. But, until Effa raised it herself late in life, after her baseball career had ended and after the civil rights movement had knocked down so many artificial racial distinctions, the subject never seems to have come up, at least in public.

Her account could possibly be written off as an effort by an elderly person, finally getting attention again after years of being ignored, to embroider her life story for a revived string of interviewers. But if so, the story of her birth clashes strongly with the remaining content of those interviews. Her memory of the Negro leagues and life in the Negro communities in which she lived was strong. Talks with others who were there and research into black newspapers and the Newark Eagle business files substantiate nearly everything else she said.

That Effa never raised the point while active in baseball and society, and actually went to lengths to portray herself as black (her 1933 marriage certificate lists her as "colored," and records Brooks as being her father) is proof of the sensitivity of the matter in those days, not a strike against her credibility. The common assumption was that if she was married to a black, lived in black neighborhoods, and ran a black business, then she was black, and that was that.

If there had been questions, her status and commitment to improving black society would have been enough to squelch them. She was as likely to extol the virtues of black society as of black baseball, as when she was quoted in 1936 as saying that the black race "does not know its own strength, and when it begins to realize what really fine things the race is capable of doing it will show rapid progress."

In truth, it does not matter whether she was black or white. If she was really white, as an adult she made a conscious, irrevocable choice to live in the Negro world. Black sportswriter Arthur G. Rust, Jr., has his finger on the most important point: "Identification is so difficult to pinpoint in this basically racist society we live in that whether Effa was really white or black seems ludicrous. After all, being black is also a state of mind, and apparently Effa thought so too." [2]

Effa and Abraham L. Manley were married June 15, 1933, in New York City, where they both then lived. It was the second marriage for both. Effa was pleased to recount on several later occasions that they met at the 1932 World Series in Yankee Stadium, which would have been either September 28 or 29, the dates of the only two Series games played in New York that year. Abe was an all-around baseball fanatic, a devoted fan of the famous Hilldale team from Philadelphia, while she professed to be less of an enthusiast about the sport than an admirer of the Yankee star Babe Ruth: "I was crazy about Babe Ruth. I lived in Harlem, which was close enough to Yankee Stadium for me to walk. So I used to go see all the Yankee games just to see Babe Ruth come up to bat and hope that he'd hit the ball out of the park."[3]

Abe, born in North Carolina in 1885, had emigrated by way of Norfolk, Virginia, to Camden, N. J., a city across the Delaware River from Philadelphia. A naturally reticent man who was long dead before interest in the Negro leagues revived in the 1970s, he never seems to have given interviews about anything but the current state of his baseball team, and so little is known about his early life.

He arrived in the Philadelphia area about the same time as numbers gambling. Introduced there from New York City in 1923, it quickly replaced policy betting as the "painless" road to wealth in the black community, as well as many parts of white society.

Abe had become fairly rich through gambling, primarily as a "numbers banker," the ultimate collector of bets and payer of winnings for at least some of Camden's black numbers players. While thoroughly illegal, numbers was extremely popular in black society. If the men running the "banks"which accepted the daily profits and paid off on the winning numbers confined their criminality to this occupation alone, they were not particularly looked at askance by the local black population. If they plowed some of their profits back into the community (and in gaming there are almost always profits in a well-run operation), they could even become socially accepted.

Gambling, laws against it notwithstanding, has always been a staple American source of amusement, a "game of skill" that has the potential to turn a profit. Beginning in the 1920s in the black urban ghettos of the North, playing the daily number stood for more than that. In black city neighborhoods it constituted a black-run investment business.

A regular player, wagering as little as a nickel or dime a day, could hope for a big, profitable win at some point. It was an incredibly precarious way to try to make money, but urban blacks in those times had limited legitimate options; the white-run banking and financial community had little or no interest in bankrolling persons from the ghettos, who generally had low incomes and little collateral.

In addition to a bet being regarded as an "investment," numbers organizations provided employment in economically depressed black communities and were also a source of credit, both by allowing regular customers to bet on the cuff and by making direct loans unrelated to their betting.

Writer Francis A. J. Ianni summarizes the meaning of the numbers game: "The numbers was a black savings bank. These people never saved any money anyhow. So they'd play a few bucks on the numbers every week. They were bound to hit a few times in their lives and when they did they could pay off some debts or buy a new sofa." [4]

As opposed to other types of lotteries, numbers had two distinct attractions. It could be played for very small bets (a nickel or less in the 1920s and 1930s), and it was easy to play. A bettor selected a number from 0 or 1 to 999, and won if it turned out to be the number for that day (based on the digits representing the volume of stock market transactions, the betting handle at a racetrack, or some other number that was publicly available and presumably beyond the game operator's power to fix).

The theoretical odds against winning were 999 to 1 (or 1,000 to 1 if the number zero could be picked), but the operators paid off at around 600 to 1. This made a well-run operation a potential source of an enormous amount of business capital in black communities, and the black numbers barons became providers of business loans unavailable from the banking community, as well as philanthropists supporting charities and churches.

Their value to the urban black communities brought about interesting treatment from the black press, which in general was moralistic about black citizens' behavior on the general grounds that misdeeds would hold back progress for the race. The editors never seemed to come down too hard on the numbers game, though. For example, the Pittsburgh *Courier,* one of the leading black weeklies in the eastern United States, would never have stooped to explicitly legitimatize illegal activities. But for years the *Courier* ran a cartoon strip called "Sunnyboy Sam," chronicling the adventures of a well-dressed, somewhat shiftless, rake who regularly got into trouble through avarice, and out of it with a quip. Whatever its humor quotient, Sam's value to readers each week may have lay more in the six three-digit numbers worked into the cartoon panels, a week's worth of advice on possible winners.

If the numbers operators were available to support both worthy black business undertakings and philanthropic projects for the community, there may have been no more natural investment opportunities than bankrolling black sports. Boxing champion Joe Louis's manager, John Roxborough of Detroit, was in the numbers business, and there was numbers money at least partially backing every Negro league baseball team in the East.

By the time Abe Manley moved to Harlem around 1930, he was a person of comfortable wealth and at least a little status in upper-class black society. He was usually described as a "sportsman," with all the high-living disdain for the daily grind that label implies. As a "sportsman," his money and fondness for a good time offset his lack of education and cultural interests.

Abe had made a very wise decision by retiring from the numbers business and leaving Camden. White mobsters moved in on black gambling in the Philadelphia area in the early 1930s, as they did in other cities. They reduced the payoffs on winning numbers and encouraged the cooperation of black numbers bankers through violence. The interlopers were generally highly organized bootleggers looking for new business opportunities as the end of Prohibition made the nation legally wet and dried up their illicit businesses. Commonly the bootleggers formed "partnerships" with the gamblers, but there is a substantial question as to how voluntary these arrangements might have been, given the violent methods and political influence available to the whites.

In Abe's case, the prudence of leaving the numbers business was unquestionable. Effa later recounted that when Abe refused to cut in some white mobsters, "they threw a bomb into the club that he operated, the Rest-A-While Club. The prosecutor happened to be a personal friend of Abe's. I've often wondered if he was on Abe's payroll, he bothered so. Anyway, he told Abe to get out of town. He had to clean up the numbers because the gangsters had come."[5]

Camden in those days was a violent place. It had been the scene of twenty-one murders in 1932, and mobsters, openly defying the police, staged running gun battles from cars on the city's streets. Like other black gambling figures who enjoyed lives separate from the numbers business, Abe Manley seems to have diversified. Much of his profits were turned into real estate investments, and with money in the bank, he moved to New York City. By the time of his marriage, at only age 48, he was described on a newspaper society page as "a wealthy, retired Camden, N.J., broker."

Effa left home sometime after graduating from Philadelphia's William Penn High School in 1916, and had also been attracted to New York. There, either because of an interest in sporting figures or through coincidence, she wound up living in the same apartment house as "Smokey Joe" Williams, a former great Negro league pitcher. Williams was retired as a player then, working as a bartender and doubling as a key contact in New York to match up prospective black players with team owners looking for talent. He could have been the key to Effa's meeting Abe, the longtime baseball fan.

Effa later told a newspaperwoman that before her marriage to Abe she "was interested in the thing that interests most women, I suppose, clothes. I spent quite a few years in the millinery business making hats, [and] had taken a little additional training in designing."

Her earlier marriage, to a man named Bush who she had met and flirted with on the beach in the New Jersey resort town of Atlantic City, had the earmarks of a typical Effa triumph. "I went after him, and I got him," she later recounted. The catching may have been the best part of the relationship, though—the marriage lasted only a short while, and Effa was fortunately available when she met Abe. Whatever his background in Camden, Abe appears to have been unfailingly good to Effa and a model of genteelness. "In 20 years, I never heard him once say 'hell,' or 'damn,' " she recalled, although several baseball men recall him using those epithets, and many others, when women were not around. He doted on his new wife, buying the first of the four mink coats she owned during her life shortly after they met. "I never knew how much money Abe had," she later recalled, "but anything I wanted, I got."

Abe also took some steps to make it clear he was the man in her life. The trip to Tiffany's for her diamond ring only took place after he made her sell a ring and brooch given her by a previous boyfriend. Then he had the stones from some men's jewelry he had acquired as security for loans to other gamblers set in a large brooch for her so her jewelry, as her minks, were all from him, and no one else.

As black newcomers to New York, Abe with money and Effa with ambition, and with an appreciation for their individual notions of the good things in life, they were at home in Harlem, the city's primary black area. In the 1930s, that community on the northern end of Manhattan was a place to behold and remember. Famous black author James Weldon Johnson wrote in 1930 that

> In nearly every city in the country the Negro section is a nest or several nests situated somewhere on the borders; it is a section one must "go out to." In New York it is entirely different. Negro Harlem is situated in the heart of Manhattan and covers one of the most beautiful and healthful sites in the whole city.[6]

The social effects of World War I, which halted European immigration while at the same time creating a pressing need for labor in northern war industries, caused a boom in the North's black communities. In Harlem, Johnson said, "old residents and new-comers got work as fast as they could take it, at wages never dreamed of."[7]

Following the Great War, Harlem was the site of economic growth. It was also the scene of the Harlem Renaissance, the outpouring of new black literary talent that spilled over into a rousing nightlife. Harlem "came to set the standard for what was modish in black urban life." [8]

Many people lived very well there, and Abe and Effa Manley seem to have been among them. Their apartment at 741 St. Nicholas Ave. was within the boundaries of the best residential section Harlem had to offer. "Sugar Hill" lay north of the main part of Harlem, pushing up against the white neighborhood of Washington Heights and both literally and figuratively looking down upon the valley in which the main part of Harlem lay. Sugar Hill was so named because it represented the sweet life in the black district, where "celebrities of all sorts—the moneyed, the talented, the socially prominent, the intellectually distinguished, the fast crowd—lived along the streets and avenues of the section." [9]

The Manleys were not a likely couple for high society, he a middle-aged black-skinned man of less than legal background and she a woman whose light skin denoted upper-class breeding but who was really from a working-class family. They were able to make an entrance into black urban high society because the postwar turbulence was changing the rules of status, as well as so much else.

While a light skin and a thoroughly upright reputation were usually prerequisites to acceptance in upper-class black society in the South and in some smaller places, this was no longer necessarily the case in great cities of the North. Black sociologist E. Franklin Frazier wrote in 1940 that

> In the large urban communities of the North, it is one's occupation, education and income or standard of living rather than family and color that determine status. Then, too, in the large city, one's social status is not determined so much by one's morals as by one's public behavior. [10]

The Manleys were at least marginal members of Harlem's black upper class, which was on a par with white society's middle class, since opportunities to amass truly great wealth were not available to American blacks in the 1930s. In several respects they measured up to Frazier's generalized description of an upper-class black family, with few or no children (none, in their case) and Effa active in social and civic affairs.

Abe's entree to black high society may have been as an "upper shadie," someone with an income worthy of upper-class status, although the wealth came from unlawful means, and without the previously requisite family or educational background. However he attained it, Abe seems to have maintained his status by avoiding the numbers business, at least as a daily participant. By the early 1930s, numbers in Harlem was controlled by the white mobster Dutch Schultz, and it would have been unlikely that a newcomer could have penetrated the existing organization. A well-documented major criminal investigation into Schultz's network, including the black operators who were beholden to him, failed to turn up Abe's name. However, it is not otherwise clear what Abe did for a living before going into baseball in 1935. Effa said that with no new numbers business, "he had nothing to do" and so could frequent the ballpark. Perhaps his investments were enough.

But there is no question what Effa Manley was doing. Sugar Hill was home at one time or another to the civil rights and black community leaders of that day, including W. E. B. DuBois, Roy Wilkins, Walter White, and Thurgood Marshall. Living among those who, along with the artists, writers, and musicians, made a lasting impact on black history, presented opportunities to work for racial equality and strengthen the black community around her. Upper-class blacks were generally the driving force in organizations and movements designed to improve their race's lot, and however she had acquired her ticket to black society, Effa picked up this responsibility as if she had been to the manor born.

By 1936 Effa had already been an officer (she always seemed to become secretary or treasurer of the groups she joined, in deference to her organizational ability) of the Edgecombe Sanitarium Renaissance Committee (a group working to reorganize and save the mortgage of that Harlem medical institution); the Children's Camp Committee of New York, and the Citizens' League for Fair Play, a Harlem-wide group that in 1934 organized the community in a successful boycott of major white-owned stores over the issue of jobs.

Effa Manley both took a turn on the sidewalk picket line and a part in the negotiations which led to the hiring of more blacks. While Harlem contained many black-owned businesses, the largest ones, which included the department stores and other large retail establishments along 125th Street in the heart of its commercial area, were owned by whites. Of these stores, the five-story L. M. Blumstein department store at 230-240 W. 125th was the largest. Blumstein's had black employees, but their work was restricted to menial jobs, such as janitorial work. Operating one of the store's elevators was the most visible job Blumstein's would offer to a black.

At a large hotel banquet one night, Effa found herself seated next to William Davis, editor of the black weekly, the *Amsterdam News,* and "we got into a conversation about how hard it was for our women to find employment, except as maids and doing housework." Davis assured her, too optimistically as it turned out, that "if you ask Mrs. Blumstein (the department store's owner), she'd hire a Negro."

A women's group grew out of that evening's dinner table conversation. It held its first meetings at the Manley apartment in February, 1934, and formulated the goal of increasing black employment in the stores. But its members had nothing except good intentions to show for their early efforts when a letter-writing campaign to Harlem ministers brought a response from a like-minded community leader, the Rev. John H. Johnson, rector of St. Martin's Methodist Episcopal Church. Blacks in major American cities were being admonished by fair-employment advocates, "Don't Buy Where You Can't Work." That was Reverend Johnson's motto, also.

In the spring of 1934 he collected Blumstein's sales slips and cancelled checks from purchases made there by the 1,000 members of his congregation. In two weeks he had accumulated proof of $7,000 spent there by blacks and made an appointment to see the management about the hiring of black women as sales clerks, jobs that were both highly visible to the buying public and fairly well paying by black standards.

Armed with his evidence, Johnson sat down in mid-May with Mrs. L. M. Blumstein, the store's owner, and her brother-in-law, William Blumstein, the general manager. They confirmed the truth of his sales-slip survey, but then rebuffed his request. The Blumsteins readily admitted that about 75 percent of their business was with black customers, but added that they were not going to hire any black salesclerks. William Blumstein pointed out to the pastor that the store employed many blacks, including the all-black elevator operator corps. While this was true, at least one of those elevator operators was a college graduate, and despite that degree would never rise higher in Blumstein's than his elevator could carry him up its shaft.

The black community's reaction was to band together into the Citizens' League, which represented 300 Harlem social, civic, and fraternal groups. Reverend Johnson was the chairman and Effa Manley, of course, was secretary. By early June pickets were parading on the sidewalk in front of Blumstein's. Effa said that, because the volunteer scheduled to walk the picket line the first morning of the demonstration failed to show up, she stepped into the vacancy. Abe, who seems to have had no special interest in the Citizens' League, drove her down to the store, she took up the sign (glad she had ordered it made of light cardboard), and the boycott was on.

As Effa later recalled, the Citizens' League "proceeded to inform the community in every way they could that Blumstein's had gone on record as refusing to train a Negro salesclerk or hire an experienced one." The league drew a reported four hundred people to a meeting on July 3, and five hundred a week later, where plans were made to continue to boycott the department store and to extend the picketing to other white-owned establishments.

A pivotal meeting was held on July 23 between the Citizens' League leaders and Blumstein's owners. Reverend Johnson, Effa, and three other league officers, lawyer Richard Carey, newspaper editor Fred Moore, and real estate magnate John Nail, were arguing their case when Effa threw in a trenchant observation of the type that would soon become familiar to baseball executives, both black and white:

> The conversation was going back and forth, and finally I said "may I say something," (I think they all had me there to say something). I said, "You know, Mr. Blumstein, we think as much of our young colored girls as you do your young white girls, but there's no work for them except to work as someone's maid, or become prostitutes." When I said that, Blumstein's lawyer almost went through the roof. "Oh, Mrs. Manley, don't say such a thing," he said. I said, "I'm only telling you the truth."

Confronted both within their offices and on the sidewalk outside, Blumstein's caved in on July 26. The store agreed to hire fifteen blacks for sales jobs by August 15, twenty more in September, and more thereafter, depending on business conditions. A victory parade and rally in Harlem on July 28 drew 1,500 people, despite a driving rainstorm that postponed it for nearly the entire afternoon.

The league then chose other targets and had further successes. A survey by the New York *Age* the following spring found that 150 blacks had clerical jobs along 125th Street. The Citizens' League in the meantime had incorporated itself, with Effa as one of the incorporators. In January, 1935, it launched its coming year's agenda with a spirited meeting in which it grilled officials of the Harlem Merchants Association for not completely living up to black hiring goals. It also appointed a committee to look into the alleged shortcomings of the city's relief bureau in regard to its promises to safeguard the interests of the city's blacks.

The league's efforts were, of course, not destined to follow a straight line to success, any more than other attempts around the country to give blacks their due. In March, 1935, five people were killed and more injured in Harlem when rioting broke out following a false report that a young boy had been killed by employees when caught shoplifting in a store which had held the line against hiring blacks. Reverend Johnson characterized the rioting as "an economic revolt against the prejudice, exploitation, the unfair practice" of 125th Street store owners who made a livelihood from Harlem's residents, yet still refused to give them jobs.[11]

On December 21, 1935, the New York *Age,* a black weekly, reported that the Citizens' League, with Effa Manley still its secretary, would reopen its 125th Street employment drive as reports of job discrimination continued. But by that time, Effa and Abe had already been proprietors for a year of a business of their own that employed blacks exclusively in high-profile jobs and always had a waiting list of eager prospective employees. The old Hilldale fan and the woman who admired Babe Ruth had taken some of their money and started a baseball club, trying to tap the rich vein of baseball gold that lay across the East River from Manhattan in the borough of Brooklyn.

Notes

1. Henry Hecht, "Woman With a Mission," New York *Post,* Sept. 15, 1975; Allen Richardson, "A Retrospective Look at the Negro Leagues and Professional Negro Baseball Players," master's thesis, San Jose State University, May, 1980.
2. Arthur G. Rust, Jr., *Recollections of a Baseball Junkie,* p. 76.
3. Richardson, "Retrospective Look," p. 158.
4. Francis A. J. Ianni, *Black Mafia: Ethnic Succession in Organized Crime* (New York: Simon and Schuster, 1974), p. 78.
5. Richardson, "Retrospective Look," pp. 157-58.
6. James Weldon Johnson, *Black Manhattan* (New York: Alfred A. Knopf, 1930), p. 146.
7. Ibid., p. 153.
8. Jervis Anderson, "That Was New York: Harlem, Part III, What a City!" *The New Yorker,* July 13, 1981, p. 38.
9. Ibid., pp. 73-74.

10. E. Franklin Frazier, *The Negro in the United States* (New York: Macmillan, 1949), p. 291.

11. New York *Age,* March 30, 1935.

Chapter 2
Opening (and Closing) in Brooklyn

The cash that the Manleys and several other baseball entrepreneurs brought to the Negro leagues in the mid-1930s may have saved organized black baseball, which had been on the ropes since the Depression had begun. What the Manleys and the others got for their money, other than alternating periods of elation and worry caused by victories and reverses on the field and at the ticket window, was a chance to participate in a watershed segment of American black history.

The Eagles, coming into existence as they did right in the middle of the 1930s and continuing on in Newark until after the integration of the major leagues in 1947, started playing in one black baseball era and finished in quite another.

By 1932 first-class black baseball played in the important cities of the East and Midwest which had white major league teams that had died from lack of funds. The 1933 season saw a revival, a six-team Negro National League spearheaded by William A. "Gus" Greenlee, a Pittsburgh numbers baron. But this revival was still underway when the Brooklyn Eagles first took the field.

The low-cost alternative to a league setup required motoring from town to town through both the North and South to play all comers for whatever money could be made. This method of play, called "barnstorming," generated the traveling stories that have become baseball folklore—of stupendous home runs and pitching heroics against local amateur teams, but also of many confrontations with the intolerance that prevailed in America's small towns.

By the mid-1940s, though, hordes of black people were coming to the ballparks to see their heroes, and the Negro league teams were successful and respectable, less dependent on traveling to dozens of small towns. Finally, there were blacks in major league uniforms, doing what those fans at the Negro league games knew they could do all along.

The Negro National League the Manleys joined for the 1935 season was actually the second black baseball organization of that name. The first had been founded in 1920 by one Andrew Foster, who dominated black baseball in his day to an extent not equaled by any other figure in the sport.

Foster acquired the nickname "Rube" as a young player in 1902, supposedly for defeating the great white major league pitcher (and fellow Hall of Famer) George "Rube" Waddell and Waddell's Philadelphia Athletics. In addition to a reputation for athletic skill, Foster was also known for his intelligence and canniness. Once he used a particularly clever trick to extricate himself from a potential game-losing situation, again against the Athletics.

With two outs in Philadelphia's final turn at bat and two strikes on outfielder Topsy Hartsell, who would at least tie the game if he were to hit safely, Foster shouted to the umpire that Hartsell had taken his batting stance dangerously close to home plate. "Why don't you make him stand back off that plate? He'll get hit," Foster yelled in from the pitcher's mound. Hartsell reacted without thinking, looking down at his feet and turning his head to tell the umpire that he was just fine, while Foster casually flipped the ball over the middle of the plate for strike three.

It was no wonder that Foster wrote in a 1908 article called "How to Pitch" that "the real test comes when you are pitching with men on bases. Do not worry. Try to appear jolly and unconcerned. I have smiled often with the bases full and two strikes and three balls on the batter. This seems to unnerve them."[1]

Foster was elected to the Hall of Fame in 1981, one of eleven men voted in primarily for their Negro league contributions. However, he holds a distinction nearly unique among the entire membership in the Hall, having excelled at all four levels of the professional sport—player, manager, team executive, and league president.

Foster's club, the American Giants of Chicago, was one of several independent black teams in the Midwest, South, and on the East Coast. They traveled around, picking up games with both black and white teams of varying skill levels, right on up to white major league squads looking to raise a little extra attendance money on their days off.

While this barnstorming remained a staple of black baseball operations throughout the history of Negro baseball, it was hard and financially risky work. The extensive travel was hard on the players. It was hard on an owner, too, when it took the team to a town where a game was rained out or where a paltry turnout would produce a share of the gate money too small to cover the expenses of getting there in the first place. The unstructured nature of independent baseball also encouraged team owners to "raid" their colleagues, enticing their better players away with offers of higher salaries.

Foster knew that if black baseball was to succeed, it needed a league structure. Preaching, as Negro league historian Robert Peterson has put it, "the need for owners to cooperate rather than cut each other's throats," he organized the top Midwestern teams into a "National League," with two teams in Chicago and six others throughout the Midwest.

It was clearly Foster's league. He was both its president and secretary, handling scheduling arrangements for all league games and charging 5 percent of attendance receipts for his work, which produced him an income of more than $11,000 in the league's well-attended first year.[2] He also engineered trades of players to create as much parity as possible among the teams, thus keeping them competitive and interesting to their supporters.

The National League rarely managed to maintain eight financially solvent teams throughout an entire season. Furthermore, despite Foster's shuffling of players, it had a distinct competitive imbalance, since his American Giants, the Kansas City Monarchs, and the St. Louis Stars divided all twelve season championships. But it continued to exist from season to season, which qualified it as successful. Even more importantly, it was run by a black man and most of its teams were owned by blacks, which could not be said for the rival Eastern Colored League. That league opened in 1923 with most of the best East Coast black teams in its ranks. Four of Eastern's six teams were owned by white men, prompting Foster to remark that calling it a colored league was like calling "a streetcar a steamship."[3]

The National League's biggest problem in the long run, ironically, was that it was too closely tied to Rube Foster. Foster became mentally unstable and began to do dangerous and bizarre things. He was seen chasing imaginary fly balls outside his Chicago home, and finally had a serious breakdown in 1926. He spent the rest of his life in an Illinois mental hospital and died there December 9, 1930, at the age of 51. Accounts at the time simplistically blamed his decline on overwork, but his disintegration had the earmarks of undiagnosed physical complications, too. Certainly his near asphyxiation by leaking natural gas in a hotel room in 1925 had a great deal to do with his decline.

Perhaps not even the great Rube Foster could have coped with the severe financial effects of the Great Depression. But it is clear that the remaining owners, unaccustomed as they were to making their own decisions, were nowhere up to the task in his absence. The first Negro National League sputtered out of existence in 1931.

Rube Foster's legacy in black sports was a substantial one, however. He became the permanent example of excellent leadership, a standard against which his successors in the Negro leagues were often found to falter. At the beginning of the 1940 season, for example, when the leaders of the new Negro National League were engaged in another of their periodic public squabbles, the Pittsburgh *Courier* resurrected Foster's reputation on its May 4 sports page and observed that "the diamond fathers of today would do much better if they'd stick a rough and ready guy in the front seat, like Rube Foster, and let him do the fighting." [4]

But while Foster was gone, the two factors that made black league baseball possible remained. These were a large pool of talented players who were effectively barred from white organized baseball and growing concentrations of black residents in the major urban areas in the North.

Black migration from the South to the North was the product of two countervailing economic forces—the decline of the tenant-farmer system in the South, which had been the black's basic relationship to the agrarian economy of that region after slavery ended, and the concurrent need for unskilled labor in the North to meet the industrial growth brought about by America's materiel needs in World War I.

In 1910, 18.2 percent of all southernborn blacks living in the North came from the Cotton Belt states of South Carolina, Georgia, Florida, Alabama, Mississippi, Arkansas, Louisiana, and Texas. By 1920, 40.5 percent of that larger group came from those states. In numbers of people, that meant more than 220,000 additional Deep South migrants. These people were a large portion of the fuel that drove the urban population growth causing the combined black populations of the four major migration targets—New York, Chicago, Philadelphia, and Detroit—to increase by three quarters of a million people during those ten years. Once begun, the tide was not stemmed by the end of the war. In 1930, New York City had 114 percent more black residents than it had in 1920.[5]

Enough potential baseball fans had finally arrived in the big cities to make league baseball possible on a long-term basis. The players had been around for years. Professional black baseball dates back at least as far as 1882, when a team named the Orions played in Philadelphia on a part-time, semiprofessional basis. Amateur black teams have been identified as far back as 1860.

Professional baseball meant the same thing to black players of the first part of the twentieth century as it did to whites: a chance to leave home and become somewhat well known and considerably better paid than neighbors and relatives who stayed behind. Not that playing baseball made even skilled blacks all that wealthy, particularly during the Depression. The average black player's salary in the mid-1930s was about $125 per month, payable only during the season. This was one-quarter of a major leaguer's pay, about equal to a run-of-the-mill minor league salary. But, as Josh Gibson's biographer, William Brashler, pointed out, "it was better than sweeping or working the railroad, where wages amounted to $60 or $75 a month." [6]

That was when a player got paid at all. Bill Foster, Rube Foster's half brother and an excellent pitcher in his own right, recalled that sometimes, "the team couldn't pay us, it was the Depression and nobody was working . . . the people couldn't go to the ball game, and our bosses promised us so much money, but they didn't have it 'cause they weren't making it." [7]

Negro league baseball tried hard to model itself on the white majors, which presented no particular problem on the field. Black ball players had been playing together and developing their skills since being squeezed out of the white leagues in a gradual process in the 1890s, and the very best blacks were always as good as the best whites.

Setting up a strong organizational and financial structure for a black league was something else, however, and the many failures made participants appreciate Rube Foster's resourcefulness all the more. Black baseball was a business, and was as caught up as other black enterprises in the general economic problems that plagued the majority of its customers, the urban blacks of the United States.

A 1940 comparison of median family incomes for white and nonwhite families in fourteen major American cities disclosed that in every city, the median white income was significantly greater than the black income, 50 percent or more in many cases. And in none of the cities did the nonwhite incomes equal a "maintenance budget" upon which an average family might exist.[8] Urban blacks, even in the North where incomes were closer to the "maintenance" line, had precious little extra cash to spend, once the necessities of life were paid for.

Not even a high school or college degree could guarantee a better standard of living for a black. In 1939 nearly 50 percent of white males 25 to 64 years old with high school degrees earned $1,500 or more a year, while not quite 10 percent of their black peers did so. Seventy-two percent of whites with four years or more of college made $1,500 or more, but only 26 percent of college educated black men reached that level.[9] Clearly, the elevator operator back at Blumstein's Department Store in Harlem was no isolated case.

The lack of disposable income led to a scarcity of investment in black businesses. The reasons given in 1932 by Dr. Abram L. Harris, a black economist, for the failure of the black housing market to thrive can be applied to most of the black economy:

> Given a general business recession (the black's) economic position, and therefore his ability to pay, become precarious. Because of the marginal nature of the work in which the greatest number of Negroes are engaged, enforced idleness and the loss of income are likely to be felt more quickly and to a relatively greater extent in the Negro population.[10]

Baseball fans without much disposable income are baseball fans who do not buy tickets to professional games. With a slim profit margin, black baseball executives became highly dependent upon changeable factors such as the weather to stay in business. They often sounded like farmers speculating in reverse about the effects of rain on their income, as when John Clark, the secretary of the Pittsburgh Crawfords, noted in 1936 that "rain in August kept many clubs out of the black."[11]

White major league teams were committed to playing half their yearly schedule in their home city, whether their followers turned up in droves or not. But black baseball entrepreneurs had a different tactic—they took their teams on the road and spread their attractions around as many cities and towns as possible, usually playing only one day or night in a location before moving on. By doing so they continually exposed their desirable product to new followers, who would be more likely to pay for what might be their only opportunity all summer to see a particular team. A prolonged absence might also elevate expectations at home and build attendance when the team finally returned.

Barnstorming from town to town had been an integral part of black baseball since the first regularly salaried squad, the Cuban Giants, began playing in 1885. The advent of organized leagues recast part of a black team's summer schedule into as many as 60 irregularly scheduled games against other league members. But the balance of the games, as many as 150 more, were independent contests in cities and towns that might be many hundreds of miles from home, with teams that were amateur as well as professional, and white as well as black.

Bart Giblin, a white New Jersey sportswriter, recalled seeing black barnstorming teams play his state when he was a youth in the 1920s:

> They would start a tour probably in Atlantic City, and they would move up the New Jersey shore. They would play in small towns like Manasquan, and Belmar and Asbury Park, and maybe go over to Trenton, and stop off in Red Bank, and play in Perth Amboy, and eventually they would get in the Essex County area, in Newark or Orange, and go on to Paterson, and then travel on into Pennsylvania. They played practically every day.

George Giles, a member of the Manleys' 1935 Brooklyn Eagles who played in 1936 for the New York Black Yankees, a nonleague squad, explained that with the Yankees,

> We were good for 200 ball games a year or more. The [white] big leagues played 154. Every holiday and Sunday we were good for four games on that day. We'd have a game at 11 o'clock, there'd be a double header somewhere that afternoon, and we'd go out to Long Island that night.[12]

Although in Rube Foster's day teams traveled in Pullman coaches to their next games, just as white major leaguers did, that mode was too expensive for the teams of the 1930s, which usually went by bus. Since the bus was the players' home away from home for days on end, comfort was a consideration. But team style entered into it, too, as owners strove to create personalities for their squads that could boost the box office take in a strange town. Shiny aluminum streamlined coaches, with bright trim that advertised any recent championships the squad had won, became common. As Negro league historian Donn Rogosin put it, "Eventually the rule hardened: the classier the team, the classier the bus." [13]

The need to maximize the number of playing dates often played havoc with the regular league schedules that were supposed to be the core of the teams' seasons. So did the fact that very few of the black teams owned their own ballparks. The best arrangement that could usually be had was to be a tenant of a white major or minor league club, which assured a black squad of a place to play, at least when the landlord team wasn't using it.

For their nonleague games, and for some teams nearly all of their contests, a more common situation was a deal with a sports booking agent. The agent, for a percentage of the gate receipts, would arrange games and reserve the parks in which they would be played, for a day or for an entire road trip. This, of course, was what Rube Foster had done for the first National League in return for his 5 percent of the gate money. But after his demise the most powerful booking agents were white. They thus became partners, either directly or indirectly, in black baseball.

Depending on whose opinion was being sought, this was either a great benefit to the league or just another example of what black writer Langston Hughes had to say about Harlem in the time of the great black literary revival, the Harlem Renaissance:

> My youthful illusion that Harlem was a world unto itself did not last very long . . . the famous night clubs were owned by whites, as were the theaters . . . the books of

> Harlem writers all had to be published downtown, if they were to be published at all . . . White downtown, pulling all the strings in Harlem.[14]

The solution for the black baseball entrepreneurs was to build their own baseball stadiums, and a few did. But for an owner to contemplate this solution would be to confront the baseball version of the vicious cycle that existed for almost all black business: construction of even a small stadium was a major capital investment, and financing was not generally available for black-owned enterprises. An owner could strive to make enough money with his team to provide his own capital, but the only way to do that was to play more games and do more business with the booking agents, thereby making them stronger.

While the Negro leagues did not qualify as superb baseball organizations by accepted standards, at the same time they were much more important than the predominant white portion of American society gave them credit for. The black baseball player always had something extra to prove. Poet and writer Amiri Baraka, who grew up a Negro league baseball fan in Newark, remembers when Satchel Paige, well into his 40s and far past his fabulous prime, finally was allowed to pitch in the major leagues in 1948.

> The papers were saying, "Is Satchel Paige great enough to pitch for the big leagues?" You see that kind of double penalization—first you're penalized by racism, and then, because you've been penalized, they want to know "How come you wasn't in the Big Leagues when you was twenty?"

But Satchel and his fellow players never needed to apologize to their black fans. Rogosin got their status exactly right.

> It was easy for historians to overlook the larger picture: Black people, crushed by segregation, desperately needed models to emulate; and they required men and

> women who cast large shadows, large enough to make known the truth of black talent. The Negro leaguers were a part of that "missing" coterie of professionals, the invisible men of American history: Black men of substance.[15]

The black stars never shone brighter each season than at the East-West All-Star Game, the showcase for the Negro leagues' best, which was played in Chicago each year. In 1934, the second East-West game was memorable, a scoreless tie for seven innings that the East team finally won, 1-0.

As it happened, the All-Star game coincided with the Chicago World's Fair, which had featured the night before a spectacular pageant of black history called "O, Sing a New Song." There were a total of 65,000 people attending both spectacles, most of them black. Pittsburgh *Courier* city editor William G. Nunn was present at both events, and he chronicled in the September 1 issue how, on those two August days in Chicago, black baseball and black history were recognized and celebrated together.

Of the game at Comiskey Park, the stadium of the white major leagues' White Sox, Nunn reported that

> We saw a baseball epic unfold itself on this historic field this afternoon. No diamond masterpiece was this game! No baseball classic! Those words are relegated into the limbo of forgotten things in describing the titanic struggle for supremacy.

The night before, at Soldiers' Field on the shore of Lake Michigan, Nunn had written:

> They made me proud that I'm a Negro, and tonight I'm singing a new song! For under the floodlights of this memorable field, with the famous "sky-ride" of the Chicago World Fair overhead . . . and with a perfect harvest moon riding majestically in the heavens, the Afro-American pageant, "O Sing a New Song" unfolded in a blaze of simple glory, which gave to some 40,000 onlookers a

different conception of the trials, tribulations and triumphs of a great and glorious race.

Abe Manley, the small-town Southern boy who had made himself rich and then had to flee for his safety before strong-arm whites, knew of trials, tribulations, and triumphs. He also had a notion of what black baseball ought to mean to his race, although he thought the men in charge were devaluing their exceptional product. In 1934 he told Effa that in his opinion the black teams were insufficiently organized, were doing too much barnstorming instead of sticking to league schedules, and in general were "going nowhere fast . . . there's a lot of talent on those teams, but it's being wasted." [16]

As it turned out, Abe was thinking about being more than just a sideline critic. "He asked me one day of my opinion about him going into this baseball," Effa remembered. "Before I knew anything, he's just making the announcement that he's going to have a baseball team named the Eagles—he even had the name."[17]

Although his ideas of black baseball's shortcomings would surface later to pit Effa and him against other factions in the Negro National League, Abe's willingness to bankroll a club in Brooklyn, playing in the Brooklyn Dodgers' Ebbets Field not far from the steadily growing black community in the Bedford-Stuyvesant area, was important to black baseball.

In the revived National League's first two years of existence, 1933 and 1934, teams from out of town would frequently play each other at Yankee Stadium or come to New York City separately for games with the area's crack white semiprofessional teams. But the league did not have any franchises in a city with 400,000 blacks living in it.

This shortage was doubly rectified in 1935, when not only the Manleys' Brooklyn Eagles joined, but veteran baseball man Alejandro Pompez returned to league play after several years absence with a Harlem team called the New York Cubans. While Alex Pompez, a native of Havana, was always able to stock his team with Cuban players out of that country's strong baseball system, the Manleys were starting from scratch. The Eagle manager, Negro baseball veteran Ben Taylor, hunted the countryside for players. His work was made substantially easier by the other teams' agreements to provide the Eagles with one or two players each, a process not unlike the expansion drafts that have stocked new major league clubs. But the results, as is the case for the fledgling white teams, were mixed, since established clubs rarely give up their best players.

The independent black teams, who had no binding agreements to keep their players with them from season to season, were also a source of talent for the Eagles. Members of the New York Black Yankees, which in 1935 belonged to no league, were particularly available once Abe's reputation for ability and willingness to pay a good salary got around. A well-known outfielder, Clarence "Fats" Jenkins (who was not rotund, by the way, and was such a good athlete he was also a topflight black basketball player in the winter) came to Brooklyn from the Harlem-based Yankees.

Although the Eagles signed some established players, several of them were past their prime and did not have long-term value to the team. At least one of those acquisitions brought a tremendous bonus, however. The Baltimore Black Sox, a 1934 member of the league, had gone out of business, and the Eagles signed one of its unemployed players, veteran outfielder Rap Dixon. Dixon was soon gone from the Brooklyn club, but he brought with him a young, unheralded pitcher. The pitcher, Leon Day, became the ace of the Eagle pitching staff and was still playing for the Manleys when they sold the franchise thirteen years later. The first year's roster also included outfielder Ed Stone, who was a regular on the team through 1943. But aside from Day and Stone, the men on the 1935 roster were not around more than a few years, at most.

Abe took his new squad to Jacksonville, Florida, for spring training and put them up at the Richmond Hotel, a first-class black establishment. The Eagles wended their way north, following the usual Negro league custom of acquiring both practice and income in a number of exhibition games in early May. They began the regular season by visiting the then-resident Newark team, the Dodgers, and pounding them 11-6 and 10-1 on May 5. Although that Newark club was to finish in last place during both halves of the National League's 1935 split season, it was still a league club, and those resounding victories undoubtedly boosted the Eagles' expectations for their own Opening Day.

They were matched with the powerhouse Homestead Grays of Pittsburgh for that first contest on May 11 at Ebbets Field, where black baseball was going to plant its flag firmly in the biggest borough of the nation's largest city. Among the clippings kept by Effa in a voluminous scrapbook was one by New York newspaper columnist Dan Parker, who described the Opening Day pageantry in what passed for complimentary coverage of the Negro leagues in those less-than-enlightened times:

> A brilliant sun was shining down on Ebbets Field yesterday afternoon when the Negro National League opened its season, but some wag suggested the game be called on account of darkness. . . . Led by a drum major with a white fur shako two inches shorter than the Chrysler tower, the players on the Homestead Grays and the Brooklyn Eagles marched out to the flagpole to the stirring martial music played by a hot Colored band which was itching to break into a blues number instead of the military march it was playing.

New York Mayor Fiorello La Guardia was on hand to throw out the ceremonial first ball. No account exists of the diminutive mayor's pitching ability, but it could not have been much worse than the performance of that day's Eagle pitchers. The Grays clobbered Brooklyn, 21-7. As George Giles, the Eagle first baseman, remembered, "they damn near killed us."[18]

La Guardia proved he was a sport, though, by staying around until the end of the bloodbath. Perhaps the savvy politician realized it would be too noticeable if he left, since despite energetic advance publicity, there were fewer than 3,000 fans in the 34,000-seat ballpark.

Opening Day, 1935, gave no indication of the success the Manleys were later to have in fielding winning teams and putting fans in the stadium seats to see them play. But one of Effa's characteristic traits, extreme and demonstrative unhappiness about failure, was displayed to baseball for the first time. She left in the third inning, went home, and had a drink of whiskey. Giles recounted that, as the Grays piled up the runs, she left the ballpark angry. "When she was displeased, the world came to an end. She'd stop traffic . . . Mrs. Manley loved baseball, but she couldn't stand to lose. I was a pretty hard loser myself, but I think she'd take it more seriously than anybody." [19]

One reason for her great dismay at the Opening Day fiasco may have been her growing personal attachment to her role as a baseball executive. While her husband labored to assemble their first team, the administrative end of the new enterprise fell increasingly to her. "I surprised even myself with my rapid progress in absorbing the lesson so vital to the successful operation of a modern day baseball organization," she later recalled. "Abe needed all the help that he could get—and immediately . . . I found that I could be of genuine assistance by performing a growing number of front office duties, along with the thousand and one other details relating to the business end of matters."[20]

The more she handled the team's paperwork, the more she felt confident about other baseball matters heretofore unknown to her. At the end of May, field manager Taylor was fired and Giles was made the Eagle manager. "Manley met me in his apartment and offered me the manager's job," Giles said. "He said, 'my wife wants you to manage the ball club.' He didn't say he wanted me; he said 'my wife' wanted me."

Giles was among the first of many male baseball men to cross paths with Effa and come away with a mixture of admiration based on her attractiveness and resentment based on her aggressive presence in their business. Giles criticized her: "she was like Charlie Finley or George

Steinbrenner [the more recent controversial owners of the white major league Oakland Athletics and New York Yankees]. They're not good for baseball. You're supposed to have some kind of class, dignity, when you get to the big leagues." But, he gave her this mixed-message stamp of approval, similar to others that would follow from baseball men trying to cope with this woman who insisted on being their equal: "She was very intelligent, she knew how to wear her clothes." [21]

Although the men in black baseball may have sometimes resented Effa Manley, the more the sport provided a role for her that first year, the more she became its advocate and, if need be, its defender. The Manleys were in the crowd May 26 for a game between the Homestead Grays and the Cubans at the Cuban's home park, Dyckman Oval in Harlem, when a Grays player slid hard into second base, colliding with a Cuban infielder who got up and slugged him. This precipitated a general brawl on the field and heated discussion in the stands.

Lewis Dial, sports columnist for the New York *Age,* reported that

> One Cuban business man was heard to say that he was through with Negro baseball. We were glad to hear Mrs. Manley, wife of the Brooklyn Eagles owner, severely censure him and just about change his mind. If there is such a thing as a lady fan, Mrs. Manley is twins, as far as the Brooklyn Eagles are concerned.

The Eagles rebounded from their Opening Day rout to humiliate the Grays, 18-9, in the first game of a doubleheader at Ebbets Field the next day. The two teams split that four-game series, which pretty much characterized the Eagles' entire season. They cruised along in the middle of the eight-team league, occasionally rising a little above the break-even level of having as many wins as losses, but as often sinking back just below that mark. When the first half of the season ended, the team had won 15 and lost 15, and was in fourth place.

In mid-June a sportswriter reported that Abe Manley believed that if he could get his hands on two more good pitchers "he feels sure he can make a race of it in the second half." [22] But those men could not be found, and the Eagles stumbled out of the starting gate when the second half began right after the Fourth of July. Although the league's practice of playing a "split season" schedule allowed the Eagles to start with a clean slate and possibly win the second-half championship, they lost 7 of their first 11 games. While they improved thereafter, they still couldn't quite struggle back to .500, and finished with 13 wins and 16 losses, in sixth place.

Despite their mediocre showing in the summer of 1935, the Brooklyn Eagles did win a championship before spring training began the next April. In mid-November the Manleys sponsored a team in the Puerto Rican winter league. It used the Brooklyn name and uniforms, but was a mix of Eagles and first-rate players from other black teams, particularly the Homestead Grays. Ed Stone was among the Eagle contributions. The Grays provided left fielder and manager Vic Harris, who also managed this squad, all-star first baseman Buck Leonard, and ace right-handed pitcher Raymond Brown. Among others recruited for the trip were the Philadelphia Stars top pitcher, left-hander Slim Jones, and infielders Ray Dandridge and Dick Seay, both soon to be prized members of Manley-owned teams.

Effa has taken credit for initiating the trip, an unusual action on her part, since she regularly gave her husband the credit for most of the important moves the couple made in their first few years in baseball. She described it as "one of my most pleasant experiences in baseball," since it not only gave the players winter employment that year and helped open up Latin America to more black players, but also resulted in the Eagles winning the winter league championship.

The team won 37 games, lost only 12, and tied 2 in Puerto Rico. In the championship game, Brown outpitched Martin Dihigo, the best baseball player to come out of Cuba and one of the Negro leaguers in the Hall of Fame.

The Eagles beat Dihigo's Alemendares team, 7 to 1, winning a tall trophy donated by the Bacardi rum company. (In 1973 Effa was pleased to donate the trophy to the Baseball Hall of Fame, although a bit taken aback by its $103 shipping cost from her home in Los Angeles to the Hall in Cooperstown, N.Y.).

The players were at least as proud of three exhibition games played on the island. In early March they hooked up with the Cincinnati Reds of white major league baseball, who were touring in the warm climes as part of their spring training. Until the major leagues were integrated, games against white teams composed even partially of major leaguers were signal events for the Negro leaguers, since it gave them an opportunity to cross the color line and show what they might do if not excluded from the majors.

They did just fine in Puerto Rico, beating the Reds twice in three contests, once by a very convincing 10-4 score. Even considering that the black team must have been in much better playing condition, having been competing all winter, the victories were important. They added incremental evidence to the eventually overpowering argument that racial discrimination, not lack of ability, kept the best blacks out of major league baseball.

But winter league play was just a sideline, and despite the Eagles' decent record in the 1935 stateside league, professional baseball relies on drawing fans to the park as well as putting runs on the scoreboard. There the Eagles had decidedly failed in their first season.

As 1935 had progressed, Effa said, "the crowds kept getting smaller and smaller. Even tiny Ebbets Field . . . was made to look like Yankee Stadium, insofar as Eagle home attendance was concerned." There were some decent crowds early in the season, including 5,000 for the May 12 doubleheader with the Grays and 7,500 for a pair of games on Memorial Day, but in general, the fans did not show up as expected.

There were several reasons for the Eagles' failure to draw fans. It was still the Depression, of course, and Effa believed that although the Eagles and their white landlords, the Dodgers, never played in Brooklyn at the same time, the Dodgers' extreme popularity siphoned cash customers away from her team.[23] But there was also another cause, in which the other Negro league teams were implicated.

The coming of the Eagles to Brooklyn put a black team in the midst of extremely fertile territory that until then had been dominated by whites. Brooklyn and the adjacent borough of Queens were the home of some of the best semi-professional teams in the East, possibly in the country. Those squads, the best of which were the Bushwicks and the Bay Parkways of Brooklyn and the Farmers of Glendale, Queens, frequently played Negro league clubs in exhibitions that provided solid paydays for the black teams visiting the New York area.

The semipros' financial affairs were in the hands of the booking agents, who had a lock on the territory. The Manleys, who had an arrangement with the Dodgers for the use of Ebbets Field that did not include a middle man, were stepping into territory recognized as the fiefdom of one Nat Strong, the preeminent agent in the East. Strong's apparent reaction to the interlopers was to continue with business as usual, which included a continuation of games with other black league clubs and semipro teams.

Self-interest ruled, as it often did among the owners of the Negro National League. Lewis Dial of the *Age* observed that the Eagles were one of two teams to be hurt the most by this practice (the other presumably being the Cubans in Harlem), since

> Teams from the league play in their territory at the same time that a league game is played in their parks. Such unfair conditions must be eliminated if the league is to prosper, as the games played in the independent parks are at less than half the admission price of regular scheduled games, thereby lessening the drawing power of the organization's clubs.[24]

The Negro National League's owners were taking advantage of their colleagues for individual gain, a theme played out all too often for the Manleys' tastes in future years.

According to Effa, "before the season was a third over, it had become quite obvious that our Eagle management was going to have to do something very drastic about the situation—or else it was a cinch we'd simply have to 'throw in the towel.' "[25] Since they didn't intend to quit, the Manleys response to impending financial disaster was to move. Instead of trying again to break new ground, they decided to put down roots in a place that until then had been pretty barren, as far as the league was concerned. They purchased the Newark Dodgers franchise from its principal owner, Charles Tyler, a chicken farmer and proprietor of a restaurant and bar called the Chicken Shack in nearby Avenel, N. J.

The Dodgers (named not after the major league team, but after Dodger's Bar and Grill, a leading Newark nightclub belonging to Joshua "Pop" Frazier, a part owner of the black team) had been in the league for two years and had never done well. The Dodgers had finished dead last in both halves of the 1935 season. An apparent financial as well as artistic flop, they reportedly lost money in 1934 and probably did little better the next year, since Tyler was willing to sell out.

The transaction was basically a merger of the two teams, although only three Dodgers—veteran pitcher Bill Evans, catcher Johnnie Hayes, and young third baseman Dandridge—became regular players with the new Newark team. Dandridge alone may have been worth whatever the Manleys paid Tyler. He played the next three years for the Eagles and parts of two other seasons later, becoming the best at his position in the Negro leagues, a distinction which in 1987 got him voted into the Hall of Fame.

Thus, by the spring of 1936, the Eagles were in Newark, beginning an intriguing infatuation between the city's black population and its own baseball team.

Notes

1. Sol White, *Sol White's Official Base Ball Guide* (Columbia, SC: Camden House, 1984), p. 107.

2. Phil Dixon, with Patrick J. Hannigan, *The Negro Baseball Leagues, a Photographic History* (Mattituch, NY: Amereon House, 1992), p. 99.

3. John Holway, *Blackball Stars: Negro League Pioneers* (Westport, CT: Meckler, 1988), p. 32.

4. Pittsburgh *Courier,* May 4, 1940.

5. Frazier, *Negro in the United States,* pp. 190-94.

6. William Brashler, *Josh Gibson: A Life in the Negro Leagues* (New York: Harper & Row, 1978), pp. 97-100.

7. John Holway, *Voices from the Great Black Baseball Leagues,* revised ed. (New York: Da Capo Press, 1992), p. 195.

8. Frazier, *Negro in the United States,* p. 611.

9. Ibid., p. 607.

10. Abram L. Harris, *The Negro as Capitalist* (Philadelphia: The American Academy of Political and Social Science, 1936), p. 169.

11. Pittsburgh *Courier,* Oct. 24, 1936.

12. John Holway, *Black Diamonds: Life in the Negro Leagues from the Men Who Lived It* (Westport, CT: Meckler, 1989), p. 67.

13. Donn Rogosin, *Invisible Men: Life in the Negro Baseball Leagues* (New York: Athenaem, 1987), p. 77.

14. Langston Hughes, "My Early Days in Harlem," in *The Negro Since Emancipation,* ed. Harvey Wish (Englewood Cliffs, NJ: Prentice-Hall, 1964), p. 107.

15. Rogosin, *Invisible Men,* p. 68.

16. Effa Manley and Leon Herbert Hardwick, *Negro Baseball . . . Before Integration* (Chicago: Adams Press, 1976), pp. 40-41.

17. Allen Richardson, "Retrospective Look," p. 192.

18. Holway, *Black Diamonds,* p. 65.

19. Ibid., p. 66; John Holway, *Voices,* p. 320.

20. Manley and Hardwick, *Negro Baseball,* p. 43.

21. Holway, *Black Diamonds,* pp. 65-66.

22. Pittsburgh *Courier,* June 15, 1935.

23. Manley and Hardwick, *Negro Baseball,* pp. 46-47.

24. New York *Age,* June 29, 1935.

25. Manley and Hardwick, *Negro Baseball,* p. 47.

Chapter 3
The Team and the Town

New Jersey's cities had experienced their own black population boom during World War I, albeit on a smaller scale than true metropolises such as New York. Between 1910 and 1930, the state's black population increased 134 percent, to 208,828, giving New Jersey a larger percentage of black population than any other Northeastern or Midwest state.

Even compared to the overall black growth rate in New Jersey, Newark's progress was exceptional. Nearly 39,000 blacks, almost one-fifth of those in the entire state, lived in Newark in 1930, although the city's total population of 442,000 was only about 11 percent of the state's. By the 1940 census, 7,000 more black residents had been counted, while the city's total population had actually decreased a bit, to a little less than 430,000. The present-day status of Newark as a predominantly black city was far from being achieved, but even then the black portion of the community was substantial, even among the city's welter of Western and Eastern European immigrant groups.

Here, too, it was the rural South that had provided the people, and the Great War the impetus, for the boom in the black population. The Northern New Jersey area, located in part directly on New York Harbor and otherwise tied to it by rivers and railroads, saw its already notable industrial base greatly increased by the demands of equipping the American Expeditionary Force which went to Europe in 1918. Newark's location on the Passaic River and the labor force provided by the influx of Irish, Germans, Italians, Russians, and Poles made it an ideal manufacturing location. It had a "vaunted reputation for making almost everything."[1] Even before the war, local boosters had named Newark the "City of Opportunity."

But while wartime demand grew, the war itself had closed down much European immigration, and some newcomers were even going home to fight for their native countries. This led to active recruitment of blacks in the South. They were glad to head north for jobs that, even though on the lowest rungs of the economic and social ladder in New Jersey, represented great improvement over their present situations.

However, the opportunities thus provided to blacks and others who came for the work also created serious social problems. The main one, which affected nearly everyone to some extent, was the population density. The city was relatively small in land area, and as it grew, it became a decidedly tight fit. The city's planning commission had stated in 1915 that "the residential possibilities in Newark have nearly reached their limit." But then 50,000 to 100,000 new war workers were added, and things got so bad that in 1919 the city government put up a tent colony for hundreds who had no other place to live.

But although the war and the prosperous 1920s provided jobs, and although Newark was a far cry from the South, there was no mistaking it for a land of equality, either.

The 1930 census revealed that of about 20,500 adult blacks in Newark who had jobs, 7,500 of them, or well over a third, were employed as domestics or in other types of personal service. While there were slightly more than that number working in manufacturing or mechanical industries, that total masked a truer reality—although black males held almost 10 percent of those types of jobs in the city, they represented a full third of the common laborers, and only 16 of 6,632 were trade apprentices. The 1,111 black women in those types of jobs likewise held unpromising, low-paying jobs making cigars and cheap clothing.[2]

Thus set up for a fall by the white economic structure, the black population of Newark saw its fortunes plummet farther than most groups when the Depression pulled the rug out from under everyone. Those who had been categorized, fairly or not, as being the least likely to succeed were, of course, among the first let go and the ones left jobless the longest when businesses shrank. Although Newark's black population had increased by 7,000 persons between the censuses of 1930 and 1940, the 13,308 males who reported having jobs in 1930 had shrunk to 7,990 ten years later. In the early 1930s, when the Depression was deepest, blacks represented one-third of all relief cases in the city, although they made up only one-twelfth of Newark's population.[3]

The combination of economic discrimination and the city's chronic housing shortage resulted in the shoehorning of a great portion of the black population into the less-desirable sections of the city. Newark at the time was divided for governing purposes into 16 wards. In 1920 its black residents were so dispersed around the city that no more than 18 percent of them lived in any one ward, and they did not account for more than 11 percent of the population in any one ward.

But this changed rapidly. One particular section, the Third Ward, an area mostly occupying a hill just west of Broad Street, the city's main thoroughfare, became increasingly decrepit and increasingly black at the same time. The Third was a mix of housing and businesses that were mostly retail stores and other small enterprises. Its overall residential population actually decreased from 1920 to 1940, while at the same time its black population grew. By 1930 almost 12,000 blacks, fully 30 percent of the city's total, lived on "The Hill" in the ward, making it the only ward where blacks were near (45 percent) to being the dominant race. In 1940, there were 16,352 blacks in the Third Ward, more than a third of the city's total and 63 percent of the ward's population.

In 1938, the city's health department reported that the Third Ward's 2,010 dwellings, mostly wood frame buildings, were crammed into an area of only about 275 acres, at about 95 residents per acre. With very few owner-occupied residences, it appeared that landlords were not investing much in their properties, since only 32 new buildings had been built there in the 15 years since 1923. Fifty-four percent of the homes were found to be at least in need of major repairs, and a fifth of those, most of them occupied, ought to have been closed, they were in such bad shape.

To John T. Cunningham, a Newark historian and former newspaperman, the reason for the Third Ward's homes' decrepitude was obvious: "They were built to be slums, back in the 1860s and 1870s when it was perfectly permissible to crowd new immigrants."

Stark tragedy could lurk in such conditions, since the buildings were often firetraps. A 1945 blaze on Broome Street killed a black father, his 4-year-old son, and his 3-year-old daughter. They lived and died in a "dilapidated, frame building, the only exits being a narrow, winding stairway—boxed in between two houses—and a rickety fire escape." One of the partners in the real estate company that owned the building told a reporter his firm had spent $90 on repairs in the 18 years they had owned the apartments, but could not recall if there had ever been a city fire inspection there.[4]

The city health department's answer to this mess was to continue to try to enforce capacity restrictions on the tenants to improve conditions in the ward, although the blacks living there had no place else to go. They also had no political clout to get conditions improved. Although Newark had wards, its commission form of city government provided only for commissioners elected at large, so the black vote was consistently diluted to the point of impotency.

White landlords often gouged their black tenants, and although a rented house or apartment occupied by a black family was much less likely to have an indoor bath, and although the median black family income in 1931 was little more than half of that earned by a white family, rents were nearly the same.

The usually bland columns of federal census data tabulated for Newark in 1940 contain a section that sums up the housing situation. Eighty-six percent of white tenant families had gas stoves (as opposed to wood, kerosene, or other less efficient, less-safer types), while only 28 percent of black tenants had them. Forty-nine percent of the white apartments contained refrigerators, but only 14 percent of the black places did. Similar comparisons for owner-occupied dwellings would have been meaningless, since there were only 388 black-owned homes in the entire city.[5]

The New Jersey *Herald-News,* one of the black weeklies published in Newark, claimed in 1939 that the status of its race in that city could be summed up thusly:

> Newark, with the largest colored population in the State, has the lowest average income, the less percentage employed in governmental work, and has no physicians or nursing students in its public-supported hospital, the largest percentage of houses unfit for habitation and is shockingly deprived of representation on policy-fixing boards.[6]

Lower-paying jobs and bad housing were only the quantifiable elements of racial discrimination. New Jersey before World War II gained the reputation among its black residents as a highly segregated state, known to them as "the Georgia of the North."[7] In more rural areas of the state, where blacks worked as migrant farm laborers, they were sometimes violently mistreated. In the summer of 1939, a group of about fifteen whites rousted seven black migrant hands out of their shack on a potato farm near Trenton and terrorized them at gunpoint. The black press did not allow the incident to be easily forgotten. This led to a series of Congressional hearings the following summer which documented conditions that included Southern black farmers being enticed north by promises of high pay, then being given as little as $2 a week in wages and forced to live in abandoned chicken houses when they reached the New Jersey farms.

A subtler incident occurred in Trenton in 1941, when law-enforcement authorities seeking to solve the "Duck Island murders," a series of nighttime shootings in a lovers' lane, came to believe that the killer might be a black man. Based on this supposition alone, the local prosecutor used driver's license records to send postcards to 1,500 black males, inviting them to stop by his office. Those who complied were questioned about the case and about any firearms they might own, and finally were requested to allow themselves to be fingerprinted, all just because of their skin color.

To be fair, Newark had no exceptional record of violence or flagrant official discrimination against its black citizens. Also, a good part of the separateness between whites and blacks was accounted for by strong neighborhood ties, as the various ethnic and racial groups in the city tended to live and socialize together. Still, the city was clearly segregated. New Jersey had a civil rights law on its books since 1921, but a survey eleven years later found that black people's "personal privileges are increasingly more limited. Segregation instead of lessening has increased." [8]

This was as true in Newark as anywhere in the state. Public swimming pools were completely closed to blacks until 1932, and thereafter open to them only during certain hours, when whites were not present. The YMCA, Salvation Army, and Boy and Girl Scouts were some of the public organizations that maintained separate, and often unequal, facilities for whites and blacks. The city's municipal hospital was closed to blacks, as was its medical staff. This may have contributed to morbid statistics such as a soaring tuberculosis death rate (as high as 700 per 100,000 for youths between 15 and 19, about 15 times that of their white peers), and a reported 36 percent infant mortality rate.

Blacks who lived in the Newark area in those days recall the subtleties of segregation, such as having to sit in the balcony or in the very back of a movie theater and being served out of a paper cup instead of a glass when going into a white-run bar. Eddie Wilkerson, who grew up in neighboring East Orange, remembered that "they had an ice cream place on Central Avenue called Delcrest and they had big ice cream cones, but the blacks had to take them out. We couldn't sit there and eat them." Monte Irvin, one of the Eagles' best players, grew up in adjacent Orange. He recalls being in a group of young blacks denied service in a restaurant right around the corner from Orange High School, from which they had graduated that very evening: "Kinda spoiled our night, you know."

Connie Woodruff, a retired black journalist raised in the city, points out that while blacks could get jobs in the city administration, hiring was stratified by color: "All the garbage collectors, the guys who throw the cans, were black, but the truck drivers were white. The first black garbage truck driver [who was not hired until 1949] became a celebrity overnight."

The discrimination was by no means a figment of blacks' imaginations. John Cunningham, who worked for the Newark *Evening News,* the city's major daily paper, recalls that one day he was working as a desk man, taking the details of a classic human interest story over the telephone from another reporter:

> A child had been left in a church, had been there two or three days. I turned to the managing editor and said, "there's a good story coming in on a kid abandoned in a church."
>
> He said, "Black or white?"
>
> I said, "Black."
>
> He said, "forget it."

But to stress this version of black life in Newark in the 1930s and 1940s is to do a great disservice to the time and place and the people who lived there, for they also recall a good side to black life in the city.

Although Irvin remembers the area's segregation, his primary recollection of Newark is that it was "just a wonderful city. A lot of the big stores were there and it was very clean and it was just first rate." For a youngster, "a good outing was to just get on a bus and go to Newark and do some shopping, or to go to Newark to the theater or for some amusement or go down to see a baseball game at Ruppert Stadium."

The Newark Irvin and others remember is one where blacks might have been poorer than comparable white families, but where they had a sense of belonging to a safe and stable community. Benjamin Hawkins, Jr., who grew up in Newark, recalled that although people struggled to make ends meet in his neighborhood, "the mothers and fathers were dedicated. They believed in authority, the policemen and the teachers and all that."

Connie Woodruff remembers Newark as a comfortable place . . .

> . . . a small, big city. First of all, it was a safe place to live, one could walk the streets in the middle of the night without being knocked in the head. Second of all, by then people were working, even at low-paying jobs. Very few people were on relief in the 1940s.
>
> There were trees in the city, there's nothing like that now. There was the continuity of families. You knew your next door neighbor, kids were not as destructive, it was not a permissive society. So it was a much better place, compared to today, when you can't sit in your house without fear. Even the politicians were better to you than they are today.
>
> The YMCAs were segregated, but we never thought of it that way. The schools were better—when you graduated from high school in those days, it was like graduating from a community college. The neighborhood taverns were places you could go to and borrow money, like the corner grocery store, not just some guy who just wanted to take your money. It was the extended family atmosphere that existed in the city. I'll always have a soft spot in my heart for Newark, having grown up there.

The black community's social structure was tied together by its churches, a number of adult social clubs, and, for the youngsters, the black YMCA on Court Street. As Connie Woodruff remembers it, "if I was going to a dance and it wasn't at the Y, my mother wouldn't let me go. The perception was that they were God fearing, nice people running the Y, so your kids could go there and be safe."

Despite existing virtually in the shadow of New York City, the East Coast center of entertainment for both whites and blacks, music and theater thrived in Newark. In addition to the eager patronage of the area's residents, the nearness to Manhattan may also have provided an advantage, for when periodic official vice crackdowns put a damper on the good times in the bigger city, business got better in Newark, only a short drive from the George Washington Bridge.

Black entertainment included a vaudeville theater, the Orpheum, and so many clubs in downtown Newark and the neighboring towns that one of the black weeklies ran a regular entertainment column, "On the Sepia Main Stem." According to Connie Woodruff, who played piano with a local group prior to her journalism career, "there were hundreds of places to go." Two enduring stars of popular music, vocalist Sarah Vaughan and stride piano player Willie "The Lion" Smith, hailed from Newark, and in addition to dozens of other entertainers with enthusiastic local followings, big out-of-town names played the city.

In the summer of 1942, for example, the Lincoln Civic Association, one of the panoply of black community organizations, organized a series of outdoor concerts at Laurel Garden, a night spot on Springfield Avenue, that featured literally the biggest names in black popular music, including the big bands of Jimmie Lunceford and Earl "Fatha" Hines and singer Ella Fitzgerald. Downtown at the Adams Theater on Branford Place, Cab Calloway, Lionel Hampton, Fletcher Henderson, Count Basie, and Fats Waller were all featured at one time or another.

Blacks in Newark, while always up against reminders of their separateness, could also see much evidence of the potential of their togetherness. When the Baltimore *Afro-American* newspaper established a New Jersey edition in Newark in 1941, the city had three black weeklies. They all energetically mined the two mother lodes of black news—what blacks were being denied by whites and what they were accomplishing in terms of "firsts" in American society.

Although they could never attain direct representation in a city governmental system stacked against them, the area's blacks did send some of their own to the state legislature. Assemblyman Walter Hargraves led the founding of the State Temporary Commission on the Condition of the Urban Colored Population, the activities and investigations of which actively led to the eventual passage of a strong state civil rights law in the late 1940s.

Blacks were consistently represented on the city's Housing Authority, an important appointed board on which to have a say, given the crying need for better housing on "The Hill." The Urban League's Newark branch was strong, acting as the blacks' Depression-era social welfare agency when the mainstream agencies would provide no help. There were several groups formed to specifically fight discrimination. Among them was the Interracial Council, composed of both black leaders and whites who joined them in opposition to the injustices of the times. The council carried on an eight-year-long effort beginning in 1938 which finally saw blacks admitted to the City Hospital medical and nursing staffs.

But in the mid-1930s, Newark had both black and white sets of most important institutions, the schools (with mostly white teachers) being one of the few exceptions. Among the varied groups were two sets of baseball fans. The city already had a good white team, the Newark Bears, a New York Yankee minor league farm club. The Bears had finished first in the International League three straight seasons between 1932 and 1934 and were perennially strong. In fifteen seasons through 1946 they never finished out of the league's first division, and won seven pennants. Now, with the Eagles open for business in Newark, black fans also had a team of great potential.

The Eagles of early 1936 performed much as they had back in Brooklyn—they cruised along in the middle of the league standings for the season's first half, never climbing too high or falling too low. The loss of three of four games to the Homestead Grays in Pittsburgh over the Memorial Day weekend killed any hopes of winning the first-half pennant race, and the Eagles finished fourth of six clubs, with a 15 and 18 won-loss record. The Manleys' club rose to second in the second half of 1936, winning 15 and losing only 11. From the 1937 season through 1941, the Eagles won more often than they lost. Although first place continued to elude the team, in the seven half- or whole-season schedules for which standings were published (the National League abandoned its split schedule in 1939 and 1940 and never got around to giving the 1937 second-half standings to the black newspapers), Newark finished second four times and third twice.

The Eagles spent most of the prewar period chasing the Homestead Grays, the team that had so soundly thrashed them in their very first game back in Brooklyn. The Grays won both halves of the 1937 and 1938 seasons (word of their finishing first in the second half of 1937 slipped out, even if the rest of the standings did not), won the full-season schedules of 1939 and 1940, and won the first-half pennant in 1941 before declining to fourth place in the second half. Even so, they beat the New York Cubans in a championship playoff and bounced back to form throughout the war years by winning both halves of each season until 1946.

This string of successes for the Grays made life in the Negro National League for all other teams an ongoing battle to see who was second best. The young Eagles' string of high finishes qualified them as about the best second-best club in the league.

By 1937 the Manleys had put together the "Million Dollar Infield" of first baseman George "Mule" Suttles, second baseman Dick Seay, shortstop Willie Wells, and third baseman Dandridge. Although the value of the combination's nickname may have been inflated by its enthusiastic followers, it sprang from the very reasonable estimation that, if the men had been white, their contracts would have commanded a great deal of money from white major league owners. The four men actually played together only two years, in 1937 and 1938, before Dandridge left the team to play in Mexico, but they are linked in the Negro leagues' oral tradition by their membership in that infield combination.

Suttles, more than six feet tall and weighing more than 200 pounds, was one of the legendary home-run threats of the Negro leagues. Catcher Josh Gibson and first baseman Buck Leonard, the power-hitting mainstays of the ever-victorious Grays, were called the Babe Ruth and Lou Gehrig of black baseball. If that was so, then Suttles was not a long step below them, capable of just as impressive slugging feats, although not quite as often.

When Suttles came to bat, fans used to encourage him to show his home-run style by shouting "Kick, Mule." In the eleventh inning of the 1935 East-West All Star Game, Suttles, then with the Chicago American Giants, delivered his most famous kick. His 475-foot, three-run homer in Chicago's Comiskey Park produced an 11-8 win for the West squad.

Seay, a Northern New Jersey native from West New York, was a light hitter, but a fantastic fielder. Except for three years in the Army during World War II, he played black baseball steadily from 1926 through 1947.

Wells, who also later managed the Eagles, had an even longer career, from 1924 through 1948. He lost no years to the war, although he did leave the Eagles twice for a total of four years to play in the Mexican League, which often offered higher salaries and better living conditions for black players. Available records show him hitting more than .300 four times and just missing that level by four percentage points another season during his six full seasons with Newark. Despite not having the powerful throwing arm that aided most great shortstops, Wells was regarded as defensively outstanding. Many black baseball historians who fervently believe Negro leaguers are woefully underrepresented in the Baseball Hall of Fame have Wells on their personal lists of those who should be admitted.

There has been some justice for the Negro leaguers, however, and Ray Dandridge was elected to the Hall of Fame in 1987. Fans and sportswriters called Dandridge "Hooks" because he seemed to rake in most of the balls that came his way. "The best way I can describe it," teammate Monte Irvin once said of Dandridge's fielding, "is that he played third base the way Willie Mays played the outfield." Dandridge was also a regular .300 hitter in the Negro leagues, and in 1951, at age 38, he hit .324 in the American Association, a step below the majors, after the color line fell in baseball.

The outfield was not as settled over this period, but the dependable Ed Stone could usually be found out there, as could Lenny Pearson. Pearson grew up in the Newark area and started a twelve-year professional career with the Eagles in 1938. He played with the team all but his final season, and had a .312 lifetime batting average. Pearson was versatile in the field, and was often the third baseman during 1939-1941, the first years Dandridge defected to Mexico.

Although Jimmie Crutchfield, who had a well-deserved reputation for excellent fielding, played centerfield for a few years in the late 1930s, the job of anchoring the outfield eventually fell to Irvin, another of those who could have been the best player ever to put on an Eagle uniform. A four-sport star at nearby Orange High School, Irvin officially joined the team out of Lincoln College in Philadelphia in 1939 (he had already been playing part time under the name of a friend, Jimmie Nelson, to protect his college amateur athletic eligibility). Irvin came to the Eagles as a shortstop,

> But Willie Wells came over to me one day, and he said "You know, we already have a shortstop on the club. I'm the shortstop, and I can't be moved, so if you want to play regularly, your position is right out there," and he pointed to centerfield.

Irvin spent 1943 playing in Mexico and 1944 and most of 1945 in the Army, but otherwise his Negro league career was spent exclusively with his hometown team. He had a lifetime Negro National League batting average of .324 and hit with power, but his black baseball career was shortened when in 1949, at age 30, the New York Giants signed him for a second career in the newly integrated major leagues. He was promoted to the Giants from the minors before the end of that same season, and played in the white big leagues until 1956. He was later a special assistant to the commissioner of baseball and a member of the committee that picked the first group of Negro leaguers for the Hall of Fame, taking his own place there in 1973.

Leon Ruffin, a light hitter but excellent defensive player, and former Newark Dodger Johnnie Hayes were the regular catchers until July of the 1939 season, when Abe Manley traded Ruffin to the Philadelphia Stars for one of the legendary catchers of the Negro leagues. Raleigh "Biz" Mackey was only about two weeks shy of his fourty-second birthday, an absolute graybeard as players' careers usually went. But Biz was probably not feeling his age, since he went on to play in the Negro leagues until he was 50.

The inability to assemble a thoroughly reliable pitching staff had been a drawback in Brooklyn in 1935, and continued to be a concern of the Manleys for the next several years. They had a great advantage, of course, in Leon Day, the kid from Baltimore who was a manager's dream. Day was an outstanding pitcher who could also hit and fill in at outfield and infield positions when it was not his turn to pitch. The best partial records assembled show Day as the winner of more than 70 percent of his games as an Eagle, including two occasions when he led the National League in wins. At bat, he had a lifetime .292 average, and he is also on most short lists of Negro leaguers who ought to be in the Hall of Fame.

In the spring of 1938, Abe scouted a Lakeland, Florida, native, lefthander Jimmie Hill, who was found pitching batting practice for white major league teams during Florida spring training. Hill had spent 1937 playing for a black team, the Albany, N.Y., Black Sox, in the otherwise white semiprofessional Twilight League. He had returned to Albany and had made the league's all-star team at midseason when Abe enticed him to Newark. Although he was only about five feet six, Hill could throw hard. His career unfortunately included a good deal of time lost to injuries, but when he was healthy, he was an important member of the Eagle pitching staff.

Another Lincoln College athlete came to the Eagles with Monte Irvin in 1939. Max Manning was also a New Jersey boy, from Pleasantville, near Atlantic City. Manning was a tall, thin, bespectacled righthanded pitcher who became a regular starter the year after joining the team, winning 11 and losing 6 in his second season. He went on to have even better years after that, showing up in the starting rotation every subsequent year the team was in Newark, except for three years in the Army during the war.

Len Hooker, another long-term acquisition for the pitching staff, joined up in 1940, remaining with the club until it left Newark. Bob Evans, who had been the Newark Dodgers' most dependable starter, continued on the Eagles staff until traded in early 1939.

The other mainstay of the pitching staff before the war was Terris McDuffie, one of the most colorful players the Eagles ever had. McDuffie had pitched briefly with the team in Brooklyn and became a regular starting pitcher in Newark in 1936. Soon he became the Eagles' number-one pitcher. He was depended upon so extensively that on July 4, 1938, after pitching a complete game victory against the New York Black Yankees in the first game of a doubleheader, he came back to relieve the second game starter with no one out in the first inning and pitched nine more innings for his second win of the afternoon.

He called himself "The Great" McDuffie, and while the New Jersey *Herald News* once lauded him as "Negro baseball's Dizzy Dean," in the same story the paper allowed as how he was an "eccentric star." [9] But "The Great" McDuffie was, in fact, very good—he won almost two-thirds of his recorded games over his eleven-year career.

Counting Ben Taylor and George Giles in Brooklyn and then William Bell and Fred "Tex" Burnett for a year each in Newark, the Eagles had gone through four field managers in three and one-half years, trying to reach their potential. Managing the Eagles for Abe Manley was never a job that had a lot of security. Effa later admitted that she did not know why her husband was continually dismissing managers, but attributed it to his "striving for perfection" But in July, 1938, Abe Manley hired an old Newark favorite, Dick Lundy. Lundy had been in charge of the Newark Dodgers in 1934 and 1935 and had been the team's regular shortstop. He then played a little infield for the Eagles in 1937 at the end of an illustrious playing career.

As far as Oliver "Butts" Brown, the *Herald-News* sports editor, was concerned, hiring Lundy was a stroke of genius on the Manleys' part, since "he has the personality, poise, intelligence and baseball acumen to compare with the best in baseball, be they white or black."[10] Lundy managed the team until August, 1941, when ill health forced him to retire, and the large and venerable Mackey took over in the first of his two stretches as Eagle manager.

By 1939, when a reported 10,000 people showed up for opening day against the Philadelphia Stars, Newark blacks had become great fans of the Eagles. Anyone who knows the affinity a community can develop for its baseball team can understand Max Manning's description of this relationship: "The Eagles were to [black] Newark what the Dodgers were to Brooklyn."

As the team on the field grew stronger, so did the relationship between the club and the community that supported it, until it far transcended the previous peripatetic history of Newark and black baseball that had existed before the Eagles came. If Abe Manley's continuous quest for the best players and managers built the team on the field, it was Effa's equally important role to establish the complementary relationship in which Newark helped the Eagles and the Eagles helped Newark.

She made sure that the team had an image of upholding the black community's best standards. Even if they had only won now and then, the Eagles might still have had a place in black Newark as fund-raisers and publicizers of the community's charities and helping organizations.

Effa, a member of the National Association for the Advancement of Colored People since before the Citizens League for Fair Play, and at one time treasurer of the New

Jersey NAACP, used game days to raise funds for the organization. The New Jersey *Afro-American* newspaper recorded a collection of $143 by the local NAACP Youth Council at a May 16, 1943, game, and the local chapter's annual fund drive (for which Effa was a co-chairman) was kicked off with a $215 collection at 1945's opening day. On opening day in 1946, volunteers with NAACP banners draped from their shoulders canvassed 8,500 fans there for the Eagles game with the Philadelphia Stars.

Other owners did this, too, but her NAACP fund-raising tactics could be quite reminiscent of the forthright Blumstein Department Store negotiator who linked young black girls turning to prostitution to a lack of retail jobs. At one point she ran a "Stop Lynching" campaign at Ruppert, selling NAACP-sponsored buttons with that hard-hitting slogan for a dollar apiece (and getting a newspaper publicity photo taken while selling one to the Newark mayor).

The Eagles worked especially hard for the institutions that promoted the welfare of Northern New Jersey blacks. As a result of one such connection, the Negro leagues exhibit at the Baseball Hall of Fame in Cooperstown, N.Y., is graced by a banner given the team by the Newark Student Camp Fund in recognition of the Eagles' efforts on its behalf.

With blacks effectively barred from the medical professions, a black hospital, the Booker T. Washington Community Hospital, was established in the city. On August 20, 1940, the Eagles played the first of periodic benefit games to raise money for new medical equipment. "This hospital is the only one in the State offering an opportunity for colored physicians and nurses to get hospital training," Effa's advance publicity noted. "This is a civic responsibility no one should shirk and everyone should be proud to meet."

The team played several games to benefit black Elks lodges, a major part of urban black social life, and also honored special achievements by individuals. John Borican was a black track star from nearby Bridgeton, N.J., who had held six world records and had won several national track titles before tragically dying of pernicious anemia in 1942 at the age of 29.

But while still at the height of his career, on August 31, 1941, he was guest of honor at "John Borican Day" at the stadium. The Manleys staged one of the Negro leagues' most attractive types of events, a "four-team double-header." Instead of the home team and a visiting squad playing each other twice, two different teams played in each game, thus exposing black baseball fans to twice as many of the well known players that they hungered to see. There were added attractions in the form of "track and field" events for the players, including a 100-yard dash competition—the winning player would race Borican. The managers of the four teams, perhaps in recognition of their burdens of command, were to compete in a wheelbarrow race.

The Eagles, once well established as an authentic sports fixture in New Jersey, were also in demand for fund-raising outside the Newark area. In 1939 Edward White, of the Urban League in New York City, wrote Effa, seeking the team for a benefit game at Yankee Stadium. Despite the existence of black teams in New York, White wrote, "we want your team as the home team because we believe it to be the most substantial organization in this section . . . also because we believe you personally interested in the work of the Urban League."

The team was also sought after to raise funds for non-black groups, such as a 1941 game in nearby Jersey City with the well-known white barnstorming team, the House of David, to benefit the local Jewish Community Center. Even when it was not playing baseball, the Eagle organization could do some good. In 1941 Effa loaned the team bus to the New Jersey Commission for the Blind's office in Newark to take some clients on an outing.

Perhaps the most interesting tie Effa forged between her team and the community was with its black youth. The Eagles had a regular "Knothole Gang" organization, which derived its name from the old-time trick of watching games for free through the holes in the pine board fences surrounding early ballparks. As run by the Eagles, it copied the practice of the white Newark Bears, allowing youngsters free admission to games. "If I had a dime to ride the bus to Ruppert Stadium and back, I went," recalls Melvin Sanders, a Newark youngster at the time. "If we didn't have a nickel, we used to ride on the back of the buses to get there, and jump off if we saw a policeman."

In 1942, Effa organized an Eagle-sponsored youth team, the Newark Cubs, on which Sanders played until he was fourteen. "She was one of the few blacks who had a little money, and she put some back into the community," he said. "Kids were robbin' and stealin', they didn't have enough to do." Sanders remembers the Cubs as "an arm of the Eagles—we were proud to be a part of the organization."

She and Abe bought uniforms and equipment for the team, while the players had to provide their own shoes and baseball gloves. They played other youth teams and eventually became the only black squad in a Newark league. There were two aspects of the Manleys' involvement with the Cubs that perfectly mirrored their roles in adult baseball. According to Sanders, they often attended the Cubs games, which were played on weekends, and when they did make these public appearances, "she was out front, while he was supportive, and took a back seat."

Effa was always concerned about doing things in a businesslike fashion, with the public impact of the players' actions always in mind. Each Cub had to sign a receipt for his uniform, which came "complete with belt, socks and cap." Furthermore, the boys had to acknowledge that:

> I promise to keep care of the suit, wash it when it gets dirty, or when the Coach tells me to, and bring it back to Mrs. Manley clean for safe keeping at the end of the season, or when I am asked for it. I promise to conduct myself in a sportsmanlike manner at all times on the ball field, and to keep in good physical condition by doing any exercise the Coach demands. I will be punctual for ball games, and will try in every way to set a high standard for boys my age.

The best way to appreciate the Eagles, as Melvin Sanders points out, was to go see them play. While the team's practice of scheduling many games with white semi-professional New Jersey teams guaranteed that it would appear at several places around the state in the course of any given season, Ruppert Stadium in Newark was the site of its most important home games against its Negro National League competitors. Playing at Ruppert meant that the best black players, the Negro leaguers, were showcased in the ballpark of a top-flight white professional team, giving appropriate, if borrowed, status to the black game.

Writer and poet Amiri Baraka recognized this. He recalls in his autobiography that "the specialist feeling was when my father took me down to Ruppert Stadium some Sundays to see the Newark Eagles, the black pro team. Very little in my life was as heightened (in anticipation and reward) for me as that." [11]

Ruppert Stadium sat in the midst of an industrial area near the Passaic River called the "Ironbound," so called because of the railroad tracks that defined its boundaries. It was primarily the home of European blue-collar immigrants who gave the neighborhood a flavor quite different from the black sections of town.

Baraka says that going to an Eagles game there, on almost foreign soil, emphasized the special quality of the experience:

> But coming down through that would heighten my sense because I could dig I would soon be standing in that line to get in, with my old man. But lines of all black people! Dressed up like they would for going to the game, in those bright lost summers. Full of noise and identification slapped greetings over and around folks. Cause after all in that town of 300,000 that 20 to 30 percent of the population had a high recognition rate for each other . . . The Newark Eagles would have your heart there on the field . . . (These were) legitimate black heroes. And we were intimate with them in a way and they were

> extensions of all of us, there, in a way that the Yankees and Dodgers and what not could never be![12]

Attending Eagle games at Ruppert, especially the Sunday afternoon doubleheaders against other black teams, was as much a social as a sporting occasion. Connie Woodruff, who also went to Eagle games with her father, then later wrote feature stories about the team when she became a newspaperwoman, remembers Sundays at the stadium as "a combination of two things, an opportunity for all the women to show off their Sunday finery, and also the once a week family affair."

> People used to come to the games with big baskets of chicken, potato salad, all the things you would have on a picnic. The women would come with flowery dresses, it reminded me of the English going to Ascot. The flowery dresses, the big hats, the hair done just right. I'm sure all those women didn't understand baseball, but it was the thrill of being there, being seen, seeing who they could see. The men who escorted them were dressed to the nines, and these women would stroll in on their arms. Who was with whom was the talk of the next week.

On opening day in 1939, the effect of all these colorfully dressed people on rookie pitcher James Walker, fresh from a semipro team in New York City, was both beautiful and intimidating: "It looked like a big cloud of flowers of different colors, and I was petrified. I had never seen this many people at one location at one time."

Eagle games were so much the expected place to be that they functioned as an excuse for some men who just wanted to get away from home and have a few drinks. John M. Dabney, Jr., of Newark (the son of one of the first black professional players in the 1880s) remembers coming out of the stadium after a game and going into a bar across the street, only to have one of the clientele quiz him on what he'd just seen a stone's throw away. "Who won, buddy?" Dabney was asked. "I got to go home and tell my wife who won. I didn't see nothing."

The relationship between the Eagles and their audience was best demonstrated by opening day, each season's rite of renewal. Effa, who handled the program, invited local and state dignitaries, who were usually white. But beginning with the opening ceremonies, which usually featured a black school band, sometimes professional entertainers from Harlem night spots and always an American flag color guard (the Attucks Guard from Newark's black American Legion post), the pageantry was almost entirely by and for the black community.

It frequently celebrated black aspirations for equality. As the country began beefing up its armed forces in 1940 to be prepared for the onset of war, the black press hotly debated two questions about Negroes and the military. One was whether or not black servicemen would actually be allowed to fight for their country, as opposed to being Navy kitchen help or Army ditchdiggers. The other was whether their invariably segregated units would be led by black officers (the Army reported in 1941 that of 88,000 regular, reserve, and National Guard officers, only 259 were black, and only six of them were Regular Army men).[13]

A result of black leaders' pressure on Washington was the mobilization of the all-black, black-led 372nd Infantry Regiment at Fort Dix, N.J. Effa's subsequent response was to invite the entire regiment, 2,500 strong, to attend opening day in 1941, and to have Mayor Meyer C. Ellenstein declare an official "372nd Day."

In 1943, Effa extended an invitation to the black members of the Free French forces at Fort Dix, organized to help retake their country. Her invitation also included a handwritten postscript to Lieutenant Beauregard, the unit commander, allowing that if there was sufficient room, the white members would also be welcome.

The celebrity picked to throw out the ceremonial first ball from the grandstands was very often emblematic of black progress, particularly in sports. In 1941, Lt. Col. Alexander Stephens of the 372nd had the honors, but in other years track star Borican and boxers Henry Armstrong and Beau Jack officiated.

In 1942, the Manleys scored a definite public relations coup when heavyweight boxing champion Joe Louis, by any measure the most famous black athlete in America at the time, agreed to throw out the first ball. A week before the game, Louis had to cancel, due to the death of his trainer and close friend, Jack Blackburn. Effa was left to report to Louis that a moment of silence for "Chappie" Blackburn was observed, and "you could hear a pin drop in the stadium." Louis finally threw out a first ball for the Eagles in happier times for both him and the team, at the opening game of the 1946 Negro World Series between Newark and the Kansas City Monarchs.

Just before the home opener, when hope was stirred in fans' hearts by optimistic newspaper stories from spring training, club owners would reestablish ties to those with special relationships to the team by way of free season passes.

Effa used the passes not only to keep in favor with the leaders of the local black community, but also to acknowledge the Eagles' debt to baseball's past, which she apparently appreciated. A regular pass recipient was Ben Holmes, a resident of the neighboring town of Orange, who, like John Dabney, Jr.'s, father, had been a member of the original Cuban Giants in the 1880s.

The pass list could also be used to reward those outside the baseball world who could be of special service to the Eagles. Dr. Walter T. Darden, a local black physician who charged only half his usual fee for treating injured players, was on the pass list. So was the Rev. Charles C. Weathers of the Pilgrim Baptist Church, who had two Eagle players under his supervision as a state parole officer.

Negro league players were often special persons in their teams' black community. The combination of athletic fame and the exotic reputation of someone who traveled a lot made the players "models of excellence and achievement in communities where few rose above the mundane."[14] The young Eagles were thus admired in the essentially small-town world of Newark's black neighborhoods. James "Red" Moore, a first baseman for the team in 1936 and 1937, recalls that "when I was there, fans would recognize us more or less as celebrities." James Walker says that "to be an Eagle meant you could do no wrong."

Francis Matthews, a first baseman who came along in 1938, after Moore left, also remembers that "we were extremely popular," and recalls with a little embarrassment a particular show of fan support during a "Ladies' Night" promotion that he might have preferred to do without:

> I fielded a sharply hit ball, and tried to make a double play by throwing it to my right as I was running. But, I threw it over the shortstop's head at second, into left field. It was the first time in my career I got booed. As I was running back to the dugout, Mrs. Smith (the madam of a local house of prostitution who was there with several of her girls), stood up and shouted, "Don't worry, baby, we're all with you."

The fans' connection with the Eagles would continue after a home game at Ruppert ended, when the team and its closest followers repaired to the unofficial club headquarters, the Grand Hotel. The Grand was a two-story black hotel at West Market and Wickliffe streets. Although it was not very large, it was one of the few commercial lodging places for blacks in Newark. Several of the players boarded there during the season, and the bar and dining room on the first floor is etched in the memories of Eagle players.

To them, the Grand was a haven, providing the kind of relaxation that comes from completely belonging. Monte Irvin remembers that "it was so good, in spite of all the segregation. You know, we had a good time when we got together in the key places." To the fans, the hotel presented an opportunity to join the ball players' special circle. According to Matthews, women looking to make a connection with an unattached ball player would sit on one side of the crowded dining room and try to get the attention of players they had seen at the ballpark. If they didn't know a player's name, they would have him paged by his uniform number.

Baraka remembers his father taking him to the Grand as a teenager after Eagles' games, where

> the ball players and the slick people could meet. Everybody super-clean and highlifin, glasses jinkling with ice, black people's eyes sparklin and showin their teeth in the hippest way possible . . . The movies I dearly dug but you never got to go behind the screen and shake hands with the heroes. But at the Grand Hotel you could.[15]

In every dedicated baseball fan there lurks that desire to shake hands with the heroes and vicariously share in their heroism. This is why there are baseball fan clubs. But in the case of the Negro leagues, the connection between the black game and the fans ran deeper, down to strata that underlay what it meant to be black, shut out of white society, but with one's own exciting people and places. The connection was rarely as obvious and dramatic as in Bill Nunn's stories from Chicago in 1934, but everyday fans in places such as Newark felt it all the same, although they might express it differently.

For Benjamin Hawkins, Jr., seeing the Eagles was a way to let off the head of steam built up during long days of hard work that simply surviving required of blacks in the 1930s. "It was like an outlet, you know, see, because a lot of times [black fans] lost interest in the National and American League, because there wasn't any blacks playing in it . . . so all the attention was centered on [the Eagles]."

Before he became one of the fans' idols himself, Monte Irvin—as a youth growing up in nearby Orange—thought the meaning of black baseball to black working men was that it was "an inspiration for the waiters, the janitors, the maintenance guys. [They would say] 'Well, goddamn it, maybe there's some hope.' In other words it gave the black people something to cheer about."

For Baraka, adulthood brought extreme consciousness of the meaning of being black, resulting in his changing of his name from Leroi Jones. In that context he thinks of some of the comically subservient images of blacks promoted by popular entertainment of the 1940s, while the meaning of the Eagles and the Negro leagues is that

> It made us know that the Mantans and Stepin Fetchits and Birminghams were clowns—funny, but obviously used against us for some reason . . . (but) we knew, and we knew, that they wasn't us. We was NOT clowns and the Newark Eagles laid that out clear for anyone to see![16]

Notes

1. Kenneth T. and Barbara B. Jackson, "The Black Experience in Newark, the Growth of the Ghetto, 1870-1970," in *New Jersey Since 1860: New Findings and Interpretations,* ed. William C. Wright (Trenton: New Jersey Historical Commission, 1972), p. 44.

2. Ibid., p. 45; Clement A. Price, "The Beleaguered City As Promised Land: Black in Newark, 1917-1947," in *Urban New Jersey Since 1870,* ed. William C. Wright (Trenton: New Jersey Historical Commission, 1975), p. 27.

3. Jacksons, "The Black Experience," p. 46; John T. Cunningham, *Newark* (Newark: New Jersey Historical Society, 1966), p. 282.

4. New Jersey *Afro-American,* April 7, 1945.

5. Sixteenth Census of the United States, *Characteristics of the Population,* 2nd Series, New Jersey (1942).

6. New Jersey *Herald-News,* March 11, 1939.

7. Lee Hagan, with Larry A. Greene, Leonard Harris, and Clement A. Price, "New Jersey Afro-Americans: From Colonial Times to the Present," in *The New Jersey Ethnic Experience,* ed. Barbara Cunningham (Union City, NJ: William W. Wise & Co., 1977), p. 80.

8. Interracial Committee of the New Jersey Conference of Social Work, *The Negro in New Jersey* (New York: Negro Universities Press, 1969), p. 65.

9. New Jersey *Herald-News,* Aug. 20, 1938.

10. Ibid., July 23, 1938.

11. Imamu Amiri Baraka, *The Autobiography of Leroi Jones* (New York: Fruendlich, 1984), pp. 33-34.

12. Ibid., p. 34.

13. *Courier,* July 12, 1941.

14. William Donn Rogosin, "Black Baseball: The Life in the Negro Leagues," Ph.D. dissertation, University of Texas at Austin, May 1981, pp. 3-4.

15. Baraka, *Autobiography,* p. 35.

16. Ibid., p. 36.

Chapter 4
Getting to Be at Home

As Newark came to be a comfortable home for the Eagles, it also became one for the team's owners. The Manleys lived in Harlem for the first few years the team was in New Jersey, but in 1938 they moved to a large apartment block at 55 Somerset Street, on The Hill. In July, 1941, they bought a handsome three-story brick house nearby at 71 Crawford St., which was large enough to provide them with an office as well as a residence.

From those locations, as well as from Ruppert Stadium and the team's general offices in the densely populated black section (first next to a beauty parlor at 105 West Market Street, then by 1938 at 101 Montgomery Street), Effa and Abe pursued their goal of baseball entrepreneurship. She also pursued a role in Newark's black high society.

Abe was easily accepted into the fraternity of black baseball owners, partially because he was a man in a man's world. But he also obviously cared for the success of his team and was willing to put his own time and money into it. In January, 1937, just a little more than two years after starting the Eagles, Abe was elected treasurer of the National League. Although in later years he was to join his wife in opposing moves of the majority of other owners, he was almost always named a league officer.

Abe was also recognized by the other owners as a serious owner in a way that might have had the most impact on those businessmen. In the late 1930s, he was one of the National League owners with the most money invested in his team. However, Abe was not just a well-funded baseball dilettante. He had the last word on all the

Eagles' player acquisitions and frequently did his own scouting and signing of young ball players.

He was respected and liked by his players, who usually referred to him by his nickname, "Cap," acknowledging he was the "captain," or man in charge, of the organization. Despite their liking for him, though, many described him as being reserved and a bit distant. He always went with the team to its spring training site in the South and often accompanied the Eagles in the team bus on their far-flung travels, even though he was not always in good physical health and the travel must have been painful.

Abe, never a devotee of good conditioning and on the way to becoming overweight late in life, would ride in the bus's front seat, across from the driver. Former pitcher Max Manning recalls noticing Manley's ankles were often swollen far beyond their normal size. "I'd feel so sorry for him. It got to the point where I'd get in and look straight up the aisle, so I wouldn't have to look at his ankles."

Abe was game for the arduous bus trips, though, and never forgot that the goal of those barnstorming tours was to play as often as possible, to paying crowds. "He hated rain," Manning recalls. The tired players on the bus "would be praying for rain, and he was up there in front praying for sunshine."

Routine business affairs while the team traveled were handled by a road secretary. For many years that was the veteran official Eric Illidge, who performed the same touring duty in the winter for the Renaissance Big Five black basketball team from Harlem and sometimes went on the road with Earl "Fatha" Hines' orchestra. Illidge was so good at what he did that, Effa said, she had made Abe promise that if he outlived her, he would take Illidge in as a full partner to run the whole business side of the team.

Despite this excellent assistance, Abe frequently took on an administrative task that symbolized he was the boss. The players were entitled to a daily meal allowance, and when the team bus reached its destination and they would file off, Abe would distribute the dollar a day "meal money." He would systematically peel off a dollar bill for each man going past, making sure, as some of them remarked, that the bills didn't stick together so a player would inadvertently get two.

At home, when he was not at the ballpark, Abe could frequently be found at the team's office or his favorite hangout, Dan's Tavern on Wickliffe Street, entertaining himself by playing poker and drinking beer. It seemed to Jocko Maxwell, a black sportswriter who covered the Eagles, that "of 24 hours in a day, I bet he played cards for 16." But, although he was a man who liked drink and entertainment, had originally made his money in the illegal numbers business, and was accustomed to swearing when provoked, Abe also had a moralistic streak. According to Effa, he fired his manager, Raleigh "Biz" Mackey, after the Eagles won the Negro National League pennant and the Negro World Series in 1946 because Mackey drank too much in public in the Newark taverns, particularly around the younger players.

Abe had given himself the unlikely role of enforcer of morals among the players, particularly the younger ones. According to Fran Matthews, "he had the Jack Armstrong, All-American boy idea about the ballplayers—no drinkin', no smokin', no women. He'd say, 'I don't want any lovers on my ball club, you can sacrifice for five months.' It looked like he was going to cry when he saw a ballplayer with a girl."

Matthews learned about Abe's rules concerning women when, right out of high school in Cambridge, Massachusetts, he joined the team in Jacksonville for spring training in 1938:

> When we left there we went to Roanoke, Virginia. All the other guys, they ran the girls off from the bus, but I was talking to a girl. Abe said, "Matthews, get in the bus." She says, "Why?" He says to her, "I hope to see you again, never." She says, "I wasn't talking to you, you old buzzard."

But while it may have been overwhelmingly attractive for a team owner to exercise the dearly purchased privilege of hanging out with the team, that was not the successful way to run a baseball franchise. Considerable administrative duties awaited the owners in their offices, chores such as arranging games and pregame publicity, ordering sporting goods, and paying the bills.

In the Eagles' early years, Effa Manley perfectly complemented her husband by taking care of these matters (including, not incidentally, much of the work that went with Abe's league treasurer's job). But then, as she became more established in the Eagles' front office and the team's ties to the Northern New Jersey black community became more important, Abe could as easily have been said to have been supporting her.

When she collaborated on a book about the Negro leagues and interviewers came knocking on her door in the 1970s, Effa always deferred to her late husband as having been the leader of their partnership. In the book, for example, she and her co-author, sportswriter Leon Hardwick, rhapsodize about Abe as "a self made expert . . . an innovator . . . a genuine student of the game." [1]

But she could relax and let her ego exercise itself, too. In 1947 she told black sports columnist Sam Lacy how the management transition really worked:

> For the first two years, Abe wouldn't let me have a word to say. . . . Then it got to a place where he would let me make a suggestion or offer a criticism, and finally, right out of a clear sky one day, he said, "Honey, I think I'll let you take over now."
>
> It thrilled me, but I wasn't sure of myself. I was scared I'd do something wrong, but he soon got rid of that fear for me. Whenever I'd show signs of hesitating about making a move, he'd simply put on his hat and coat and go out and get into the car and drive off. [2]

Recognition from others in the nearly all-male world of baseball came to Effa gradually, but steadily. Although her abilities were only acknowledged by baseball men in terms that made it clear she was not really one of them, words of meaningful praise came as time went on. The "lady fan" applauded by the New York *Age* in 1935 for sticking up for black baseball at the Dyckman Oval had, by 1939, become "the country's no. 1 female baseball fan . . . her hubby owns the high flying Newark Eagles." In 1941, fellow owner Cumberland Posey of the Homestead Grays wrote that "Negro baseball owners can take a few tips from the lady member of the league when it comes to advertising."[3]

With the increasing awareness that she was a real member of Eagle management came news photographers who pointed out her unusual position in the baseball world, taking her picture in the otherwise male sanctuary of the team dugout. A photo probably taken in 1941 shows her in her familiar role, impeccably dressed and seeming to cast a shrewd, executive eye on her players on the field.

But another picture taken in 1938 captures the other face of her baseball life, the sheer enjoyment of being involved in the game. A young photographer from the New York *Post* had approached her to pose, and after initially demurring, saying "It's Mr. Manley's team," she relented. "The boy was in tears, he said 'Mrs. Manley, if I go back without your picture, I'm going to be in the doghouse.'" No one wanting to publicize the Newark Eagles would ever leave Effa Manley's presence disappointed to tears, so she posed in the dugout, not in her usual fashionable jacket and hat, but in an Eagles team jacket and cap, in which she looks very comfortable and not in the least under duress.

Her official position with the team was business manager, which essentially put her in charge of nearly everything concerning the Eagles that occurred in Newark except for the actual playing of the games. Playing schedules had to be arranged, since the slate of league games put together by the owners before the season started covered less than half of all the games each summer. Every time the team went on the road, it needed accommodations, sometimes in a different locale each night for up to two weeks. If the Eagles had arranged a game, they were responsible for getting the contest publicized through the newspapers and by placards in local businesses.

The team had to be equipped, and the Manleys insisted on a level of quality approaching that of the major leagues. That meant, according to 1939 invoices in the team files, $16.45 for a complete uniform, $6.76 for gloves, from $1 to $1.75 for bats, and about $10 a dozen for baseballs. Then the uniforms had to be cleaned ($21.55 for the club's entire wardrobe at Uneeda Cleaning and Dyeing Co. in Newark), and the team bus, without which most of the season's schedule couldn't be played, had to be maintained.

New contracts with the players had to be negotiated each spring, and then, of course, payroll had to be met every two weeks. Abe's blanket rules on behavior notwithstanding, the young men who made up the Eagles, many from rural areas and all making more money than they ever had before, frequently needed individual help in coping with their new status. This could require management of part of their paychecks to ensure bills were paid and money sent home to families.

All this was done with an office staff that usually consisted of Effa, her longtime secretary, Carrie Jacobs, Illidge as road secretary, a bus driver, and, after the first few years, a part-time publicist. Those who were involved with the team characterize Effa first by describing her as a hardheaded businesswoman. Profit margins in black league baseball in the 1930s were slim, if they existed at all, and alert cash management might determine if a season ended in the black or the red. Ways to economize that would not result in shortchanging the players, thus spoiling their morale, were welcome at the Eagles' office.

For example, in 1939, the A. G. Spalding Co. informed the Eagles that 8-ounce flannel baseball pants were selling for $8 a pair, but that the firm had available for the first good offer 23 pairs that had been made for the New York Yankees but had shrunk slightly in cleaning. "We'll take them," Mrs. Manley replied in a matter of days.

Both Manleys shared at least one common trait. They were penurious in their business dealings, while living comfortably in their personal life (Abe drove a Lincoln, and Effa furnished their home with Oriental rugs and always owned at least one fur). The late Othello "Chico" Renfroe, who was an Eagle spring training batboy in his youth in the mid-1930s, then played against them in the 1946 Negro World Series on the Kansas City Monarchs, regarded the Manleys as simply "tightwads," although he otherwise thought well of them.

It was a tribute to their ability to run an operation that would make players want to be Eagles that they could do so even while guarding their dollars. Monte Irvin, one of the best players ever to play for Newark, had acquired a significant reputation as an athlete at nearby Orange High School. Abe, naturally, pursued his services, but Irvin, who was also being courted by black professional teams in other cities, asked about the possibility of a signing bonus. "Oh, we don't do things like that," Abe replied. "It should be an honor and a privilege for you to play for the Eagles, since we're a local team and do a lot for the community." Manley's pitch worked—Irvin signed with the club, without any bonus. He says he figured he would get the money later in salary increases, and at least by Negro league standards he did, when he became a star for Newark.

Abe and Effa's thrifty approach to baseball was best illustrated by their attitude toward the ball itself. A team could go through hundreds of them in a season as they were hit into the stands and scuffed up so badly that they could not be used anymore. But both Abe and Effa resented profligate waste of the balls. Irvin recalls that during one at bat, Fran Matthews fouled several pitches off into the stands, and Abe sent word down to the manager to tell Matthews to either strike out or hit the ball safely—"the next time one goes in the stands, its going to cost him whatever the ball costs." Often the portly Abe would jump from his seat in Ruppert Stadium to give chase to a foul ball hit into the crowd, hoping to recover it before a fan did, and thus return it to the Eagle ball hoard. "That man worshipped baseballs," Irvin laughs.

In her book, Effa also lamented the high cost of baseball's most indispensable element and complained about umpires who didn't appreciate the value of a baseball. "Balls not only were lost when hit into the stands, but umpires have a habit of throwing balls out of the game once they become scratched." [4]

Away from the ballpark, the Manleys could not have been more different. Effa liked parties and had many acquaintances among entertainers (pianist Eubie Blake and Broadway lyricist Andy Razaf were among them). She also forged her own social relationships with sports figures, including Bob Douglas, owner of the Renaissance Big Five basketball team, runner Borican, and Joe Louis.

Louis was invited twice to throw out the ceremonial first ball at important Eagle games. Effa definitely had high regard for him, and they seemed to have done mutual favors for each other. She recalled that when she went to Cleveland in 1947 to see Larry Doby, the Newark Eagle who integrated the white American League, she was unable to find a good room at the best black hotel in the city (her position as Doby's previous Negro league employer would have prevented a quiet arrival at a white hotel), so Louis turned his suite over to her. "We were good friends," she said, and sealed her evidence of the relationship with "he started in business the same year we did."

She clearly wanted to be upwardly mobile socially, while Abe was clearly disinterested. "The guy was a professional baseball man, and that was pretty much his life," Newark sportswriter Jerry Izenberg remembers. But Effa's high-profile way of life, plus her good works, brought her in contact with Newark's black upper class. She could successfully sell commodities other than baseball, and was a leader in local fund-raising and membership drives for the NAACP, the Urban League, and the Boys Club.

Her elegance did not go unnoticed, either. Harriette Hardy Everett remembers Effa Manley as the fashion example to which the younger women all aspired. Effa would sometimes turn up in "Sally's Chatterings," the social column in the local black weekly, the New Jersey *Herald-News*. An account of a sorority gathering in 1941 mentioned "the charming Effa Manley, a symphony in grey and dubonnet topped by a lavish grey krimmer caracul coat." "Sally" had also gone to an Eagles game in 1939, and gushed:

> "God Bless our lovely women" thought your columnist, as well as the Newark Eagles on last Thursday nite when, beautifully attired in navy sheer frock with lace top bodice, through which peeked a wide band of pale pink ribbon, wearing a navy baku hat with pale pink and blue ostrich feathers, and a mist gorgeous silver fox cape, Effa Manley [and several others] wildly cheered the game.[5]

In Harlem and the black enclaves in the other big cities in the North, one could now earn one's way into black high society, instead of having to be born into it. In Newark, that was less true. Effa's looks alone, set off as they were by her light skin, were partial qualification for a place in the city's black leadership (it's clear that she was not telling the story of her illegitimate birth in those days). But acceptance did not come that easily. According to Izenberg, who was a teenager when the Eagles were still in Newark, Effa's advantages, "her complexion, the perception of her having money and her show business contacts" worked for her.

But, he says, the reason she was in town at all—the Eagles—worked against her, because baseball was not high-class enough.

> The kind of people who followed that ball club, they were never going to get into society. She was always going to be "that woman who owned the baseball team," and the people who were going to go down and see that team play were the people who didn't have access to the cotillions or the Spring dance at the YMCA. It sounds to me as if she walked a social tightrope.

Her efforts rewarded her and aided black Newark at the same time. But, despite her nimble balancing act on the edge of Newark's black upper crust, total acceptance seems to have eluded her for reasons that included her relationships with Abe and baseball, as well as the unyielding portions of her own personality. Connie Woodruff, whose family belonged to Newark's black society, recalls ambivalence in her parents' social set about the light-skinned Effa, the society pretender, and down-to-earth Abe, the "sportsman":

> In the black community, there was a very definite caste system. Effa, being the color she was, with her husband very dark, partied sometimes with a different group of people, and shifted back and forth between high and other society.
>
> I can see her raising funds for upper class causes, she would like to be associated with the doctors, lawyers and teachers. But she was not an overly friendly lady, at least to females, and she was not an easy person to get next to. You just didn't make friends with her. The only reason you called her [the familiar name] "Effie" was that you were at the baseball park and you were spending money to see her team. Other than that, she was "Mrs. Manley" and he was always "Pop Manley." You always saw a lot of people around them at the baseball games, but you couldn't say anybody was really their friend.
>
> We were not thinking in terms of public relations at that time, but she was the ultimate public relations expert for what she did. She knew it was smart to show up at certain things and places, and give the aura of involvement. Since real light, bright people were held up as the symbol of success in those days, she probably liked that, too. The roar of the crowd, the applause, you know.

Effa's no-nonsense business manner alienated many people who might otherwise have been closer to her. One of them was J. Mercer Burrell, a black lawyer in Newark who led the American Legion color guard at the Eagles' opening day ceremonies. In 1941 the Manleys hired him to do some legal work for the club, and subsequently he and Effa became involved in a dispute over a six-dollar difference in his fee. Burrell, apparently frustrated with Effa, lectured her in a letter that comes uncomfortably close to capturing the least attractive part of her personality. "It isn't the question of the money involved, but I am not happy when I am being held cheaply by those in whose interest I have never failed to extend my very best efforts," Burrell wrote. "It seems to me that your gratitude goes out for sycophants and 'yes men and women,' rather than individuals who try and render to you honest, loyal and efficient service. One does not hold real friends by such methods."

The elegant, acid-tongued, very light-skinned Effa and the quiet, very dark Abe certainly must have looked less than compatible. Connie Woodruff's opinion is that "they never looked like they went together, they looked like Mutt and Jeff."

Recollections of Effa include accounts of her attraction to some of the players on the Eagles, particularly the irrepressible Terris "The Great" McDuffie. Effa, Abe, and McDuffie took the facts of this alleged triangle with them to their graves, but it was no secret that Abe and his star pitcher were far from the best of friends. Illidge, the traveling secretary, recalled riding alongside Manley on the team bus to Pittsburgh to play the Homestead Grays, with Abe muttering that "when I get there, I'm going to trade that son of a bitch McDuffie to [Homestead owner] Posey." That deal was never made, but in August, 1938, Manley did get McDuffie out of his life for awhile, engineering an obviously one-sided trade that sent his top starting pitcher to the Black Yankees for rookie pitcher Slim Johnson.

That wasn't MacDuffie's last hitch with the Eagles, however. During World War II, he came back to Newark to finish his career and also worked a raise out of the Eagles for the start of the 1945 season. To again have MacDuffie around— once after his wife and now his money—may have been too much for Abe. At the beginning of the season, Manley ordered manager Willie Wells to start the pitcher against the Baltimore Elite Giants, although it was Wells's considered opinion that McDuffie wasn't in condition to pitch in serious competition. The Giants hit the ball all over the park, but Abe wanted McDuffie kept in the game to absorb a humiliating defeat.

Wells defied him and shortly thereafter resigned as manager and was traded to another team.

The combination of the Manleys' appearance of incompatibility and her reported interest in other men leads to a potential conclusion that Effa, having found a rich benefactor, was using Abe primarily as a source of financial support. She said, much later in life, that "Abe never stinted in what I wanted," although she always expressed great respect for him.[6]

But Max Manning, the former Eagle pitcher, says his judgment of the Manleys is that, in its own way, their relationship was a good match.

> From what an outsider could observe, they got along perfectly. Even if she used him, as some say, as long as he was happy, what difference does it make? Life's about being happy, and as long as Abe could play cards at Dan's Tavern and gamble, he was happy. He had a solid interest in the team, but he left most of it to her, she was by far the most capable. Maybe that's why he married her in the first place. He might have suckered HER in.

The responsibilities that the Manleys and other Negro league owners had to meet to ensure successful balances in both their scorebooks and checkbooks divided into three categories. These essentials were to find good players, draw up a schedule for them, and make sure they got sufficient creature comforts (including a regular paycheck) to keep them happy and playing well. To the extent these are things all professional baseball owners had to worry about, they put the Negro league magnates at least symbolically in the company of their white peers. To the extent black owners had to work harder at these things, their extra efforts told of their organizations' shortcomings, both self-inflicted and imposed by white society.

On the Eagles, putting the team together and finding replacement parts when needed was Abe Manley's job. A white major league club would have its own staff of talent scouts traveling around to the amateur and semipro baseball fields of America to find players with sufficient potential for the big leagues. If a major league club signed a player to a contract and he needed more experience, it had agreements with minor league teams, some of which might be owned outright by the big league club, to give the man a chance to prove himself.

Scouts and farm teams, of course, cost money above and beyond the expenses of putting the main team on the field. Normally this was cash that the Negro league teams did not have. The team officials would look up some prospects in person, as Abe did around New Jersey and when he was traveling with the Eagles on road trips, but they often gave players tryouts based only on tips from "word of mouth" networks of amateur coaches and former players.

With his longtime involvement in black sports in both the Northeast and the Atlantic Seaboard, Abe Manley had as good a set of connections as anyone. Oscar Charleston, who in the 1920s and early 1930s had been one of the best, if not the best, player the Negro leagues ever produced, frequently wrote the Eagles. Bill Yancey, a professional basketball and baseball star who played shortstop for the original Brooklyn Eagles, later ran the government sports program for the Republic of Panama and recruited outfielders Archie Braithwaite and Victor Barnett from winter baseball in Central America for the team in 1944.

Some of the Manleys' scouts were considerably less well situated in baseball than Charleston and Yancey. The Eagle files contain a 1947 telegram to Effa Manley that illustrates the perils of recruiting on a shoestring. Someone with only with the initials C.E.P. (possibly Eagle catcher Charlie Parks) wired, HAVE GOT BOY. CANT LEAVE UNTIL FRIDAY. WILL COME TO NEWARK. PLEASE SEND $25 AT MY EXPENSE. CLOTHES IN PAWN. PLEASE WIRE AT ONCE. After Abe's death, Effa speculated that he had at least partially financed the Eagles' talent searches by forgiving IOUs from baseball men who had found him players. "We didn't have a paid scouting system, but when Abe died, I found a whole lot of notes," she said.[7]

Sometimes young players would take the initiative and write to the Eagles, seeking a tryout. That is how the team found Fred Hobgood, a regular member of its pitching staff during World War II, who wrote a joint letter with another aspirant, James Waters, from Kinston, N.C., in 1941:

> We would like to seek a job or a tryout with your ballclub. We are now at the ages of nineteen years old, we have had two years of experience with a semi-pro club which were the state champions . . . Frederick Hobgood, pitcher, has record of 19 victories and 2 defeats, has excellent control, bats and throws on left side, neither has habits of smoking or drinking.

While this approach worked well for Hobgood, a more usual result was foretold in a letter from Abe to an amateur coach who had recommended a player. "It would be impossible to carry every ball player who applies to training camp, we could not take this risk unless a man has been very highly recommended by some one whose opinion we respect."

Given the precarious financial underpinnings of many black baseball teams, there were almost always good player acquisitions to be made from clubs which had dropped out of the Negro leagues, gone out of business altogether, or broken an implied contract with a player by not paying him regularly. The Eagles acquired Willie Wells in 1936, when the American Giants of Chicago dropped out of the National League, but in February, 1942, the Manleys passed on the opportunity to sign Reece "Goose" Tatum, a renowned black professional basketball player but mediocre outfielder and first baseman who marketed himself via a postcard after his 1941 team failed to regularly pay his full salary.

The many black teams operating in lower-level leagues, or completely independently, were also fruitful sources of players for the Negro major leagues. Players could be acquired either through outright sale of their contracts or by releasing them to the big clubs in exchange for continued good will that could include the chance to have a well-known National or American league on its own schedule as a big box-office draw.

Although they could not afford full-fledged farm systems, sometimes the National and American league clubs were able to set up working agreements with individual teams, as the Eagles did at different times with two North Carolina teams in the Southern League, the Winston-Salem Eagles in the late 1930s and the Asheville Blues in the mid-1940s.

Clubs outside the two top black leagues were usually not protected by agreements keeping the National and American teams from raiding them for players, and if dealings with them were not supported by gentlemen's agreements between the owners, interesting things could happen. Abe Manley seems to have been capable of both straightforward and nefarious deals. His acquisition of eventual star outfielder and pitcher Johnny Davis from the Mohawk Colored Giants of Schenectady, N.Y., in 1940, was marked by a cordial exchange of letters with Mohawk owner Henry Bozzi (the deal was substantially complicated by the fact that the young Davis was on parole in New York State for a youthful crime, and arrangements had to be made to transfer him to the Reverend Weathers' supervision in Newark).

In 1939, however, Abe had written Willie Riddick of Norfolk, one of his main contacts for the annual Eagle barnstorming tour to the Virginia Tidewater region, giving him explicit instructions on how to circumnavigate local baseball owner J. Brady Johnson and heist one of his players:

> I want you to go and get me a Ball Player who is playing with the Norfolk Black Tars. His name is Tuttie Braxton, and he is an infielder. Do not let Brady Johnson know you are trying to get this boy, as he might try to stand in your way . . . You take him to the train, buy him a ticket to Newark and put him on the train, also give him taxi fare from the station here in Newark to my office . . . I will send you a check right back as soon as he arrives.

Abe Manley seemingly would go anywhere to find a good player. In 1939, he inquired of the warden of the New Jersey State Prison in Trenton about the availability of a prisoner to whom Abe was willing to give a tryout, assuming he would want "an opportunity to re-establish himself."

But for all the work of the Manleys' far-flung network, New Jersey itself was probably the most fertile ground for recruits. Many of their best players came from the Newark area or not too far away. Three eventual major leaguers, Irvin of Orange, Larry Doby of Paterson, and Don Newcombe of Elizabeth, grew up near the ballpark, and Manning, a mainstay of the pitching staff, was from Pleasantville, near Atlantic City. Lennie Pearson, a good hitting outfielder and infielder with the club for several years, grew up in the Newark area after his family moved there from the South, and Charles Biot, from East Orange, started his career with the Eagles before being traded.

Irvin and Doby were college athletes when they began playing for the Eagles, and protected their amateur status at first by only appearing in games outside the Newark area, playing under assumed names. Irvin called himself "Jimmy Nelson" after a friend he admired, and Doby played as "Larry Walker." According to Irvin, "many athletes did the same thing at that time; the communication wasn't what it is today, and you could get away with it."

The reason men could play for the Eagles under assumed names and not get detected was because the club spent a great deal of time barnstorming on long road trips, jumping between cities that had no connections with the Negro National League, other than that an enterprising booking agent had set up a game there.

Each team in the National League could count on up to sixty games a season with other league teams, but that only amounted to forty-five or fewer playing dates, since many games were doubleheaders, and this was not enough opportunities to generate sufficient income. A team played about three league contests a week, which left plenty of time for the extra games that put business in the black in good years or narrowed the red-ink margin in bad ones. The opponents could be other league teams, in exhibitions that might or might not count in the league standings, or top semipro teams.

The Eagles did not play as often as some of the other Negro major league teams like the Homestead Grays, who logged as many as 200 games in a season, counting spring training and postseason exhibition games. Former Eagle players recall a workload of about 150 games a year, almost exactly the same number of games played by a white major league team at that time. However, the white majors began play earlier in the year and finished a little later, a difference of about a month, all told. They also generally played three or four consecutive games in a visiting team's city before moving on, unlike the Negro league teams, which were almost constantly in motion. The white teams usually went from city to city by Pullman sleeper, while to save on transportation costs and ensure travel unrestricted by segregation, Negro league teams usually rode their buses all night, if necessary, to the next ball game.

The resulting demanding schedule for the black players was summarized in a 1939 newspaper account of a two-week round trip for the Eagles. The article featured the tongue-in-cheek headline, "Ball Player's Life Is Soft:"

> The team left Newark last Saturday and played at Wilmington, Del., in the afternoon then went to Baltimore that night. Sunday motored to Richmond, Va., played two games and returned that night to Baltimore. Monday played twilight game in Bellfonte, Pa., and then drove into Buffalo, arriving at 5:30 a.m. Played night game there and then jumped 250 miles to Pittsburgh, Pa., after game. Played in Pittsburgh Wednesday and Altoona, Thursday and returned to Pittsburgh after game. Friday played in Canton, Ohio, and motored back to Pittsburgh after game, where team played Saturday. Played two games in Indianapolis, Ind., Sunday and back to Columbus after game. Rained out in Yorkville, Ohio, Monday and played in Akron, Ohio, Tuesday night

> and left there after game and rode 650 miles to Newark. Played Grays here Thursday, Friday in Tremont, Pa., back to Philadelphia for two games with Stars on Saturday and then to Newark for two games Sunday.[8]

Some partial schedules in the Newark team files indicate the team had at least 100 actual playing dates a year, with several of them doubleheaders. Every season would feature a road trip, usually paired with another National league team, to Abe Manley's old stomping grounds in the Virginia Tidewater area. In 1942, for example, the Eagles and Grays set up a southern swing with games on August 7 in Easton, Maryland ; August 8 in Milford, Delaware; August 9 in Richmond; August 10 and 13 in Norfolk; August 11 and 12 in Newport News, and August 14 in Portsmouth.

In the mid-1940s, more interleague competition developed between the Negro National and American leagues, which gave the National League teams from the East opportunities to set up similar midwestern trips. In 1944, Chicago booking agent Abe Saperstein put together an eleven-day trip for Newark that started them out in Dayton, Ohio, on June 6 and sent them as far west as Davenport, Iowa, sandwiched around what must have been a lucrative four-day stay in Chicago.

When the Eagles were not playing other Negro league teams, they most often competed against the good white semipro teams in New Jersey, Pennsylvania, and New York. That region teemed with excellent clubs composed of part-time players who were as anxious to book games with the Negro league clubs as the black clubs were to play them to fill gaps in their schedules.

Just having a Negro league team for an opponent was usually enough of a draw for a local semipro club, although some teams promoted themselves with an extra effort. One offer the Eagles received, but apparently did not take up, was from the Wilkes-Barre Miners, a team from the Pennsylvania coal fields that, presumably with the ballpark lights out, "puts on an act with coal miners' helmets and lamps before the game."

The semipro teams, even without sideshows, made up a part of baseball culture in the first half of this century that has been lost almost as entirely as the Negro leagues. Bart Giblin, a former New Jersey sportswriter, describes the state of baseball in New Jersey in those days:

> In that period there was no television, and baseball was the main summer recreation for men. . . . Every town in this area had a baseball team and probably more than one, because there was more fellows to play. But they always had one very good team in each town.

The ball fields of New Jersey have produced well over 300 major leaguers, including well-known players such as outfielders Doc Cramer, Goose Goslin, and Joe Medwick; third baseman Bobby Brown, currently the president of the American League; catcher Jeff Torborg, the recent manager of the New York Mets; and pitchers Hank Borowy, Jim Bouton, and Al Downing. The best local teams were the ones the Eagles played. They filled the gaps in the league schedule by playing in Belmar against the well-known Braves, as well as in Metuchen, Red Bank, and other places where fans would pay to see their local heroes try to beat the Eagles.

The New Jersey team the Eagles played most often, and relished beating the most, was the East Orange Base Ball Club. East Orange was a fixture in each year's Eagle schedule—the two teams played six times in 1938, for example, each winning three. The white team was formidable, since it frequently contained members of the best semipro team in the region, the Bushwicks of Brooklyn.

The Bushwicks were run by an immigrant cigar maker named Max Rossner. He also owned Dexter Park, where the team played. The ubiquitous Nat Strong, the booking agent who for years controlled Negro league scheduling in New York City, was one of Rossner's partners. The Bushwicks, playing the other top-notch semipro teams and all the Negro league teams that were located in the New York area or came there to play league games, often drew from 10,000 to 20,000 fans to Sunday doubleheaders at Dexter. Dexter had lights, and many night games were on each year's schedule.

Hall of Fame pitcher Whitey Ford; Borowy, the New Jersey boy who later starred with the New York Yankees and Chicago Cubs; former Yankees' pitcher Lefty Gomez; Dodger outfielder Gene Hermanski; and longtime infielder Billy Jurges were among those who played for Rossner, either before going on to the majors or after their big-league careers were over, or in Hermanski's case, while stationed in Brooklyn with the Coast Guard during World War II. In those years professional white baseball paid better than the black version, but had nowhere near the stratospheric salary schedule of today's game. Many players who were probably good enough to have played professionally had good jobs in New York, especially at defense plants during World War II, and were actually better off going to their day jobs, then playing ball nights and weekends.

The Bushwicks; the Bay Parkways, a Brooklyn team run by Rossner's brother Joe; and the Farmers of Glendale, Queens, were dependable money-making dates on Negro league teams' schedules. The black teams' games with those squads received almost as much publicity in the sports pages of the black weekly newspapers as did the league games. The semipro teams may not have been of overall major league quality, but there were always familiar names in their lineups, and victories over them provided incremental evidence to what blacks always knew—they could play among the best white teams and players, if only given a chance.

But the Eagles never played a single inning against what should have been their natural rivals, the Newark Bears, although Abe reportedly issued at least one challenge to the white team. People close to the Eagles who were asked about this missed opportunity are insistent on two things—it was the Bears, or their parent Yankees, who would not allow the competition, and if a game had taken place, the Eagles would have had an excellent chance of winning it.

Jocko Maxwell, a black radio sportscaster and newspaper sportswriter who covered the Eagles, says not only did the two teams not play each other, players of one team never even showed up to watch the other's games or practices. As for competition between Newark's two pro teams, Maxwell says the Eagles would have been willing, but "the Bears would not touch the Eagles. The Yankees would not allow it. They actually despised the Eagles because the Eagles had a better club, and everybody knew it."

Effa Manley claimed to know what lay at the heart of the Eagles' success. "Ball players have a word they use, I realized it is the most important word in their vocabulary," she said. "They say they're 'satisfied.' Without it, you've just got a guy in a uniform. Our players actually enjoyed what they were doing."

Keeping a player "satisfied" in the Negro leagues paid off in more ways than just ensuring he gave his best effort on the field. While a black ball player could not enter white organized baseball, there were always opportunities beyond the team that might currently have him on its payroll. In fact, since organized baseball strictly enforced the reserve clause written into each of its players' contracts preventing them from going into an open market to seek a better deal, it can be argued that black players actually had more freedom of movement.

Leagues in Mexico and other Latin American countries frequently shopped for Negro leaguers who would leave their United States' commitments to go south. Players also often took advantage of what they claimed to be broken contracts with black teams (usually fractured by missed paydays) to look for a better situation stateside. Furthermore, despite frequent earnest pronouncements by the officials of the Negro National League and its sister American League that the "raiding" of team rosters by other clubs would not be tolerated, some of that went on, too.

The result was a limited erratic free market for good black players. But if the main attraction in this market was money, there were other lures, also. The difficulties involved in completing a Negro league team's season, particularly the incessant traveling, made teams such as the Eagles, who provided good road accommodations and regular paydays, attractive. Effa made a point of noting that "we were proud of the fact that players for the Newark Eagles' organization never were forced to wait for their paychecks. Paydays were the first and fifteenth of every month during the season, and we diligently met this deadline promptly, in all instances."[9]

If that does not seem to be such a notable accomplishment, consider this account of Charles Biot's. Biot, another of the fine athletes from Northern New Jersey, was signed by the Eagles out of East Orange High School in 1939, but was traded that same season to James Semler's New York Black Yankees.

There, Biot experienced another type of Negro league operation:

> Semler, he wouldn't pay me my money. I got $160 per month, so Jim took me in the back room and talked me into him paying me $80 every two weeks. Then he started cutting me each time, $50, $45, he was underpaying me. He owed me over a hundred dollars, which was a lot of money in those days. Semler was making money, but he was slick with it, he was holding out on the younger players.

In addition to promptness, the Eagles also had the reputation of being one of the better-paying teams in the National League, as the Manleys' desire to keep their players satisfied won out over their penurious natures. A successful season for an Eagle usually meant a pay raise the following year, although Effa zealously guarded the team treasury so that salary progress for the individual was as hard-earned as it was nearly inevitable. By such tactics were the precarious profit margins in Negro league baseball maintained. Max Manning recalls that in dealing with Effa on salary, "we were often at odds, rubbed each other the wrong way. If you held out, she'd let you hold out, to see who would be the most stubborn person. I guess this happened with most of the ball players on our team."

Annual contract negotiations usually commenced around the first of March and were opened by Effa mailing each player the Negro National League's standard player contract, with the Manleys' salary offer filled in on the dotted line. If the offer was acceptable, all the player had to do was sign the contract and mail it back.

To return a contract unsigned, with a demand for more money, was to engage Effa Manley in open financial warfare. Among her weapons were an excellent memory for what the player had accomplished the previous season (particulary his failures) and, to avoid directly insulting her own employees, a practice of inferring that the player, a person of sound, reasonable mind, was under the unfortunate control of someone giving him terrible advice.

Negotiations with pitcher Len Hooker in 1941 included this letter to his Raleigh, N.C., home:

> Dear Leniel:
>
> First of all, I was quite surprised to receive your contract back unsigned, and with the curt notation "terms not satisfactory." I cannot believe it was your idea. I cannot even understand you permitting it to be done. If some one feels you need advising, and they are no doubt acting in good faith, I am sure if you had told them the entire story of your year with the Eagles, they would have felt you had been treated more than fairly.

Hooker, Effa reminds him, was given an unsolicited $25 a month raise in 1940 after getting off to a fine start, a reward made "because the management felt you were working hard and were a real help to the club." However, she points out, in the second half of the season he was considerably less successful. He won only two games after July 15, although the Eagles gave up seven runs in one of them and nine in the other. "I do not give you credit for either of these victories. The other pitchers were just worse than you," she adds.

The lecture then closes with a pep talk and a final demand that is nearly parental in tone:

> I will be only too happy to have you worth a big salary. After all, a good pitcher is a valuable man. When you rate more money you will not have to demand it. The smart thing for you to do will be to be ready to join the club when we leave for camp. Get in condition, and make a reputation for yourself. We are leaving April 3rd for camp, and I expect you to sign the enclosed contract, return it, and be ready to meet the bus in Raleigh about midnight that day.

With the younger players, Effa's negotiation stance as a sort of surrogate parent was even more pronounced. When twenty-one-year-old Larry Doby, from nearby Paterson, failed to come to her office to discuss their contract differences in 1946 she wrote him that . . .

> having met your mother, I know you were not raised this badly. There is only one conclusion to reach, that is you are being very poorly advised by someone both stupid and ignorant of baseball conditions.

When another local product, seventeen-year-old pitcher Don Newcombe from Elizabeth, turned down her original offer in 1944, she corresponded with his parents, Mr. and Mrs. James Newcombe, letting them know that:

> I long ago developed the feeling no ball player is indispensable. I am writing you because I know no one is more interested in his future than you, his parents. If you care to discuss the matter with me further, I will be glad to talk to you. Whatever happens, I wish Donald the best of luck, but I do hate to see him getting off so completely on the wrong foot.

Her tenacious negotiation pose could be overcome, however, and in 1941 Max Manning succeeded with an approach that combined dignified sincerity and a veiled threat:

> Owing to the dissatisfactory conditions of the contract I received, I am returning it. This is my third year with Newark and although I have not been phenomenal I do think that I represent more at this time than is indicated by the salary you offer. . . . A Negro baseball player's life is a hard one. He has to make money while he is still young and spend it wisely. Likewise he must obtain his salary however and where ever he can. This is an old story but it becomes more ominous each new year of Negro baseball. I am not trying to be spectacular or big time. This is an honest request for an honest salary. I remain yours for a hasty agreement.

Manning explains the importance of his philosophical digression into a player's hard life: "She knew I was pitching well, my record was good, and that was when Pasqual (Jorge Pasqual, a wealthy owner in the Mexican League who often recruited Negro leaguers) was raiding. She said, 'I don't want to lose him.' "

Just a few days after Manning sent his letter, he received an uncharacteriscally low-key reply from Effa, granting his raise. "I know this is a little unusual, to have the increase granted so readily, but I do not feel that I want to enter into any long drawn out discussion on the matter," she said.

Her relations with the players beyond business duties such as contract negotiation were a mix of formality and personal concern that reached the category of "mother hen" behavior with some. (Among other things, she fended off young women admirers. The team received a lot of mail for individual Eagles from females, and Effa was not above keeping the letters, thus in her mind keeping her players from unprofessional distractions.) Above all, it was clear that she appreciated loyalty toward the team and would repay such an effort in kind.

Generally, she was considered to be aloof from the players, although she and Abe were always perceived as having personal favorites on the squad. Manning, who readily admits he got along as poorly with Effa in his playing days as he got along well with her husband, recalls that "she kept the team more or less in its place. She kept us at bay." For example, she would come to the Grand Hotel where the players had congregated after a game, but instead of joining in the camaraderie that usually accompanied a team gathering there, would merely greet those who might be gathered on the front porch, and go on inside to dinner.

If Abe tried to police the team on the road, Effa was its conscience and its advisor at home in Newark, setting standards that were probably tougher than those Abe required on the bus trips. "Mrs. Manley was the disciplinarian of the team," James Walker recalls. "She would call you in and tell you how to dress, what to do, who to associate with. When you had your problems, if they were personal, you went to Mrs. Manley, and she was very understanding, as long as you toed the line."

These requirements earned her a compliment from fellow owner Cumberland Posey of the Homestead Grays, who said in 1943 that the Eagles were one of only two teams in the Negro National League that successfully maintained discipline among all its players.[10]

In 1937, the players gathered in Chicago for the East-West game announced they would not play if the owners did not pay them more than the $50 each was then getting for participating. It had not eluded the players that the team owners were taking away four-figure sums from the gate receipts, while paying the star players a relative pittance. Effa, in Chicago for the game, confronted the men from the Eagles. She was visibly angry as she tried to persuade them to go ahead and play, which all of the players did, after negotiating a raise. "We didn't hear any more about it, but she was angry, though," said pitcher Leon Day.

In truth, she didn't like to lose, and she didn't like her team to lose, either. Not all of the black society figures whose company she desired to join may have cared about the Eagles' won-loss record, but she knew enough about baseball, or perhaps about life, to value victories. One day in 1941, a bitter loss to the archrival Homestead Grays brought out her frustration, which she attempted to dispell as only a non-player can, by castigating the man who had beaten her club. The Eagles had been vanquished by the best that day, as Josh Gibson, the premier home-run hitter in black baseball, hit a three-run homer to wipe out a Newark lead before hometown fans at Ruppert Stadium. Effa accosted Gibson outside the ballpark. "How dare you do a thing like that? You broke everybody's heart," she chided.

This brought a sterling rebuke from Gibson, all the more telling because it was true: "Miz Manley, I'm known to break hearts."

She may also have wanted to win so badly because in those days the Newark Bears almost always won their league's pennant, and she strove to model the Eagles on the white version of the sport, in an attempt to validate the quality and value of the black game. She couldn't do this on the field, and there was no stopping Josh Gibson while sitting in the stands, but she could replicate the trappings of white baseball.

For example, as Izenberg points out,

> The mayor of Newark, if he chose not to be re-elected, could ignore the Bears home opener. But she elevated the Eagles to the point where the white mayor of Newark was always at their opener too, and always sat in Effa Manley's box. That was very important.

Not all of Effa's efforts were appreciated by the team, though. One of her habits that made her unpopular with some players was her tendency to interfere with the team's field manager during games. "She was loud, and if the pitcher was going bad you could hear 'get him out of there'," Matthews remembers. "She wanted everyone in Newark to know she was in charge."

Among the stories about her that have become part of Negro league folklore is one about her demanding that Terris McDuffie be the starting pitcher for a certain game, so he could suitably impress a group of visiting women acquaintances. The story, from an age when a woman chief executive in any kind of undertaking was rare, shows not only her assertiveness but, unfortunately, that she approached baseball from a "woman's point of view." Manning, for one, thinks such tales are mostly apocryphal: "She had nothing to do with actual field operations, she was strictly a business person." There are also stories about her actually sitting on the bench with the team, "but if they're true, I wasn't there."

Manning also recalls an old story that has Effa actually giving signs to the players, in one case by crossing her legs to signal for a bunt. In this particular tale, she forgets what she's doing, keeps her legs crossed, and sets off pandemonium on the field as one obedient batter after another lays down a bunt. "As we went along, the story changed to Abe doing this. He sat there with legs crossed and went to sleep and nodded. Everybody kept the hit and run on (the tactic signaled for in this version of the story) for an entire inning until they realized he had fallen asleep. This is how tales come up."

More accurately documented than her supposed attempts to interfere on the field are instances in which Effa got involved in the personal problems of players, doling out salary advances or occasionally outright small gifts of cash, along with advice that seemed to come more from an older relative than an employer.

The team files contain a postcard from the North Carolina wife of an Eagle who had not been sending any of his salary home to support her and their child, along with Effa's reply that although the team was currently playing in Baltimore, "I will talk to him when he gets back, and will see that he sends money to you every pay day from now. I am enclosing you a Money Order for ten dollars. Hope you and the baby are both well."

In 1945, a mainstay of the Manleys' 1930s teams, former manager Dick Lundy, wrote for help. Leg injuries had forced him to retire a few years before, and he had gone home to Jacksonville, Florida, unable to either play baseball or work full time at his other occupation as a porter at the Jacksonville railroad station. In October his mother had died, and he wrote his former bosses, seeking to borrow $50 to help pay her funeral expenses. Effa promptly dispatched the money to him.

Perhaps the helping relationship that took most of Effa's time, and tried her patience the most, was that with lefthanded pitcher Jimmie Hill. Hill lived in his hometown of Lakeland, Florida, during the winter, where his life seemed to be especially trouble prone, if not sometimes disastrous. He married young, and his first baby died at childbirth. He once was arrested for getting involved in a bootleg liquor scheme, and he had health problems. He detailed all these woes in letters to Effa during the off-season, invariably concluding with a request for a $10 or $25 loan from the team until spring arrived.

Then, in April, 1941, after having hit the Manleys up for some more cash, this time in the form of advance travel money to get to spring training, he did not show up in camp. This earned him a blistering letter from Effa:

> Well, James:
>
> I don't know when I have ever been more surprised and disappointed, than when I learned you were not in camp. . . . Such behavior as this makes me wonder if you have real good sense. I have been more than an employer to you, as you well know. . . . I have come to the conclusion that I have pampered and petted you entirely too much. I do not like the thought of doing a complete about face and getting as mean as I have been nice, but such conduct as you are now displaying is what causes such things to happen. . . . I expect you to be in camp not later than this Tuesday. . . . Regardless of what has caused you to behave so badly, I expect you to get yourself together, and start showing some signs of good sense. You know you are not getting any younger. By this time you should be getting more money than you are and should be a real star. That cannot happen until you make up your mind to act like a man, and not a child.

Both the giving and the criticizing stemmed from her pride in the team and from her realization that a woman's touch might not be at all out of place in this masculine pastime. In addition, as far as she was concerned, the touch was going to be that of a successful woman.

Manning believes that

> Although there might have been some male owners who would have done something like send money to Lundy, it's more typical of a woman to have this compassion. As a mother hen, she would take care of some guys if they needed it. There were some she felt that she'd just as soon not, but there were some she sort of favored, would do just about anything for them to help them out. She wasn't all hard nosed, there was compassion and feeling, particularly in terms of players who made contributions to the success of the club and welfare of the newer people in the organization. She felt it was no more than right.
> Plus, there was the fact that people would talk if they knew she didn't help out a destitute former player. So there's two ways to go on it. She had a lot of pride in the organization and the success it would have, and in the public opinion about the team. She didn't want anything with a black mark on it.

Notes

1. Manley and Hardwick, *Negro Baseball,* p. 40.
2. *Afro-American,* Jan. 25, 1947.
3. *Courier,* July 8, 1939 and April 26, 1941.
4. Manley and Hardwick, *Negro Baseball,* p. 51.
5. *Herald-News,* July 22, 1939 and March 8, 1941.
6. Richardson, "Retrospective Look," pp. 192-93.
7. Ibid., p. 176.
8. *Herald-News,* Aug. 19, 1939.
9. Manley and Hardwick, *Negro Baseball,* p. 50.
10. *Courier,* Dec. 11, 1943.

Chapter 5
The Business of Black Baseball

Effa Manley grasped the notion that success in professional baseball depended as much upon presenting her team positively as it did upon winning games. This put her well beyond most of her fellow owners. No one associated with the sporadically profitable, relatively unsophisticated world of black baseball used the term "marketing," but that is what she was doing.

Those extras that she wanted from her Eagles—a team that looked good and behaved itself off the field—helped make their games spectacles of which Newark's black community could be proud. It may have looked to players and fans as if she were applying a woman's touch to a man's sport, but it would have been more accurate to say she was applying a businessperson's touch to a pastime that often sorely lacked that approach.

Her insistence on details began with the players themselves. According to Max Manning:

> She was very meticulous about how the team looked. On the road was one thing, but in Newark, you always dressed properly. She didn't want to see you sloppy. If your shoes were muddy, she'd remark about it. The uniforms were always meticulous. When we went on the road, there was always a package of clean uniforms. When we came back, our white uniforms (worn for home games) were as clean as can be.

Effa herself later boasted about the quality of the Eagles' outfits, but characteristically made her insistence on quality a point of economy, not style:

> We did indeed buy only the best quality merchandise. Our reasoning was that it would be sheer folly to do otherwise—in view of the fact that the constant sliding and "having to hit the dirt" . . . placed an undue strain on the clothing they wore.[1]

If sliding into bases and other wear and tear on the diamond took a toll on the high-quality uniforms, she was capable of taking steps to make her team look better equipped than it really was. A 1943 team roster in the Eagles' business files bears the following typewritten notation, probably made either by Effa or at her orders: "Give the new pants to the infield, Ruffin (Leon, a catcher) and Davis (Johnny, who sometimes pitched)." Those players, when in the field, would be located closest to the fans in the grandstand, and consequently would look as sharply outfitted as possible. The outfielders, stationed on the relatively vast turf out past the bases, away from most of the customers, would presumably have to put up with any worn-out pants.

Maintaining the team's stock of uniforms was also made easier by one of her standing rules that in one way treated the grown-up Eagles like the teenaged Newark Cubs. Just as the youths had to sign a form promising to keep their suits in good condition and return them at the end of the season, the men were told not to expect their first paycheck of the spring if their complete issue had not been turned in at the end of the previous year.

To the extent she could make them behave, Effa liked the Eagles' fans to toe the line, also. Newark fans didn't particularly have a reputation for unruliness, but the celebratory nature of a baseball game did occasionally carry some of them away. The bar across the street from the stadium didn't help matters, either.

In 1942, she worked in conjunction with city officials and Fred R. Clark, editor and publisher of the New Jersey *Guardian,* one of the black weekly papers, to crack down on drunken ballpark behavior. In early June, when the season was just beginning, Clark editorialized on the *Guardian*'s front page about the adverse effect on the race of bad conduct in the stands. But Clark also called on city Public Safety Commissioner John B. Keenan to request the police precinct judge for that part of the city be instructed that "whoever is arrested at our ball games for mis-conduct (sic) will be immediately locked up and held in jail overnight without bail until he faces the judge the next morning, who will greet him with a severe fine." Anyone picked up who was found with a concealed weapon could be held on more serious charges for the grand jury.

Effa wrote Clark that she liked his work and thought it important. "I understand the conduct of the Colored fans all over the country is pretty bad, and we [the National League owners] decided a lot of it is due to the fact that there is so much drinking at the Ball games," she wrote Clark. "Mr. Posey said in Washington they have made a ruling, anyone seen drinking from a bottle will be escorted from the Park and his money refunded to him."

Order in the grandstands was of sufficient importance to Effa that at least one season she recruited her own undercover security men to help her enforce it:

> At one time in Newark the crowds were getting a little too noisy for me. We always used ballpark police (the Bears' regular employees) but they were old, Lord have mercy if anything would break out. So I personally hired some men on the side they didn't know about, who worked in the taverns. One day my men picked up an unruly fan, and the ballpark help were very angry when they found out.

In that case, she went to the police court personally to plead for punishment, and unruly fans "realized I had the cops and I would go to court against them."

Despite the periodic policing problems, getting the use of Ruppert Stadium was one of the best moves Abe and Effa ever made on the Eagles' behalf. It was not always easy for the Negro league teams to find first-class home fields. Unable for the most part to afford their own stadiums, the clubs were often lucky to make a steady arrangement with a white professional team for use of its park when it was on the road.

The quality of the fields in the Negro league varied widely. Yankee Stadium in New York was the grandest location in the East, but it was not a home park for any of the Negro National League teams, and was used only on special occasions. Cumberland Posey, the resourceful owner of the Homestead Grays, had acquired permission to play not only in Forbes Field, the Pittsburgh Pirates home, but in the Washington Senators' Griffith Stadium, where, beginning in 1940, he tapped into a fabulously rich vein of black baseball fans in the national capital who had no team of their own.

But if the game were against the Philadelphia Stars, it would probably be played at the team's home field at 44th Street and Parkside Avenue, where smoke from Pennsylvania Railroad trains pulling into and out of the nearby yards often obscured play, and the playing surface was rough. Randy Dixon, a black sportswriter, claimed that fans should be issued overalls and gas masks when they attended a game at 44th and Parkside.[2]

If the opponent was the New York Cubans or New York Black Yankees, the game might be played anywhere in the metropolitan area. During most of the Eagles' tenure in the league, neither team had a dependable home park. The Black Yankees settled for awhile in Downing Stadium on Randall's Island in the East River, but it was far from ideal. For one thing, it had no grandstand roof to shield patrons from the hot sun. The Yankees and Cubans were as likely to stage games across the Hudson in Northern New Jersey, particularly Hinchcliffe Stadium in Paterson, as in New York City.

The Eagles' predecessors in Newark, Charlie Tyler's Dodgers of 1934 and 1935, the Newark Browns of 1932, and the Newark Stars of 1926, did not have the use of Ruppert, and played in places that were clearly inferior. One of them was Sprague Field, located in a factory section of nearby Bloomfield, where a laundry building was so close that a ball hit on its roof was only a ground-rule double, not a home run. Another was Newark Schools

Stadium, basically a football field, which had an even more acute baseball dimensional problem—the fences were so close at the foul lines that a ball hit over them counted only as a double. There was also the Meadowbrook Oval at South Orange Avenue and 12th Street, adjacent to Fairmount Cemetery. Although Fairmount was to be Abe Manley's eventual resting place, the neighborhood's ballpark did not meet his standards while he was alive.

Ruppert, on the other hand, was the real thing. Built in 1926, it was still pretty new. Important for a team that did not have first choice of playing dates there, lights had been installed for night play back in 1932, before many major league parks, much less the ones Negro league teams played in, had them. Ruppert Stadium was a full-fledged baseball stadium built for minor league baseball. Located on what was then still meadowland on the eastern edge of Newark, in the lowlands bordering the Passaic River, it was named after Jacob Ruppert, the beer baron who owned the New York Yankees. The Yankees owned the stadium, where its Bears farm team played. John Cunningham, who attended many games there, remembers it as "a good place to watch baseball, like an undersized Fenway Park."

Jerry Izenberg, another Newark journalist who began his career in the era of the Eagles and Bears, says, "the seating capacity was listed at 12,000 something, but it was actually much larger. The record crowd for the park was about 22,000. What they would do was put a rope across center field, and stand people out there." Management could do this, Izenberg said, because for a minor league park, the center field dimensions were large—the fence was 410 feet from home plate, a distance more likely to be found in a major league park. But the foul lines were each only 305 feet away from home plate, a tantalizing distance for power hitters such as Suttles and Irvin.

There were some drawbacks to the location. Amiri Baraka recalls that the stadium's locale had a characteristic defining it as part of industrial Newark—it smelled bad. "They're always talking about toxic waste like it was recent," Baraka joked in an interview. "Newark was always toxic waste capital of the world. But that was part of the ambience of Newark."

The smoke from the dump fires that passed for solid waste disposal in those days sometimes blew across the field and interrupted play. Typically, Peter Strauch, a former umpire recalls, the Manleys were loathe to have a game called on account of smoke until after five innings had been played, so that the contest would have lasted long enough to be declared official, and they would not have to give the fans their money back.[3] One night in 1947, when royalty from the Bears' parent Yankees was in attendance in the person of President Larry MacPhail, dump fires could be seen burning outside the park.

The fact that the park was so far from the residential parts of the city eventually proved a drawback to white and black teams alike, when television and other forms of recreation competed for the baseball fan's dollar, but a streetcar line ran by the stadium, and when the trolleys gave way to buses, there was a stop two blocks away that served three different routes from downtown. Up until after World War II, that was sufficient to bring black fans down from The Hill.

The Manleys acted to become tenants at Ruppert Stadium immediately upon moving from Brooklyn, forging a deal with George Weiss, the Bear's vice president, and Ray L. Kennedy, their secretary. The arrangement, formalized in an annual lease, was, in the context of those agreements between organized baseball clubs and Negro league teams, a fair one. In general, however, the white teams had a tremendous upper hand over the otherwise homeless black teams, and the Bears-Eagles leases show that, also.

The 1939 document, preserved in the Eagle files, ensured the Bears a rent of 20 percent of the gross attendance receipts for doing little more than opening the ballpark gates. Virtually all overhead expenses related to game days were the Eagles' responsibility. They had to pay the ticket sellers and takers, the ushers, the ballpark police, the scoreboard operators, and anyone else needed to put on a game. Mostly the Eagles hired the same men who worked for the Bears in those capacities, at a total outlay of $100 or more per game. If the game was at night, a $65 charge for use of the lighting system was also tacked on. All these expenses came out of the Eagles' home-team share, ordinarily 50 percent of the gross gate receipts, and did not affect the Bears' 20 percent rent or the visiting team's 30 percent gate share.

Admission prices for 1939 were set in the lease at 40 cents for adult bleacher seats, 65 cents for the grandstand, and 85 cents for a box seat. Children under 12 could get into the grandstand for 25 cents and the bleachers for 15. The contract gave the Eagles a chance to distribute as many as 200 free passes for "Ladies Day" games on a frequent basis.

The lease gave both the Bears and the Eagles the chance to pull out of the agreement if it were financially unsatisfactory, but neither ever did. The Eagles' ability to draw fans (mostly black but some white) put money in the pockets of both parties. Reliable attendance and financial information for the Negro leagues is as hard to come by as complete player statistics, but the Eagle files recovered in Newark contain four years' of nearly complete Ruppert Stadium attendance and receipt data that make partial reconstruction of the team's finances possible.

In 1939, for example, the Eagles had fifteen home dates in Newark between May 14 and September 6 (they played twenty-two games there in all, including seven doubleheaders and their appearance in a four-team doubleheader). The team averaged 2,176 paid admissions for each playing date, but on the eight Sundays (which included five of the doubleheaders) the average paid attendance was 3,480. Attendance was up markedly in fifteen Ruppert dates in 1941. The average was 2,696, and eight Sundays brought in an average of 4,293 people (including 11,674 for the home opener May 11 against the Cuban Stars of New York City).

Cum Posey, the owner of the Homestead Grays and also a regular sports columnist in a Pittsburgh black newspaper, reported in 1940 that "by much hard work on the part of Mr. and Mrs. Manley and the full cooperation of the sports writers of Newark, Newark became the leading Sunday city of the league in 1939."[4]

In 1939, the Manleys netted just less than $7,000 from games at Ruppert. They made $10,230 in 1941. Neither was a fabulous total, as professional baseball income went, but in the perspective of Negro league finances, it meant that the Manleys were able to cover from a half to two-thirds of their whole season's player payroll from those games, leaving their 30 percent visitor's shares at other Negro league parks, plus the income from their numerous other games against semipro opponents, to pay for the rest of the team's expenses and perhaps turn a profit.

In later years Effa always stated that Negro league baseball had been an overall losing proposition for her and her husband, costing them $100,000. No balance sheets are available to back that up, but from what can be pieced together season to season, it is plausible. The Manleys' experience basically paralleled that of the other National League owners of that period. The mid and late 1930s were difficult times in which to turn a profit. The leading edge of a wartime boom in attendance started to show up about 1940, and, when things seemingly couldn't be any better financially, the bottom dropped out in 1947.

For the Eagles, there was no question that 1935 in Brooklyn was a money-losing season. After moving to Newark, the team remained incorporated in New York State as the Brooklyn Eagles Baseball Club, and its state corporate tax returns for the 1936 and 1937 seasons show continued losses. For the twelve months ending September 30, 1936, the Eagles took in $14,583.90, but spent $23,615.50, a loss of $9,031.60. The following year, income was up, to $20,551.27, but expenses were $24,684.05, and they lost $4,132.78. By then the club officers (Abe was officially president and treasurer, Effa was vice president and secretary) were owed $13,003.48 in outstanding loans. The team's assets consisted of $139.10 worth of cash on hand, bank deposits and office furniture.

The 1938 season was apparently no better. The Newark *Herald* reported in mid-season that the Eagles had dropped $10,000 in the first two months of play, as atten-

This studio portrait was Effa's favorite portrait, which often illustrated society page stories about her. *(National Baseball Hall of Fame)*

Abe Manley, the Eagles' president; manager Raleigh "Biz" Mackey; and Bill White, a team employee, stride purposefully along a foul line at Ruppert Stadium in a publicity photo. *(Lawrence D. Hogan)*

Posters like this one advertising an Eagles' game against the New York Cuban Stars were an important part of Negro league advertising. Placed in groceries, retail stores, and barber shops in the black sections of cities, they quickly and economically spread the word of upcoming baseball attractions. *(Lawrence D. Hogan)*

This newspaper cartoon lampoons the attempt by Effa and the Eagles to acquire the services of the great pitcher Satchel Paige, who ignored the purchase of his contract by Newark in 1938 to play instead in Latin America. The characterization of Effa by black baseball's males as a "glamour girl" is present here, too. *(Effa Manley scrapbook)*

An enterprising *New York Post* photographer persuaded Effa, somewhat against her will, to strike this pose in the Eagles' dugout wearing a team cap and jacket in 1938. Ordinarily, she dressed very fashionably when in public, even at the games. *(National Baseball Hall of Fame)*

George "Mule" Suttles, one of the great home run hitters of the Negro leagues, played for Newark during nine seasons and also managed the team in 1944. *(Lawrence D. Hogan)*

This photo shows the 1941 Eagle pitching staff at the beginning of the season, when the international troubles that became World War II had not yet actively involved the United States. Before the war was over, Leon Day, Max Manning, and Jim Brown would all be in the armed forces as Newark, like the other black teams, had to find replacements for many of its veteran players for the war's duration. *(Lawrence D. Hogan)*

This is the first known photograph of the Manleys' baseball team, taken in spring training in Jacksonville, Florida, in 1935 when they were the Brooklyn Eagles. Not all the players are completely identified, but important to Eagle history are Ben Taylor (back row, extreme left), the first manager; George Giles (back row, sixth from left), the first baseman who became manager during the season; and Leon Day (front row, extreme right), who pitched for the Eagles for several years. (*Lawrence D. Hogan*)

The Eagles drew more than 13,000 fans to Newark's Ruppert Stadium for this 1942 Opening Day game. Ruppert was the team's home park when not in use by its regular occupants, the Newark Bears of the white International League. Many Negro league teams had identical arrangements with white ball clubs, since few black owners could either afford or get financing to build their own parks. (*Negro Baseball . . . Before Integration*)

Pitcher Leon Day is congratulated by his catcher, Charlie Parks, after his Opening Day no-hit game which began the Eagles' 1946 championship season. *(Lawrence D. Hogan)*

The official team photograph of the 1946 black world champion Newark Eagles. Pictured are (back row, left to right) Monte Irvin, LF; Johnny Davis, LF, P; Lennie Pearson, 1st B; Len Hooker, P; Maxwell "Max" Manning, P; Cecil Cole, P; Rufus Lewis, P; Larry Doby, 2nd B; (middle row, left to right) Leon Ruffin, C; Warren Peace, P; Jim Wilkes, CF; Bobby "Cotton" Williams, P; Bat Boy; (front row, left to right) Selton (Last Name), SS; Charles Parks, C; Clarence Israel, 3rd B; Raleigh "Biz" Mackey, C; Bob Harvey, RF; Leon Day, P. *(National Baseball Hall of Fame)*

Four key members of the 1946 Negro world championship Newark team pose in front of the team bus before heading South for spring training the following year. From left to right are outfielder Johnny Davis, secondbaseman Larry Doby, outfielder Monte Irvin, and firstbaseman Len Pearson. *(Lawrence D. Hogan)*

Max Manning, a New Jersey native who joined the Eagles out of college in 1939, was a key member of the team's pitching staff through 1949. *(Lawrence D. Hogan)*

Effa's continual efforts to have the Eagles recognized by more than Newark's black community eventually made the team's Opening Day festivities a "must" appearance for white politicians. Here Mayor Vincent T. Murphy throws out the first ball. Abe Manley is standing to the mayor's left. *(Lawrence D. Hogan)*

Although there was often acrimonious competition between the Negro National and American leagues, Effa was on excellent terms with Dr. J. B. Martin, the president of the rival American League and owner of the Chicago American Giants. This photo dates from the 1948 joint league meeting at which the Negro National League went out of business. The Eagles, sold at that time by the Manleys to Martin's brother and another man, joined the American League when the National disbanded. *(Negro Baseball . . . Before Integration)*

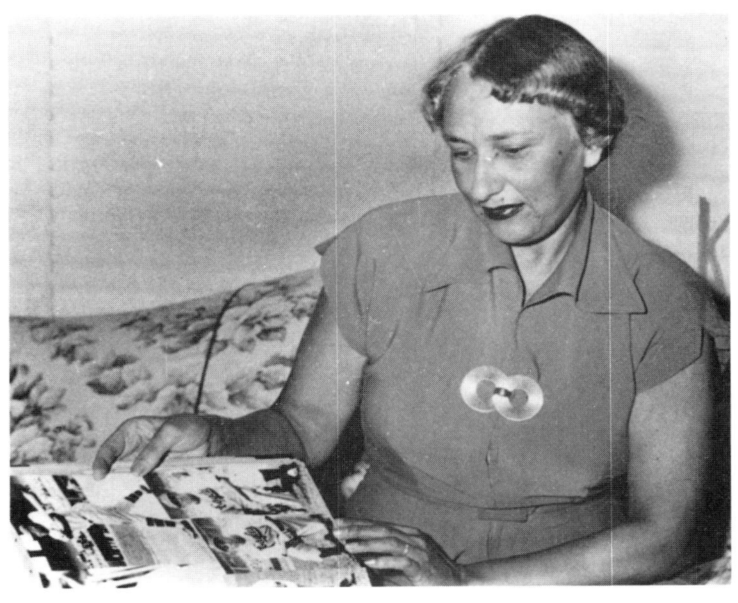

Effa pores over the voluminous baseball scrapbook she had been keeping since 1935. This picture was probably taken around 1950, after she and her husband, Abe, sold the team and got out of baseball. *(National Baseball Hall of Fame)*

dance at league games was generally poor.[5] Small wonder, then, that at the beginning of the 1939 season, when the New Jersey Unemployment Compensation Commission questioned why officers' salaries had not been included on a required report, Effa replied that "the simple fact is that the business has lost so much money each year that the officers have been unable to receive any salaries."

Early in the 1940 season Randy Dixon wrote that "the Manleys, (Affable Abe and Effusive Effa) have written some $63,000 in red ink to learn that organized baseball is a business and not a lark."[6] A figure that detailed could only have come from the Manleys, and it shows they were both aware of and concerned about their losses.

There is also evidence that, while continuing to put a successful facade on team operations, Abe and Effa were pinching pennies behind the scenes. In August, 1940, the Workmen's Compensation Bureau in New Jersey decided against the Eagles in a case brought by pitcher Darltie Cooper, who had suffered a broken foot in May while running out a ground ball. It came out in the hearing that the Eagles did not carry mandatory workers' compensation insurance. When J. W. Kent, the hearing officer, informed Effa of that obligation, she began to plead poverty. "What if I don't have the money for the compensation insurance?" she asked. "Then," the clearly unimpressed Kent replied, "you go to jail." At that point, reported American Negro Press reporter Irvine I. Turner, "Mrs. Manley is said to have twirled about and left the courtroom."

That was also the season that she cut costs by reducing the salaries of the team's administrative personnel. In July, she informed Jerome Kessler, the team's part-time publicist, that he was going to be taking a pay cut. "Yesterday was the smallest crowd we have ever had while playing in Newark, and it is a matter of cutting expenses or ceasing to operate," she wrote.

Defense work in northern industries started to increase in 1941, even before the United States actually went to war, as the federal government reacted to the worsening international situation by increasing supplies to its armed forces. As had happened in World War I, more manufacturing jobs in the North drew blacks from the South. In short order, many of them became Negro league fans, and the clubs that continued to put a good team on the field began to make money.

Sportswriter Art Carter reported in the off-season following 1941 that the Eagles grossed $50,000 the previous season (two and one-half times their reported income in 1937), "of which 10 percent must have been profit."[7] Again, one or both Manleys were a likely source for this information, which is confirmed in a personal letter sent by Abe to attorney Samuel P. Orlando of Camden, N. J., a few months later. "We made a little money with the base ball last year and are in front a little ways this year," the letter reported. A little bit of success had not turned the Manleys' heads, however, as the note continued, "but of course we are expecting anything to happen any day."

Although team finances were beginning to look up in 1941, the Manleys acquired some "insurance" against a return to fiscally losing baseball. Before the season began, they acquired additional capital from a silent partner, Percy Simon. Simon, from Abe's old Norfolk, Virginia, home, was known as a promoter of black sports in the Virginia Tidewater area. In this capacity he also functioned as one of the Manleys' informal network of talent scouts.

The deal was done quietly. No team member or anyone else associated with the Eagles during those years who was interviewed for this book was aware that Simon had apparently helped bankroll the team. But in April, 1941, Effa notified federal Social Security officials in Newark that the team had "been sold to a Mr. Percy Simon." Some of the disputed legal bills that occasioned J. Mercer Burrell's stinging reproof of Effa the next year were for work accompanying the sale.

Few details of Simon's involvement with the team can now be discovered. He certainly did not have a hand in the day-to-day operations of the club, or the players and others would have remembered. He appears to have gotten his investment returned in the form of a salary. The Eagle files contain some of the quarterly Internal Revenue Service forms on which the team had to report its salaries, and he is listed in 1942 and 1943 as a team employee. The report covering the first half of the 1942 season shows him being paid $300. The pair of forms spanning the entire 1943 season have him down for a total of $750.

Simon seems to have severed connection with the team in 1945, when the Manleys instructed lawyer Burrell to restore their names as owners of the Newark Eagles Baseball Club on the trade name certificate on file with the State of New Jersey. It's not clear, however, how profitable Simon's bailout investment was for him, since in 1945, Effa was advising him on the payment of withholding taxes: "You should not have to pay any tax until you get all the money back you have invested."

From very beginning of her partnership with Abe, Effa was in charge of promoting the team. While Abe was capable of creating considerable personal good will, he appears to have had little talent, or probably even interest, in more formal public relations. Effa, on the other hand, while capable of riling people with whom she disagreed, understood that a word-of-mouth reputation was not nearly enough to draw fans to see her team.

The Eagles always touted their games through advertising placards placed in local businesses. This was a tried and true method for the Negro leagues that today seems quaint—more appropriate for school bake sales than professional baseball. But the Negro league games were targeted foremost at the homogeneous black neighborhoods, where people tended to shop and otherwise congregate in stores patronized mostly by members of their race. Since the tiny Eagle office staff (usually just Effa and secretary Carrie Jacobs) could not possibly handle placard distribution, Effa would hire out the job. J. Dory Laramore, a regular Eagle contact in Trenton, was sent 100 placards in advance of the 1940 home opener, and was promised five cents for each one passed out. Effa reminded him in her accompanying letter what a generous deal he was getting, since in Newark the team only paid three cents per poster.

Once the fans were in the park, the game itself was pretty much the only attraction. Special souvenir and giveaway events were unknown, although celebrities popular among blacks were often invited and advertised. Jerry Izenberg recalls that Effa, through her show business connections, could often entice singer Lena Horne to come to Ruppert Stadium, and would also feature performers from the famous Cotton Club in Harlem.

There would be additional competition on opening day, as players tried to win prizes, usually men's clothing, for recording the first hit, run, and extra-base hit of the season. Fran Matthews recalls one opener when, batting leadoff for Newark in the bottom of the first inning, he hit a home run, thus outfitting himself nicely with a single swing of the bat. "I got $100, suits, hats, clothes, from the stores which had prizes for the opening day firsts. It was against Dave Barnhill, who told me 'you young so and so, you'll never get another hit off me.' And I didn't."

Effa clearly was not content to just get as many Northern New Jersey blacks as possible to see her team. Although its success is debatable, she clearly had a campaign to bring whites in to see the Eagles. In 1939, for example, she urged Murray Halpern, of the Adler Shoe Company in Newark, to advertise at the stadium, since "we are planning a big campaign for the Opening Day to try and get white people interested in coming to our games."

The attempt to get whites in baseball-mad Newark interested in the Eagles probably had something to do with her employment of Jerry Kessler, the team's only white employee. Kessler started doing advertising sales and publicity work for the Eagles in 1936, while working his way through Newark University. Later, he became a lawyer with a practice in the city, but continued to do publicity for the Manleys until entering the armed forces during World War II.

Kessler did yeoman work for the Eagles as a publicity man, and in 1949 was Effa's attorney when she blocked the Brooklyn Dodgers' signing of Eagle star Monte Irvin without paying her any compensation. But, despite Kessler's good work for the team, other blacks frowned on her decision to give work and money to a white. In 1940, when Effa and Abe championed a Harlem newspaper publisher for league president, they not only faced severe opposition from other owners, but wandered into the continuing war between New York City's black papers. A columnist for the opposition weekly commented snidely "Speaking of onholy alliances, how about the one between the Negro publisher of a Negro newspaper who hires white printers and the Negro owner of a Negro baseball team who hires a white press agent??" [8]

As Kessler was leaving for service with the Navy in 1940, a Manley ally, Oliver "Butts" Brown of the black New Jersey *Herald News,* applied to handle Eagle publicity. He pointed out that (with his editorial support) the Manleys had been pushing to have the league divest itself of its white booking agent influence and become truly run by blacks. Having had Kessler on their payroll during this period had been a drawback, Brown said.

In a letter to Effa, he argued that "no white publicity man could be of much assistance to you in the many things you hope to do to improve the condition of Negro baseball. In fact, he would be a detriment. The only spot you were vulnerable in your fight for Negro domination of the league was the fact that you employed a white publicity man."

Perhaps because of this appeal, his steadfast support for the Manleys in the cutthroat world of the Negro league owners, or his influential position in the Newark black community, Brown was in fact hired to do publicity for the team during the war. The lines between black newspaper sports journalism and the Negro leagues were sometimes blurred. Arrangements existed that would be considered conflicts of interest today, and Brown collected $100 a month for publicity work while also writing about the club and the league for his newspaper.

Ordinarily, the attention of the black newspapers was vital (and from the owners' perspective, worth paying for), because an unspoken but very solid barrier existed between black baseball teams and the white-owned and managed newspapers that served their cities. In general, coverage of the Negro leagues was sparse to nonexistent in the mainstream papers, and was left almost entirely to the urban black weeklies. As early as the Eagles' first year of existence in Brooklyn in 1935, Effa had discovered that "it was next to impossible to get much space in the white metropolitan dailies."[9]

In Newark, though, Effa broke through that wall. As white sportswriter Bart Giblin recalled, the black clubs "were never written up much by the local papers, until later when the Newark Eagles became more prominent, and Effa Manley got pretty good publicity from the Newark *News*." The now-defunct *News* was the leading paper in Newark, but in addition to wangling coverage there, Effa had a connection that also got attention from the city's other daily, the *Star-Ledger*.

Black radio sportscaster Jocko Maxwell, who had a close connection with the team, was a member of a family that had several members working for the *Star-Ledger*. His father, William Hunter Maxwell, his brother Emerson, and his sister Bernice were all employees, and Jocko would make sure that Eagle box scores and game accounts made it to the paper's sports department after home games at Ruppert.

When the black teams did break into white sports pages, they often found themselves being treated unequally. Effa noted the

> practice of the majority of white sports writers (at least those few who did bother to make an occasional appearance at one of our games) who persisted in writing condescendingly of the players, and the crowds. It was obvious that—from their attitude—they were convinced few, if any, of the black players coming under their scrutiny were good enough to perform in the white professional leagues.[10]

Irvin, an all-sports star at nearby Orange High School as well as a Negro league all star with the Eagles, testifies that conditions in Newark were just that way:

> It was a strange way of writing. When a black guy would do something, it would be very derogatory, "this burly, ebony something, did this or did that." Not a complimentary writeup, as if they almost hated to say something good. I used to get on them about it, but they said that's what their editor wanted.

A fine example of this was one piece of the coverage of the Eagles' debut in Brooklyn. New York *Daily News* columnist Dan Parker, in what was generally a complimentary account of the opening day game, led with: "A brilliant sun was shining down on Ebbets Field yesterday afternoon, but some wag suggested that the game be called on account of darkness." The column, illustrated with a couple of line drawings depicting the players, umpires, and fans in minstrel-style blackface, was headlined EBBETS FIELD GOES HIGH YELLOW.

This often was the layer of burlesque that had to be waded through to get at coverage of the Negro leagues, although the publicity-starved club owners undoubtedly saw it was better than none at all. Effa, in fact, clipped the Parker column and put in it her scrapbook. She was inclined to add her own editorial notations to the scrapbook items when she was particularly pleased or displeased by a piece, but didn't comment on this one.

Whatever the tenor of coverage in the newspapers they read, white fans would come to see the black players, although more would come to see a Negro league team play a white semipro squad than to watch two black squads. Eagle games against the Bushwicks and Bay Parkways of Brooklyn and the East Orange Baseball Club were a dependable source of income for the club, second only to the games against Negro league opponents. Games between two black teams could expect only a limited white audience. This was true in most black baseball venues, but in Newark the annual success and popularity of the Bears probably cut into white Eagle attendance, also. While the two never played in Ruppert Stadium at the same time, the continual ability of the International League team to draw fans must have pretty much consumed the white baseball dollar in the Newark area. In 1932 the Bears, finishing first by 15 1/2 games, drew an outstanding 342,000 fans. Between 1932 and 1938, they put almost 1.5 million in the park. The 20,569 who attended a game against Toronto on May 2, 1937, were trumpeted as the largest crowd ever to attend a Newark sporting event, but that record didn't last long. A year later there were 23,610 (somehow, nearly twice the supposed normal capacity of the park) for a May 22 doubleheader against archrival Jersey City.

White attendance at an Eagles game at Ruppert appears to have averaged between 5 and 10 percent of the crowd. But whether that turnout was a lot or a little depends upon who is asked. Jocko Maxwell, a regular at the park, estimates that

> Attendance was 80, 90, 95 percent black. White fans did not support the Eagles, and you can quote me. You could have 7,000 fans down there and you wouldn't have 500 whites. We had the racial stuff, whites in Newark at that time did not want to be associated with the blacks, particularly on their pleasure time.

Monte Irvin, on the other hand, remembers the 10 percent white attendance as "quite a bit." Bob Harvey, an outfielder with the club from 1944 on, said the Eagles had "a good white crowd, people who liked baseball."

Considering that blacks were by far the primary constituency for Eagle games at Ruppert, Effa's unceasing efforts to publicize her team and get whites to the ballpark were extremely successful. This was particularly true since the Eagles probably had the smallest black population base of any team in the Negro National League.

In 1940 there were 45,760 blacks in Newark proper, but less than 20,000 more in the immediate adjoining communities in Essex, Union, and Hudson counties. In all three counties combined, there were 104,622 blacks, only 5.8 percent of the total population. While the Eagles would advertise their games in more distant cities such as Trenton, it is unlikely that fans were able to come that far to regularly attend Eagle home games. New York City's many black fans were nearby, of course, but the competition for the baseball dollar that had driven the Manleys across the Hudson in the first place continued unabated in the metropolis, and if enough blacks would not go to see the Eagles play in Brooklyn, they would not likely have traveled to Newark.

This is a very rough calculation, but if most prewar fans of both the Bears and Eagles are assumed to have come from members of the teams' own races, and if most of them are assumed to have come from Newark and its immediate environs, then the wildly popular Bears' annual average attendance of a little more than 200,000 from 1932 through 1938 represented about 1 of every 3.5 white residents. The Eagles' 32,646 drawn to Ruppert in 1939, by comparison, is 1 for every 2 blacks in those same communities.

It is no wonder that Effa felt confident enough to chide Cumberland Posey in 1939 when he requested payment of booking fees for a series of barnstorming exhibition games he had scheduled between the Eagles and his Grays. Effa retorted that the trip had not been all that profitable, the Eagles grossing only $1,042.06 in 10 days, with heavy travel expenses. "You have come to Newark only two days this season and received $1,007.50," she pointed out. "The reason for this big difference is I have taken a town to play in, and worked hard to build it up."

Prior to the war, however, the truest summary of black baseball's financial affairs was that "underfinanced and overextended, few, if any, Negro league franchises registered profits." [11] After the Negro National League got back on its feet in 1933, success seems to have been defined by the avoidance of red ink, the general state of affairs for the years that led to black baseball's near collapse in the depth of the Depression.

Black sportswriter W. Rollo Wilson, who should have had some accurate information on league finances, since he was doubling at the time in the largely figurehead role of National league commissioner, wrote about the 1933 season that only one club had made money, and "fellows like Bob Cole (owner of the Chicago American Giants) and Gus Greenlee (of the Pittsburgh Crawfords) lost thousands." Wilson said of 1934 that the owners were "putting the money 'on the line' this year, knowing they cannot win but willing to sacrifice now for a future which will pay dividends."

After the season, Wilson reported that "few, if any clubs made any money" but that "the losses of other clubs were surprisingly small." To Cum Posey, who also had a regular column in the Pittsburgh *Courier*, this translated into success. The year was one of the league's best seasons, he argued, since "no club made as much as the best clubs in the 1920s, but none lost as much as those in bad years."[12]

Similarly, Posey summed up 1935 as "not a glorious financial success . . . but Negro baseball as a body grossed more than has been grossed by Negro clubs since 1930."[13] A statement coming out of the league meeting on January 28, 1938, asserted that "for the past seven years, Negro League Baseball and Negro Independent Baseball has operated at a loss." Financial records were reportedly produced at the meeting to support this sweeping conclusion, but since the prepared statement was to be mailed to the league's players as a warning to expect salary cuts for 1938, it is not surprising that no specifics were quoted. Rainy weather disrupted the league schedule in 1938, leading to more financial loss, but Posey noted with satisfaction that the league, which derived all its income from team dues and a share of game receipts, had paid off $1,000 in debts.[14]

Just as the Manleys had done and Rollo Wilson had predicted, the other owners in the league hung in, took their lumps, and for the most part were still in business when profits began to turn up. In 1941, "baseball had one of its most profitable seasons . . . and it is felt that only limitations and priorities caused by the war will halt the organization from carrying out greater programs."[15]

By 1941, Negro league baseball was a $500,000 business, according to a newspaper piece Effa Manley wrote for the black papers that summer. Her method of calculation was simple, and appears accurate: each team spent about $40,000 per season on player and staff salaries and a host of overhead costs such as park rentals, equipment, and transportation between games. There were six teams each in the Negro National and American leagues, and multiplying their number by the average team outlay brought the total to almost $500,000. Adding the five-figure spending from the annual East-West all-star game to that total pushed the amount of cash the black leagues were spending over the $500,000 mark.

In her book, Effa expanded this estimate, figuring that "the numerous barnstorming professional and semi-pro teams—which played across the country from April through October—further demonstrated that Negro Baseball was a multi-million-dollar proposition in those days."[16] But her estimate of what the league teams spent in 1941 shows how much better off the black side of professional baseball had become in just a few years. Posey had written in 1937 that the National League spent only about $175,000 for its operations, a full 30 percent less than Effa credited it with four years later.[17]

Of course, while this outlay was clearly a matter of pride to Effa and other officials of the Negro leagues, by no means did this money all go to America's blacks. Most of the park rental fees and nearly all of the expenditures for baseballs, bats, and uniforms went to white team owners, booking agents, and equipment manufacturers, who may otherwise have competed fiercely with one another, but had a near monopoly on where, and with what, the black game was played.

Financially speaking, a Negro league team's season could have wildly varying peaks and valleys as it motored around, mixing league games in recognized home parks with games against other league teams on neutral ground (which might or might not count in the league standings) and contests against semipro teams. The weekend games in big cities, where at least one of the teams had a following, were the potential big-money days. The other contests provided returns that approached the infinitesimally small, but owners were paying the players' salaries anyway, and out on an extended road trip, any game that at least defrayed expenses was welcome.

Buck Leonard, the longtime Homestead Gray first baseman who is in the Hall of Fame, has described the relative importance of the games in his team's mixed schedule:

> We'd play the Edgar Thomas Steel Mill team, and over in Braddock they had a team. We'd start at 6:30 and play as many innings as we could get in before dark. The Grays would get \$75 to \$100 to play the game. For the whole team! But Sundays and weekends were the days you really expected to make enough money to pay off your players. Those were the games you played in Forbes Field, Griffith Stadium, Yankee Stadium and those parks. They were called "getting-out-of-the-hole" days.[18]

But the small-town games played on the way to a big payday in a big city pallpark could be frustrating, and not always very profitable. The management of the visiting Negro league team and the local squad would divide up the cash receipts at the end of the game so the blacks could be on their way to the next stop. The arrangement would often give the winning side the bigger share of the gate, but it could be hard to collect the extra share.

Buck Leonard recalled an instance when the Grays had to overcome not only the local opposition, but the umpire hired by the town team:

> One time we were playing in a town outside Norfolk, Virginia. Every time we got in front the umpire would fix it so they'd tie the game. In the ninth inning we were leading by a couple of runs; our owner went in there and got the 60 percent. They tied the game in the last of the ninth inning; he went back in there and they split the money. We went out there and we got in front again; he went back in there and we got the 60 percent. They tied us again, and he split the money again. We were getting ready to go back out on the field again when we said,

> "Wait a minute, there's no way in the world we're going to win." We said, "Let's split it and we'll play no more."[19]

Financial records of these thousands of road games played in obscure towns by Negro league teams are even rarer than accountings from their major sources of revenue, their home games, and the black sports pages seldom reported on the outcomes of these contests, much less their attendance. But a few shreds exist in the Newark Eagle files that show how tough it was to make a living between the bigger paydays. In 1936, for example, the Eagles and the Homestead Grays played a series of April exhibition games, both to get their players in shape for the coming season and to help defray the expense of spring training in Florida. On April 14 in Jacksonville, only 251 people paid to see the two teams play, and the Eagles pocketed only $89.55. Five days later, on a Sunday, 614 showed up, and the Newark share rose to $238.85. But the very next day, in Atlanta, attendance was back down to 250, and the Manleys were paid only $95.50.

Fortunately, the Negro leagues' most popular and lucrative attractions every season were able to provide support for all the teams. The chief one was the annual East-West game in Chicago. Each team in the Negro National and American leagues got a share of the net gate receipts, and since attendance at the all-star gala could top 50,000, the size of the subsidy was significant, at least by black baseball standards. In 1941, for example, Newark's East-West share was $1,977.76. To illustrate its impact on the team's finances, that year it sent three men to the game, Monte Irvin, Lennie Pearson, and Jimmie Hill. Together they made $545 per month, and the money the Eagles received from that single game was enough to cover their salaries for nearly the entire four months of their 1941 contracts. It could be said that the all-star game gave the Manleys the services of their three best players for nearly nothing that year.

Beginning in 1946, the two leagues added a second all-star game on the East Coast. While it was never as well attended as the main one in Comiskey Park, it did serve to boost the shared pool of dollars even higher. In 1946, the pair of games produced more than $28,000 for each league, more than $31,000 in 1947, and more than $23,000 in 1948, the National League's last year of existence. While at least the National League saw to it that its share was also used to stabilize the league treasury by deducting outstanding team dues and other expenses, there is no question that the all-star receipts remained a major source of income for the teams.

Second only in popularity to the all-star games were the next biggest display of Negro league talent, the four-team doubleheaders pitting a different pair of squads in each of the two games. This provided twice the number of well-known players for an afternoon's watching, and when a four-team doubleheader was held in a place where black baseball fans abounded, such as in Yankee Stadium in New York City, some of the best attendances of the year could be expected.

A doubleheader matching the Pittsburgh Crawfords and the Philadelphia Stars, then the Chicago American Giants and Black Yankees, drew 27,000 at Yankee Stadium as early as 1934, and many of the four- team features topped the 20,000-fan mark. So popular were games there that the host Yankees, who were making money steadily from the Negro leagues off the usual rental agreement based on gate receipts, even donated the "Jacob Ruppert Memorial Cup" in 1939 (the colonel had died earlier in the year) to the black team that won the most games at their park.

Although Yankee Stadium was not home to any of the Negro league teams (despite one of the New York entries calling itself the Black Yankees), playing there became a regular part of the Eastern black baseball season. The first black game at the stadium was held in 1930, when the Lincoln Giants of New York and the Baltimore Black Sox drew 18,000 fans. The first four-team doubleheader there was in June, 1932, and certified the location as a winner for the Negro leagues. Eddie Gottlieb, the white sports promoter and part owner of the Philadelphia Stars in the Negro National League, recalled that it rained steadily in

New York from Friday through the morning of the Sunday event.

> We went to the ballpark —it was still very cloudy and threatening—and tried to figure out whether to open the gates or not. We finally decided we would and see what happened. About 12:30 the people started coming, and they stormed the gates, knocking over ticket boxes. . . . We immediately put everybody to work who could sell tickets. We wound up with about 24,000 people in spite of everything.[20]

Probably the third best money-making situation, at least in the National League, was the dual hometown identity of the Homestead Grays. Always popular in their native Pittsburgh, beginning in 1940, the Grays also played a number of games in Washington, D. C. That city had a large black population (nearly 190,000 in the 1940 census) with an appetite for baseball. The Grays, motoring back and forth on the 260-mile axis between Pittsburgh and the national capital, played home games in both Pittsburgh's Forbes Field and Washington's Griffith Stadium. They always drew well in Washington, but the World War II urban population boom that fueled Negro league attendance was especially prominent there. Crowds of 20,000 or more were frequent for Grays games, and the club drew 125,000 fans in Washington alone in 1941. The 30 percent of the gross gate receipts due each visiting National League club from the Atlantic Seaboard must have substantially bolstered many a southern road trip.

Not surprisingly, players' salaries generally followed the curve that described the team owners' climb out of red ink. The reserve clause in white major leaguers' contracts that bound them to one team until traded or released was meant to be the way business was done in the Negro leagues, also. But the opportunity to leave for a summer in Latin American baseball, plus frequent breaches of the reserve principle among black teams in the states, added an element of free market opportunity for the players and helped them capture some of the growing profits.

First, however, the players had to share in the losses. In the 1920s, before the first Negro National League collapsed, players made about $150 to $200 a month, on the average. But it was reported in 1938 that the average salary was only $115.[21] By the all-around good season of 1941, the players' lot had improved significantly, at least in Newark. The 22 player contracts for that year found in the Eagles' files average $145 per month.

While the amounts of money involved are pitifully small, Negro league players were relatively well off in the context of what black workers could expect to earn before the war. A 1932 study determined that the median weekly pay for a black male worker in Newark was $20.44, which came to $87.60 a month, less than even a journeyman ball player could earn during the summer.[22]

Getting paid in the spring, fall, and winter was a different matter. From early April, for a month or so before the Negro league season officially began, a player could at least expect to be fed and housed by his team while in spring training. In the fall he might continue barnstorming in the South with his teammates or players from other teams (sometimes playing teams of white major and minor leaguers). Latin America, where baseball was played year-round, might beckon in the winter, or there were a limited number of slots in a winter league in Southern California which usually fielded a black team. Otherwise, players had to fend for themselves.

Negro league ball was a financial tightrope, and Abe and Effa Manley walked it with all the other owners. Other than earning a reputation for paying their creditors and players on time, they handled their money pretty much the same as the other owners. But at least one of the Eagles thinks they could have done better. Monte Irvin, a special assistant to the baseball commissioner after his Negro and major league careers, recalls that the players themselves urged the Manleys to spend money to better establish their team. Of the Eagles' dependence on a rented home field and arrangements with booking agents for games elsewhere, "we told her, why don't you build your own stadium, avoid booking agents. There's plenty of land here [down by the Passaic River, anyway]. But she didn't want that kind of responsibility."

Irvin says there was even a way to prevent players who had experienced popularity and good pay in the Latin American winter leagues from leaving the Eagles to also play there in the summers. "We all used to congregate at the Grand Hotel there on Market Street; we said to the Manleys, 'you should buy this hotel, fix it up, enlarge it, and the guys will have something to do in the winter. They won't have to go away.'" The advice, however, went unheeded. "I said, you can OWN Newark, as popular as we were," Irvin remembers. "They were wonderful people, but penny-wise and pound foolish."

Perhaps the Manleys, although well-off, didn't have enough money to make such major investments. Then again, since they had ambivalent feelings about the Negro leagues' survival up until only a few years before the postwar decline of black baseball, such investments may have never felt safe. Or maybe the answer is as simple as Irvin says it is, and they lacked the vision to go with their baseball and business acumen.

But even if Effa was, indeed, pound foolish, Irvin can testify from experience how she was penny-wise. After the 1948 season, with the aid of lawyer Jerry Kessler, she fought off an attempt by Brooklyn Dodger President Branch Rickey to sign Irvin to a Dodger contract in a deal that offered no compensation to the Eagles. Soon after, Kessler negotiated Irvin's sale to New York Giants and their president, Horace Stoneham, for $5,000. This was a small sum, given Irvin's ability, but about all the Eagles could get for his contract—the Negro leagues had little bargaining leverage in the face of the popularity of major league integration. Effa gave her attorney half of the purchase price as his fee, turned over half of the remainder to the man to whom she and Abe were selling the club, and kept the rest herself.

Irvin, who went on to play seven seasons with the Giants and had a key role in their 1951 pennant season, argued with her at the time that "I've been on the payroll all these years, why don't we just split the money? She said, 'No way. I'm going to buy myself a fur stole. I owe it to myself. You're going to make a lot of money in the majors.'"

Then, in 1979, Irvin met Effa at a Negro league reunion in Ashland, Kentucky. She showed up wearing the stole she had bought thirty years before with the Irvin sale money. It was still in good shape, and Irvin joked with her, "You got a pretty good deal."

"Not as good as Horace Stoneham got," she retorted.

Notes

1. Manley and Hardwick, *Negro Baseball,* p. 51.
2. *Courier,* Feb. 17, 1940.
3. Asbury Park (N.J.) *Press.*
4. *Courier,* April 27, 1940.
5. Newark *Herald,* July 9, 1938.
6. *Courier,* May 11, 1940.
7. *Afro-American,* Feb. 28, 1942.
8. *Age,* March 2, 1940.
9. Manley and Hardwick, *Negro Baseball,* p. 44.
10. Ibid.
11. Jules Tygiel, *Baseball's Great Experiment: Jackie Robinson and His Legacy* (New York: Oxford University Press, 1983), p. 23.
12. *Courier,* July 14, 1934; Sept. 15, 1934; Nov. 17, 1934.
13. Ibid., Feb. 15, 1936.
14. Ibid., Sept. 10, 1938.
15. *Afro-American,* Feb. 14, 1942.
16. Manley and Hardwick, *Negro Baseball,* pp. 52-53.
17. *Courier*, May 15, 1937.
18. Holway, *Voices,* p. 259.
19. Ibid., pp. 264-65.
20. Arthur G. Rust, Jr., *Get That Nigger Off the Field* (New York: Delacorte Press, 1976), p. 50.
21. Paul M. Gregory, *The Baseball Player* (Washington: Public Affairs Press, 1956), footnote on p. 129; *Courier,* June 4, 1938.
22. Interracial Committee, *Negro in New Jersey,* p. 91.

Chapter 6
The Manleys for Reform

The Negro National League owners represented the full spectrum of types who ever had gotten involved with professional black baseball. There were the career baseball men, some of whom dated back even before Rube Foster had founded the first league; men who had invested riches made in other businesses, frequently gambling, and, although Foster surely would not have invited them in, white sports promoters to whom a Negro league team was just one more horse in a large stable of sports investments. (See Appendix A for descriptions of these owners.)

Some of these men (they were all men, another reason Effa Manley often upset them so) were good businessmen, and some were profligate. Some were reticent and others flamboyant. It sometimes became an important issue that some were black and some were white. Each of the team ownerships stood for one or more of the disparate groups that made the Negro leagues distinctive, which went a long way toward explaining why league meetings resembled a convention of Byzantine princes.

These petty fiefdoms that were the league ownerships were defended by their principals with ready responses to both real and imagined grievances by mixing and matching their allegiances to suit their current interests.

The initial site of most disputes was Pittsburgh, which was never quite big enough to hold both Cumberland "Cum" Posey, chief owner and operator of the Homestead Grays, and William A. "Gus" Greenlee, owner of the Pittsburgh Crawfords and primary founder of the league in 1933. Their feud was the dominant relationship in the league until Greenlee suffered financial reverses and dropped out after the 1938 season.

For public consumption, each would provide plausible reasons, other than their intense turf battle, for not getting along. For example, in 1934, a much-awaited Labor Day weekend series between the Grays and Crawfords was canceled. Posey blamed it on Greenlee's selfish reaction to the Grays' decision to play an August benefit game in Forbes Field, the major league Pittsburgh Pirates' home park, rather than at his Greenlee Field. Nonsense, Greenlee replied in the press; the series fell through because Posey selfishly refused to commit 5 percent of his gross receipts from the series to the league treasury, thus depriving the league of part of its operating revenue.

If there was nothing else for the two to fight about in public, Posey could always resurrect the charge that Greenlee and the others running the 1935 East-West game had padded expenses and deprived other league members of their rightful share of profits. Greenlee's response, that those who had gone to extra lengths to make the game a success deserved extra money, was reasonable. But his argument was partially undercut by the fact that one of the other all-star partners, Robert Cole of the Chicago American Giants, had been called to task by the other owners for failing to account for league funds while league treasurer.

Continuing suspicion in the East about the handling of the East-West receipts in faraway Chicago resulted in Effa Manley's first official mission on behalf of the league. She was sent in advance of the 1937 game to review the financial arrangements, with instructions to withhold the players picked from the Grays, Eagles, and other Eastern clubs if it were not clear that each would share equitably in the proceeds.

The loss of the Crawfords and the addition of the New York Black Yankees and New York Cubans brought changes in the lineup of interests that were pulling the league in various directions. For one thing, the Battle of Pittsburgh was over—Posey had outlasted his opponent. But admission of the two New York clubs and the reduction of Pittsburgh's representation to one team split the six members evenly between the New York metropolitan area and the rest of the Eastern Seaboard states. It also added another white man to the power structure in addition to Eddie Gottleib of the Philadelphia Stars, as William Leuschner's close ties to James Semler's Black Yankees made him a regular at league meetings.

By 1940, the Manleys, Semler, and Alex Pompez of the New York Cubans had formed an informal New York area alliance that blamed President Tom Wilson, owner of the Baltimore club, for most of the league's ills and was, in turn, accused of trying to take over the league. But this alliance had its limitations, since one of the Manleys' strongest beliefs was that the white booking agents held too much power over affairs. Pompez and Semler, both lacking regular arrangements for home parks, were heavily dependent upon the agents, particularly Gottleib and Leuschner, and could only go so far in opposing them.

Earlier, Posey appeared to be happy to coexist with the booking agents, but by 1941 he, too, thought them too powerful. He summarized the chances of wresting Yankee Stadium scheduling rights away from Gottlieb in a letter to Abe and Effa that December: if the Gottlieb-Leuschner business arrangement extended to Leuschner getting half of the Yankee Stadium booking fees (as he suspected), then "we could not count on Pompez vote, as Pompez could not afford to fall out with Leuschner." Posey added that Semler would side with them if he got five dates of his own to promote at Yankee Stadium. But this created a sort of chicken-and-egg dilemma, since the dates could only be his if successfully taken out of white hands. Tom Wilson, Posey reported, "would go along the way the rest of the league wanted it done," which was an exceptionally safe position, given the deadlock facing the rest of the membership. At any rate, Gottlieb didn't lose his Yankee Stadium rights.

If rivalries among the National League owners were not enough, from 1937 on there was the competition of the Negro American League, founded to organize big league black baseball in the Midwest and South, from Chicago and Kansas City all the way down to Atlanta and Jacksonville. There should have been no reason the two leagues could not have operated in harmony, as did their white counterparts, except that there was no black equivalent of Kenesaw Mountain Landis, white baseball's commissioner. The black leagues had no overall chief. Instead, they tried to iron out their differences in joint league meetings that frequently failed to achieve even moderately long-lasting solutions.

There were also clashes of major league egos that, not surprisingly, involved Cum Posey. Posey held J. B. Martin, president of the American League and Robert Cole's successor as owner of the Chicago American Giants, in very low repute. The Pittsburgh owner publicly charged that Martin "rules like a dictator."[1] Privately, Posey told the Manleys that Martin was "the biggest four flusher and liar I have met in all my years of baseball."

Martin had faced up to serious police harassment of his drug store business in Memphis in 1940 (it was alleged that in addition to being black, he had also made the mistake of being a prominent Republican in a town run by Mayor Ed Crump's Democratic machine) and then had succeeded in elective politics in his new Chicago home. With these credentials, he probably was not too intimidated by Posey. He was friendly with other National League owners, especially the Manleys, and doesn't seem to have had any interest in a vendetta against the National League.

But since Posey's Grays were the westernmost team in the National League and depended upon games in the Midwest for a good portion of their income, the American League represented a threat to him and co-owner Rufus Jackson that would not have scared the other National teams. This was especially so since his sphere of influence as a booking agent in Western Pennsylvania rubbed up against that of the American League's white agent, baseball and basketball empresario Abe Saperstein of Chicago. By 1941, Posey definitely considered Saperstein a danger. He used his column to proclaim that "it is up to all who have any interest in organized Negro athletic enterprises to stop Saperstein, [Syd] Pollock [a Saperstein associate] or any others who are attempting to monopolize them."[2] Cum Posey had not painstakingly constructed black baseball's most successful dynasty, the Negro leagues' version of that era's New York Yankees, by ignoring threats.

The inherent tension between pitcher and batter that forms the core of baseball's attraction had an off-the-field counterpart in the Negro leagues. Scrambling self-interest conflicted with the acknowledgment that there was more opportunity and security in a league operation, or the owners would not have been together at all. Small wonder that, as it was reported in 1936, a league meeting was so tense that "every view put forward by any member appeared to be a challenge to the other members."[3] Under the circumstances, Tom Wilson's easygoing presidential manner may have provided the grease that kept the league's parts moving in an approximation of unison. "Let bye-gones be bye-gones," he said, to end wrangling at one meeting, "and lets get together and make some money."[4]

Abe and Effa Manley were never advocates of the Tom Wilson School of Baseball Management. Effa recalled that at the time the Eagles were founded, Abe considered the Negro leagues poorly organized—"everything was run in a permissive, self-defeating, and entirely unorthodox manner."[5] Husband soon won wife over to his point of view, or perhaps the other owners drove her there.

At the first league meeting of 1937, "Mrs. Manley, who is rapidly learning the business end of the baseball game, addressed the members and in no uncertain terms, expressed her disapproval of the way the members conducted league business." She then contrasted what she saw as current faults with the "wonderul future possible for Negro baseball if conducted in a businesslike manner."[6]

Notes from 1941, in Effa's handwriting, which were found in the Eagle files in Newark, give a strong clue as to the wide range of league business she thought needed attention. The collection of jotted words and phrases, perhaps made in advance of a league meeting, suggest she was ready to question just about every aspect of the operation. "Gottlieb," "Yankee Stadium," and "Saperstein taking players" are clear references to relations with the white booking agents; "teams play same number of games" refers to the chronic problems in creating a balanced league schedule; and "chairman" and "financial statements" refer to an issue always on her mind—the need to appoint someone other than club owners as the league's chief executive to make the entire operation more businesslike and profitable.

Women executives were rare in American business in the 1930s, even rarer in professional baseball. Although Maude Semler would sometimes help her husband with the Black Yankees, and Ethel Posey would inherit the Grays from her late husband in 1946, a woman who actually held major decision-making power over a Negro league team was unknown, except for Effa Manley. She would have had an enormously difficult time even getting her views heard when the owners convened, except that however suspicious they would have been of her, they liked and accepted her husband just as much.

In 1936, the Eagles' second year in the Negro National League, Abe was made the league's vice president. He became treasurer in 1937 and, except for the 1942 season, held the office until the league went out of business in 1948. It was well known that Effa did nearly all of the work required by the position, and they became accepted essentially as co-treasurers, although the male-dominated owners' group would only bestow the title on Abe.

He seemed to be able to keep above the bickering that invariably consumed the league meetings. In fact, Posey wrote in the middle of the 1936 season that "Mr. Abe Manley is the one now in the league who we are certain is for the best interest of the league and its members." [7] If Effa's participation was all right with Abe, then it was all right with the other owners, too. As confident as she eventually became of her own abilities to run a baseball team, Effa had no doubts about how she got her start: "In the beginning, men owners were a little disturbed at women in the picture, but not for long. They saw how important I was to Abe, and everybody was crazy about him."

Effa eventually began to garner her own compliments, the ungrudging ones coming from people who were not necessarily in the National League power structure. Frank A. Young, sports editor of a major black weekly, the Chicago *Defender,* wrote her in 1940, saying, "I find you very gracious and ladylike, and knowing more baseball than some of the so-called baseball experts who have been in the game for years."

Since they always agreed publicly (apparently usually in private, also) about what was best for the league, the Manleys began to be recognized as a single voice for putting black baseball on a more organized basis, one more closely resembling the white major leagues.

Having suffered a particularly galling setback in 1940 over their claim of rights to the famous pitcher Satchel Paige, they angrily threatened to quit the league. This occasioned a letter from Michael Iannarella, an employee of Gottlieb's Philadelphia sports promotion business, urging them to stay. "Negro baseball will certainly miss someone who has fought to clear up the mess and muddle that has infested the league," he wrote them.

Eventually, the National League owners came to recognize that, in those situations where they could agree that their common financial self-interest was at stake, Effa was a valuable representative. They had sent her to Chicago in 1937 to monitor the East-West money, allowed her to keep the league treasury, and in 1943 put her in charge of setting up a series of benefit games for the Army and Navy relief funds.

But Wendell Smith, of the Pittsburgh *Courier,* noted, in praising her appointment, that Effa's counsel was not always welcome.

> She has always had her hands in the baseball broth, but the other cooks were never willing to try her recipe for a better all-around menu for the Negro National League . . . she has been the No. 1 thorn in the vulnerable sides

> of the other owners, simply because she is a woman with ideas and aggressiveness.[8]

In her old age, Effa minimized the male opposition to her taking a seat among the owners and specifically said they had not been prejudiced against her. In her book, she said the biggest problem was an undercurrent of uneasiness at the first few meetings. "It seems the gentlemen weren't quite sure just how freely to act with a female sitting in on their business confabs." [9] She also recalled an apologetic telephone call from Cum Posey simply because he had used profanity at a league meeting.

For whatever reasons, she was being disingenuous. Two of her former players, Monte Irvin and Max Manning, remember otherwise. Irvin says her insistence on more foresight was very unpopular, at least when it came from her. "The Negro league owners were all going in their own directions—nobody had any intelligence but her, they were jealous of her looks, jealous of her money, just naturally resentful." Manning's opinion is that at league meetings "I believe there was a lot of resentment about her when she left [the room]. They recognized the woman was sharp and could see things they couldn't see, and they resented it."

One thing that Abe Manley wanted to see, and that Effa also supported, was full black control of Negro league baseball, for they not only took their baseball seriously, they took its blackness seriously, too. "Abe had been waging a one-man war against the booking agents from the first day he entered the picture," Effa wrote. "Abe always took the unwaverable position that league teams should do their own booking . . . but he fought a losing battle. The tentacle-like grip of the booking agents proved almost impossible to break." [10]

The battle of black and white control of the Negro leagues had existed back in the beginning, when Rube Foster monopolized play in the Midwest and whites, led by Nat Strong, ran the East. By the late 1930s, the situation was much less clear-cut and was curiously mixed in some ways. Blacks and whites worked together to produce segregated Negro baseball, and to some extent it could be said that each needed the other. The black side supplied the players, of course, and entrepreneurs such as the Manleys, Posey, Greenlee, and J. B. Martin were present in such numbers as to make white domination of the ownership side impossible.

Nonetheless, the white booking agents held the "high ground" in that they controled the playing fields, without which there could be no professional ball. Promoters such as Gottlieb, Abe Saperstein, and Leuschner had standing agreements with the semipro clubs that the Negro league teams depended upon as nonleague opponents. In Gottlieb's case, he also had locked up Yankee Stadium and Shibe Park, home of the Philadelphia Athletics, when the Yankees and As were playing out of town. There was no way a Negro league team could have a profitable season without coming to these men for playing dates and giving them a share of the gate receipts.

It should be noted in the booking agents' defense that the best ones provided a real service for their share of the money. If Ed Gottlieb Sporting Enterprises booked a game for a team, its owners had little more responsibility than to make sure their players turned up on time. Mike Iannarella, at Sports Poster Service, a Gottlieb subsidiary, made sure that tickets and window posters were printed and newspaper publicity, including photos of the club's star players, was in the hands of the local press in advance of the game date. The agent's entire package of services was a major factor in keeping Negro league clubs' front office staffs small—if a black team had as many as half a dozen employees, including secretaries and a bus driver, it had a big staff.

Gottlieb, who with Pompez was one of two Negro league owners named in the 1970s to the special committee that selected the first nine Negro leaguers to the Hall of Fame, had also faced major league baseball's closed door. In 1942, the Philadelphia Phillies were up for sale. Gottlieb, acting on behalf of Dr. Leon Levy, who owned a Philadelphia radio station, among other investments, tried to find out discretely if the league had any problems with Jewish ownership of a team.

According to New York *Times* columnist Walter "Red" Smith, Gottlieb recruited sportswriter Bob Paul to put the question to National League President Ford Frick, but when Paul sought an appointment, Frick "said he had to catch a train for Chicago." When Paul, at Gottlieb's urging, pressed for a meeting on the train, Frick replied, "I've come to the conclusion I cannot discuss anything about the sale of the Phillies. So don't bother meeting my train." The league took over the Phillies when the owning Nugent family could no longer afford to operate them. It then hastily negotiated a sale to lumberman William Cox and repented when Cox was banished from baseball for betting on games. Gottlieb would have been general manager of the Phillies if Levy had been allowed to buy the team, but instead he found his baseball career lay with the other outcasts, the Negro leaguers.

The booking agents themselves might be subtly barred from the major leagues, but at their level, they had power. To go head-to-head with them could mean financial disaster. Black owners in the East in the mid-1930s did not have to think back too far to recall John Drew. He ran the Hilldale club in the Philadelphia area in the first years of that decade, refused to do business with the agents, and consequently found it difficult to get the games with semipro clubs that he needed to fill out his schedule. Webster McDonald, a player and manager in Philadelphia black baseball for years, recalled that Drew "said he would sit down and pay his ball club for the season even if he didn't play a ball game, rather than play an exhibition game [booked by a white]. So he finally dropped out." [11]

Ed Bolden, who moved back in charge of black baseball in Philadelphia when Drew folded his operation, took precisely the opposite tack. He made Eddie Gottlieb his partner, and the two ran the Philadelphia Stars. McDonald, who managed the team, said that "when other clubs were hitting it rough, our ball club was playing every day."[12] Although Bolden was always listed as the club's president, at least one other Negro National League executive, Richard Powell of the Baltimore Elite Giants, believes that the Stars became virtually Gottlieb's team as he acquired more and more of a share in return for the loans he made to Bolden.

Abe and Effa Manley were not alone in regarding the booking agents as an unwelcome and damaging influence on the league. Before a pitch had been thrown in the 1935 season, Posey had made a veiled attack on Gottlieb and Leuschner, the inheritors of the power that had belonged to the late Nat Strong. The purported object of his ire was the Black Yankees, still an independent team backed by the booking agents and often scheduled in competition with the Negro league teams. "There are powerful forces in Eastern baseball, with unlimited measures," Posey wrote ominously.

> These forces stretch out like an octopus; they will attempt to ensnare the various club owners by devious methods, but all these methods have one object, the destruction of the League. The Black Yankees are one of the tools by which these forces hope to crush Organized Negro Baseball just when [it] is strongest, and thus crush it for all time.[13]

The league, of course, was not crushed, but the agents' influence remained weighty. The Brooklyn Eagles suffered directly from the competition in 1935. Nat Strong had been a part owner of the Bushwicks, the crack semipro team in Brooklyn, and his agency arranged their games, creating substantial competition for Eagle home games. That other Negro National League teams would accept bookings with the Bushwicks on the same days the Manleys were trying to draw fans to Ebbets Field in the same borough of New York City shows just how embedded the need for white money was in the league structure, and how futile it probably was to try to drive it out.

When it came time to reminisce about her long career in baseball, Effa again painted herself as more conciliatory than she had been when the league was in flower. She maintained, when in her seventies, that she was not in full agreement with her husband's opposition to the agents. "I thought those other men had experience, but when I saw what his attitude was, I didn't pursue it any further. He was probably right, but I was thinking about the financial result," she temporized. [14]

The surviving league owners and officials who read those words must have been incredulous when they thought back to the league meeting of February 4, 1940. There Effa campaigned against Gottlieb, insulted Posey, and set the black baseball world on its ear for a few weeks.

The 1940 annual meeting, held in Gottlieb's offices in Philadelphia, had little that seemed controversial on its agenda, but the Manleys, Pompez, and Semler had a recipe for trouble—they wanted Tom Wilson out as president. They nominated Dr. Clilan P. Powell, publisher of the black New York weekly, the Amsterdam *News*. But the Grays, Philadelphia Stars, and the Baltimore Elite Giants (representing every league official except Abe) backed Wilson, throwing the election into a 3-3 tie. With the leadership decision deadlocked, the meeting began to fall apart because of the underlying issue of the teams from the New York area—they wanted Gottlieb stripped of his lucrative rights to promote their games in Yankee Stadium.

Baltimore *Afro-American* sports editor Art Carter reported:

> In a fiery speech, Mrs. Manley insisted that her reasons for seeking dismissal of Wilson were based on the league president's approval of an agreement whereby Gottlieb, as a private booking agent, collects 10 percent on promotion of games in Yankee Stadium, the loop's most profitable promotions. She assumed the position that the league was a colored organization and that she wanted to see all of the money kept within the group.

"This thing is bigger than any of us here," she reportedly said about Negro ball. "It isn't just a question of my team or your team winning, or of who'll make money next season and who won't. This matter has developed into a race issue." The argument got hotter, with Effa blasting Posey, Wilson, and Bolden for giving up future advantages for blacks in return for profits now from Gottlieb.

An *Amsterdam News* clipping in Effa's scrapbook reported the meeting ended when Effa "hurled epithets at Cum Posey [who] left the meeting in a huff, vowing that he would never return as long as Mrs. Manley was the Newark Eagles' representative." Posey, the pioneer of Negro baseball and scion of an established black Pittsburgh family, must have been truly incensed, because before he stormed out, the acid-tongued Effa had called him a "handkerchief head," a derogatory slang term for a black who was routinely subservient to white authority.

Despite some unladylike behavior, Effa's opponents still treated her like a woman. Posey charged that Effa "took advantage of her sex in the deliberations," and the *Afro-American* cropped her likeness off the left end of the group photo of the owners and ran it separately, labeling her the "Stormy Petrel" of the league.

Posey remained incensed. On February 17 he used his column to defend the Yankee Stadium deal with Gottlieb, pointing out that the booking agent had been able to reduce the fee for the use of the park from $3,500 to $1,000, as well as cut the Yankees' operating charges in half and negotiate a better rate for liability insurance. The Grays owner claimed Gottlieb's negotiations with the Yankees had saved the league members $10,000 in 1939. Gottlieb, in return for $1,100 in booking fees, had enabled the clubs to take home $16,000 in profits. "The promoter took all the headaches, the league clubs walked into the stadium, and twenty minutes after the game was over, walked out with their shares," Posey claimed.

To show the folly of abandoning Gottlieb, he contrasted the Yankee Stadium profits with some failed promotions Semler had put on in the city-owned stadium on Randall's Island, located in the East River in New York. According to Posey, three games put on by Semler in 1938 had netted only an average of $12 each for the teams, "and it took two days after each game to argue over and pay bills."

But Posey would not be satisfied with merely a rational, dollar-based rebuttal. He had been embarrassed in public, by an aggressive woman, no less, and he would try to get even. He allowed that at the league meeting "we have never heard so much senseless chatter and baying at the moon as was done by one party." He further accused the guilty party of performing for the benefit of "a prepaid crowd of New York sportswriters." Her picking on Gottlieb brought "a race issue" into the meeting, which was "a disgusting exhibition for a lady."

For good measure, he accused Effa of skimming profits from a four-team doubleheader in Newark in 1939. Then, having denounced her for dragging race into the argument, he played the other side of the race card himself:

> We wonder if the Negro sports scribes who made the "Cook tour" to Philadelphia and heard the irrational outburst concerning race pride know that the Newark Eagles pay a publicity man [Jerry Kessler] $50 a week, and this publicity man is a white man?[15]

The usually affable Tom Wilson was also heard from. In a February 11 letter to black sports editors, he characterized Effa's proposals on Doctor Powell and Yankee Stadium as "idiotic." He continued, "it does not make sense to have a woman, who positively does not know the first thing about baseball, tell experienced baseball men how to conduct their business."

A personal letter to Effa on February 17 shows Posey still angry, but at least able to apply a little humor to the situation. "All this mess at the league meeting was not necessary . . . you admit you don't know anything about the game, but still get mad and insulting with everybody who disagrees with you." Referring to his contention that Effa had a sympathetic relationship with the metropolitan New York black sportswriters, Posey added that

> When you have the writers of New York and Newark write about me, I think, "well, that gives President Roosevelt a rest from them." When I write about you,

> then think of the space you are taking up, which could be alotted to Eleanor. I always try to remember, to learn how to dish it, you must first learn how to take it.

If Posey and Wilson thought their offensive would quiet Effa, they were wrong. She pointed out in a letter to Art Carter that the dispute over Yankee Stadium bookings (to which she and Abe had not assented when the deal with Gottlieb was struck in 1939) was only one of several complaints about league operations.

> The public and the ball players are entitled to a better break. The only way this is possible is through the adoption of sound business policies and an impartial set of officers. This is my position, and I shall continue to take this stand.

The fact that a woman had stood up in a men's forum and demanded reforms did not go unnoticed. An acquaintance, Mrs. Olivia M. Rudolph of Charleston, S. C., wrote, asking Effa to "accept my congratulations on the stand you took at the 'Philly' meeting. It takes real courage to hold your own against such strong men."

The attempt to replace Wilson came to naught when the league meeting was continued on February 24. Pompez, stating it was "in the best interest of the league" to resolve the deadlock, suggested retaining all the 1939 officers. Although Semler, who stood to gain a great deal financially if he could get control of Yankee Stadium, resisted what was probably intense pressure from Gottlieb and Bill Leuschner, Pompez's survival skills in a tight spot included knowing when to retreat to a safe position.

The tempest did not die down without some further pointed motions from Abe Manley, however. He tried unsuccessfully to have Posey replaced as secretary by baseball writer Al Monroe, and attempted to have the practice of reimbursing officers for official traveling expenses ended. Buster Miller, sports columnist for the New York *Age,* thought that:

> Like all reformers [the Manleys, Semler, and Pompez] fell into the common error of trying to accomplish all their reforms at one swoop. A long time ago, one of our Broadway Balzacs wrote: "A chump is a guy who just can't wait." The reforming league owners couldn't wait, and now they are likely to lose their fight.[16]

Having fought and lost on principle, the Manleys then proceeded to lose money because of their stand. The Eagles were shut out of Yankee Stadium promotions completely in 1939 and 1940, not returning there to play until Memorial Day, 1941. The agents would withhold playing dates from the Manleys to inconvenience the Eagles, as well as keep them from the most profitable venues. Outfielder Bob Harvey recalled, "they would have us travelling 300 or 400 miles at night for a game, when they could do better than that." Dick Powell, of the Elite Giants, definitely recalls that "the Manleys were not in Gottlieb and Leuschner's good graces" but eventually were let back into important dates because the other club owners demanded the Eagles' presence. "Someone like [Douglas] Green [of the Elites] or Pompez would say to Gottlieb or Leuschner, 'hey, look now, we need so and so, to have a balanced league.' "

Publicly, relations between the Manleys and the booking agents and their supporters eventually returned to a state of civility, to such an extent that Randy Dixon reported in the Pittsburgh *Courier* before the start of the 1941 season that the "feuding Manleys and Gottlieb have figuratively kissed and made up."[17] But throughout her career as an owner of the Eagles, Effa never abandoned the position that Negro league baseball would be a stronger institution if it were not beholden to whites.

In 1944, she completely identified with the black race in commiserating with B. B. Martin, owner of the Memphis Black Sox in the Negro American League, about one of his league's teams, the white-run Indianapolis Clowns. The Clowns, who often burlesqued Negro baseball by dressing in grass skirts and painting their faces to look like "cannibals," were regarded in many circles as a disgrace to Negro baseball. But their owner, Syd Pollock, had close ties to Abe Saperstein, and so was immune to the criticism. Effa told Martin that problems with the Clowns did not surprise her, "as those people never did want baseball to get too high class, and all these sort of things help to keep it down."

Although the idea of a permanent home for the Eagles in Brooklyn was in the past, the Manleys continued to try to showcase their team there. They still ran afoul of the agents, who not only booked teams into Dexter Park to play the Bushwicks, but were also trying to monopolize Ebbets Field when the Dodgers were not playing there. In 1944, Effa secured Ebbets for a July 4 game with the New York Cubans, only to find that Leuschner's Nat C. Strong Baseball Enterprises had rented the park two days before, for a Cubans-Kansas City Monarchs contest. Leuschner absolutely refused to permit both games to be advertised together, and left Effa with the impression that he "was trying to tie the Brooklyn park up so all the teams would go in there under his promotion."

Effa countered by making the Fourth of July game a special war bond rally day (the Eagles were also promoting war bonds in Newark on July 2) to increase attendance. "The first thing I have to do is try to make July 4th a success, so we will be able to get the dates we want in Ebbetts [sic] Field, so the teams will not have to pay booking fees," she wrote Wendell Smith. However, although the bond sale went well, attendance was only about 3,000 in head-to-head competition with the Brooklyn semipro teams. By now, Effa was getting used to these setbacks. "In the baseball [world], we learn to take things like this just as we do rain, etc.," she wrote a friend.

But not getting her way seldom made Effa Manley reconsider her views. In a mostly conciliatory letter written to settle a minor financial disagreement with Gottlieb, Effa observed, "you have all the ability necessary to put Negro Baseball on a permanent paying basis. But in order to do this, Negro Baseball must come first, and Ed Gottlieb second. Is this too much to hope for?"

Dependence on playing fields controled by others led directly to the Negro leagues' most obvious shortcoming when compared to white big league baseball. The neat, arithmetically balanced schedules that have always existed in other professional leagues never existed in the Negro National or American circuits. Former player Charles Biot observes that this gave them the reputation of being "organized and disorganized" at the same time.

There were several reasons for this state of affairs. For starters, the clubs had to work around the home schedules of the teams that owned or otherwise had first claim on the parks. For example, making the Eagles' home schedule every year began with the Manleys obtaining a copy of the Newark Bears' home slate. Even then, other events could intrude upon the black clubs' plans, as when a Rocky Graziano-Tony Zale prize fight at Ruppert, which figured to pack the park, knocked out a scheduled Eagle game.

Rained-out games, easily rescheduled as doubleheaders or on open dates in the more organized leagues, could create both scheduling and financial havoc for Negro league teams. The two teams that had been canceled could probably get together again that season, but the meeting might not be in the same location. "Rain checks," passes given to the fans who had paid for the canceled game that allowed them to get into the rematch free and let the teams keep the gate receipts from the rainy day, were impossible to issue. If the game couldn't be rescheduled, or if it had to be played in a less-profitable location, money was lost forever.

Many Negro league teams had favorite well-paying, nonleague opponents (the Bushwicks, for instance) and would forsake league games for a chance to play their nonleague rivals. They might show lack of discipline in other ways, too. Art Carter, of the *Afro-American*, criticized the Grays in May, 1941, for featuring an exhibition game a week before the scheduled start of the season as their season opener. Such erratic behavior was "one of the big reasons the Negro National League fails to do any better than it does" with its fans, Carter wrote.

In the National League, balanced scheduling was a goal, but one to be achieved within rather broad parameters. The rule for 1942 was that each team must play each of the others a minimum of eight to a maximum of twelve times, and each team must play at least forty games. In 1945, Effa wrote John Collins of the Brooklyn Dodgers' front office that "for the first time we are playing each other nearly an even amount of games. This is some improvement."

Actually, there could be, by organized baseball standards, enormous deviations in both the numbers of games played by the teams and the numbers of home games each played, even before rain outs started to disrupt the formal schedule. An examination of schedules published before the first and second halves of play in various years shows the following: In the second half of the 1935 season, the scheduled games for each team ranged from twenty-six for the Eagles down to fifteen for the Philadelphia Stars. In the first half of 1943, the Baltimore Elite Giants were supposed to play thirty-two games, while the St. Louis Stars, in their only half-season in the league, were only committed to fifteen.

In general, the teams with the most secure home park situations played as the home team more than the others, either at their usual home fields or at neutral sites, where they got the strategic advantage of batting last and possibly taking the larger home-team portion of the gate. Philadelphia, which didn't have to share its sooty 44th and Southside diamond, had twenty-eight of its forty first-half games in 1939 scheduled at home, as well as thirty-nine of all its fifty-four games in 1943. The Grays tended to get this scheduling break, too, and after they became established in Newark, so did the Eagles. In contrast were the more or less "homeless" Cubans and Black Yankees. In 1943, only five of the Yankees thirty-four games were to be home contests, and the Cubans were supposed to be the home team only seven of thirty-nine times.

With scheduling that uneven further interrupted by rain outs and other changes, it was even difficult to tell at times who was in first place. In 1936, Tom Wilson's Elite Giants claimed the first-half championship, which was awarded on the basis of won-lost percentage, only to be challenged by Ed Bolden on behalf of the second-place

Philadelphia Stars. His position was that the Giants could not claim the title until they had played two postponed games against the Stars. Two Philadelphia wins in those games would give that team the best percentage. Wilson's response was that the first half was over, and his team had won. The identity of the first-half champion was not decided until near the end of the second half, when the Elite Giants and Stars did finally play the games, and the Giants won them to "preserve" their title.

The twice-yearly league scheduling meetings resembled bazaars. An owner went to one armed with as many prearranged lucrative dates as possible, in order to have bargaining chips toward achieving the best possible deal for his team. Actually, working out a balanced schedule never really seems to have been a goal of the league, as Cum Posey once indicated when he advised Effa during the winter of 1945 to line up potential dates at the Dodgers' Ebbets Field before she went to the league meeting. "That gives you a trading front at the schedule meeting, as the meetings when schedules are made really are trading fronts."

While the major restraints on the Negro leagues came from forces outside their control—mainly segregation and the resulting lack of access to capital with which to build ballparks—many, if not most, of their other problems stemmed from the lack of an influential, impartial force at the top of the organization. The white major leagues, besmirched by serious gambling scandals, had hired federal judge Kenesaw Mountain Landis in 1920 and given him far-ranging powers to run their game. Judge Landis wielded that power enthusiastically, and while he may or may not have been right in individual cases, there was no question of who was in charge.

The Negro leagues had no Landis, or even independent presidents of the individual leagues. The Negro National League attempted to employ an independent commissioner in 1934, hiring sportswriter W. Rollo Wilson. Wilson kept the job only one season, however, and was replaced in 1935 by Ferdinand Q. Morton, a New York City civil service commissioner. Morton made a grand entrance at the March 14 league meeting in Philadelphia—while the owners conferred, the door to their meeting room was thrown open and someone intoned "Gentlemen, the new commissioner."[18]

Posey had made the commissionership look important in 1937, describing him as a one-man arbitration board, with the final say in disputes, and "the public's representative in baseball." But less than three years after having been hired, Morton was out of a job. The official league version was that the commissionership had been "temporarily" set aside by the owners, pending negotiations with the Negro American League about hiring an overall commissioner. The truth of the matter was that Morton had exceeded his miniscule authority. He had called the owners together for a league meeting, but Gus Greenlee, the most powerful owner at that time, told the others not to show up, and Morton met only with himself. Shortly thereafter, he was dumped.[19]

Major R. R. Jackson, of Chicago, who in his political career had been both a city alderman and a state assemblyman, was the independent president of the American League for three years, 1939 through 1941, but the owners in the Midwest eventually decided they had no use for him, either.

The National League had no offices of its own, existing piecemeal in the headquarters of Abe Manley, Tom Wilson, and its other officers. Until after World War II, its financial situation was often perilous—in April of 1942 its cash balance was down to $159.23. Team dues, the main source of league income, often were not paid in full, and, ironically, the most dependable source of income came from the booking agents. From 1939 on, the agents paid the league 20 to 25 percent of the fees they collected for booking league teams.

The league's representatives on the field—the umpires—could not always keep control, either. Ordinarily only two umpires were hired for a game, one to work behind home plate and one to work the bases, although white big league baseball had gone to four regular umpires years before. Some years, only three umpires were on the league payroll, and were supplemented by locals hired by each home team. Without strong league support, the umpires were frequently challenged, and sometimes abused, by players and managers. In 1937, President Greenlee fined three managers $25 each and three players $10 each for fighting with umpires, but that minor sort of discipline did little good.

A more likely scenario was the disputed league championship playoff in 1934. The losing Chicago American Giants protested one of their four losses because when Jud Wilson, a player for the Philadelphia Stars known as one of the meanest men in black baseball, struck one of the umpires, he was allowed to stay in the game. The umpire had, in fact, ordered Wilson ejected, but Wilson refused to leave and the ump, intimidated, let it pass. Eventually, Rollo Wilson did nothing about the Giants' appeal, either, even though he had been present in the crowd when the assault happened, and the Stars had won the playoff series by that single disputed game.

Occasionally, the umpires fought back, as when E. C. "Pop" Turner knocked Eagles' manager Dick Lundy out during a game in 1940. Lundy had come off the bench to argue a decision, when "suddenly the manager and umpire started throwing punches, and Lundy was felled by a right to the jaw." [20]

The Manleys never doubted the need for someone in charge who had no financial stake in any individual team. "I still say, as I always have, our baseball needs a Commissioner," Effa wrote to Pittsburgh baseball man John Clark. "It is not fair to Negro Baseball, the players or the Negro race, but what can be done until the Negro owners decide to stick together, and put such a man in office."

From 1939 on, rarely a season went by without the Manleys putting forward the name of an independent candidate to be either National League president or commissioner of all Negro league baseball. Their nominees were always men of substance, often with significant sports backgrounds. Dr. Powell, whose nomination set off the Philadelphia firestorm in 1940, was an x-ray specialist in New York, in addition to running the *Amsterdam News,* and in 1943 was the first black appointed to the New York State Athletic Commission.

In 1942, Abe and Effa were solidly behind Joseph Rainey, a former newspaperman, a Pennsylvania state athletic commissioner, and a Philadelphia court magistrate. Rainey later would be president of the Philadelphia NAACP, and in 1948 defied Birmingham, Alabama, police commissioner Eugene "Bull" Connor by speaking on civil rights to a racially mixed crowd at the Southern Negro Youth Conference.

But the most distinguished Manley candidate was William H. Hastie. Hastie had resigned a federal judgship in the Virgin Islands in 1939 to become dean of the Howard University law school. He then became an aide to the secretary of war, Henry Stimson, in 1942, but quit that position the following year in protest of Jim Crow conditions throughout the Army Air Force. This protest by no means doomed his career in the Roosevelt and Truman administrations, and in January, 1946, he became the first black appointed governor of the Virgin Islands. In keeping with Judge Hastie's qualifications, the Manleys put him up in 1939 not to be National League president, but to be commissioner of both leagues.

None of the Manleys' nominees, nor anyone else outside the circle of owners, for that matter, was to wield any important power in big league black baseball until after World War II, when the entire institution was in irreversible decline. Not that the owners did not occasionally say they favored the concept—Posey reported to the Manleys in 1941 that Tom Wilson was in favor of an overall commissioner, and Posey put himself on record in 1943 as favoring league officers without financial interests in any team.

But their individual agendas made real progress on this front impossible. For example, a few lines after telling Abe and Effa that Wilson would go for a commissioner to unite the league in the East and the one in the Midwest, Posey added that Tom "wants the commissioner to be a man who leans toward the East."

Posey, active in politics and amateur athletics in the Pittsburgh area, did not favor Rainey because "I don't think he has proven consistent in politics or athletics." Besides, Posey was known to favor Judge William C. Hueston, a fellow official in the black fraternal Elks order. The Grays' owner had no more success in promoting Hueston's candidacy over the years than the Manleys did with their various men. This was in part because Hueston had been Rube Foster's successor as president of the first Negro National League. The league declined and fell under his administration, although there probably was not much he could have done about it, with the Depression going on and Foster disabled.

However, the main reason the Negro leagues never got their own Judge Landis (or even a moderately effective fellow such as Albert "Happy" Chandler, the judge's successor) was because most of their representatives didn't want one. Oliver Brown, whose observations on league affairs in the New Jersey *Herald-Journal,* were some of the most accurate of all the black sportswriters, named names in 1944: Posey, he said, wouldn't want anyone who would make him play by the rules; Gottlieb and Saperstein saw their booking commissions disappearing under the control of a powerful black leader; Tom Wilson and J. B. Martin wouldn't want to give up their control over the annual East-West game, for which they got about $2,000 apiece each year.

"You will never get a commissioner until these men put aside their selfishness and place the interest of organized Negro baseball first," Brown wrote. "They haven't the vision to see that they are standing in their own light, for the more efficient the league is run, the more money all will make."

In 1945, the two Negro leagues came fairly close to electing a commissioner at a June 12 joint meeting. The American League nominated Robert Church, and Posey put up Judge Hueston. It took nine of the twelve team votes to elect the first commissioner, but Church could get only seven, the rest going to Hueston. Voting was split along league lines, with one exception—Effa, representing the Eagles, voted for Church.

Finally, in 1947, Tom Wilson was voted out and the National League elected an independent president. Effa got her wish, not only in having the office created, but in getting to pick the man to fill it. She was instrumental in the selection of Rev. John Johnson, who had picketed and negotiated with her at Blumstein's Department Store in Harlem thirteen years before.

Johnson had gone on to achieve other equal rights victories, and his election was a move to give the league greater credibility with the recently integrated white major leagues, the cooperation of which was going to be necessary for the black leagues to survive. Johnson was the right man, but his arrival came too late—in two seasons his league would go out of business.

The most noticeable way in which the Negro leagues differed from white organized baseball was the black clubs' lack of binding ties over their players. Players frequently deserted one team for another between seasons, and sometimes "jumped" all the way to Latin American leagues. White professional ball had had rules against such jumping since the late nineteenth century, and the rules had evolved into a standard "reserve clause" in player contracts. The restriction kept players under contract to their teams even after a season was over, and at the same time prevented other teams from making "raids" on other clubs by offering more lucrative salaries.

Although the Negro leagues purported to operate under the same rules, the reality of team-player relations was that players often switched teams, even when a contract had been signed. Bill Yancey, who played for eight different black teams, including the Brooklyn Eagles in 1935, acknowledged that the black leagues had contracts with their players, "but we didn't pay much attention to them. You signed up for a year . . . but if you felt like jumping the next year, you jumped . . . that's the reason I played for so many clubs. If I was unhappy I said the hell with this and I jumped." [21]

The willingness of some players to disregard their contracts was buttressed by the fact that they usually could get away with it. Much jumping was from one black league to another, and there was no overall commissioner to nullify the move. But the players had some justification that did not exist in the white major leagues, or in most of the minors, for that matter. The precarious financial position of Negro baseball inevitably meant that some weaker teams would miss making payrolls during times when poor gate receipts dried up their cash flow.

Ball players, both white and black, had no job security beyond what their bodies could earn them on the diamond, and as far as Negro leaguers were concerned, a club that could not pay its players had not earned their loyalty. This position was even acknowledged by the Negro National League, which allowed any player not paid in full by November 1 for the previous season to become a free agent, able to sign with any other club.

Self-interest among the black owners being as strong and unfettered as it was, a player looking for a greener ball field usually found one, as a club on a more solid financial footing took advantage of a weaker one. This never happened in Newark, though. If a player wanted to jump the Eagles, he had better make the long leap to Latin America. Abe and Effa Manley would not tolerate contract breakers on their team. Their policy of always making payroll was their best defense. When Effa reminisced about the loyalty of "satisfied" players, this is primarily what she meant. By always having salaries available when they were owed, even if it meant going to the bank for a short-term loan, the Manleys were able to eliminate the most likely reason for a player to break one of their contracts.

But, as might be expected, they did not rely upon defense alone to protect the Eagles. If they suspected they were losing a player, they took steps to prevent it. Fran Matthews recalls that in 1942 he turned down a contract with the Eagles to stay at home in the Boston area, where he had a well-paying defense job at the Watertown Arsenal. In his spare time he played for a crack amateur team, and caught the eye of the Kansas City Monarchs when that Negro American League team barnstormed through Massachusetts.

Matthews played well enough to be invited to accompany the Monarchs to Washington to play the Homestead Grays, but at the park, "just before the Star Spangled Banner, here comes Cum Posey with a telegram from Effa, stopping me from playing." Effa was well within her rights, since by white major league rules, a player was a team's property until the team, not the player, severed the contractual relationship. Somehow, she had found out what was going on, and stopped it cold.

Nor would the Eagles go after other teams' players. Just before the start of the 1939 season, Abe received a letter from Raymond Brown, ace of the Homestead Gray pitching staff. Brown informed Manley he had not been able to come to terms with the Grays, and that Posey had given him permission to try to make his own deal with another team. Abe's reply, which certainly had Effa's approval, if not her direct participation, was not to Brown, but to Posey and Rufus Jackson.

> I have before me a letter from one of your important men, Raymond Brown, applying for a position on my Ball Club. I think in this case Gentlemen it is ridiculous to refer him to some other Club, as we are all in one Organization, and should try to strengthen the Organization. In the case of the man in question, you are as much able to meet his demands as I am, or any other Club. You should offer him what you think you can afford to pay and leave him to accept it, or else stay out of baseball so far as organized Negro Baseball is concerned. I think that this will be the only way of dealing with the ball players, if we expect to have any Organization.

While the Manleys were not necessarily opposed to the borrowing or lending of players to fill out teams for exhibition games, if a game was on the regular schedule, they expected rosters to consist of only the teams' own players.

They made that point forcefully in 1944, when they protested the award of the first-half pennant to the Homestead Grays.

The Eagles had finished a close second to the Grays, so close that reversal of a single Homestead win over Newark would give the Eagles the title. That was just what Effa had in mind when she protested the second game of a July 2 doubleheader, which the Grays had won behind the pitching of star lefthander Roy Partlow. The trouble was, Partlow was the property of the Philadelphia Stars. He was stationed in the Washington area with the Army, and unavailable to travel with his team. There was an understanding that he would be available to pitch for any National League team playing in the Capital, so the Grays recruited him for that game. But Effa and Mule Suttles, then managing the Eagles, protested before the first pitch was thrown, claiming that Partlow's availability extended only to nonleague games.

The Eagles wanted the game forfeited, but the Grays claimed they had the right to keep the victory. Characteristically, Tom Wilson compromised, ruling later that month that the game be played over. Making their point did not help the Eagles in the end—they lost the replay in mid-August, 8 to 4, and still had to settle for second.

Despite the Manleys' successes in having player contracts enforced, they lost one of the best players they had ever pursued, pitcher Leroy "Satchel" Paige. The Eagles' long-running attempt to enforce what the Manleys believed to be a valid contract with the brilliant pitcher has been obscured, partly through Effa's own statements, by hints of a sexual liaison between the two. In a 1978 interview, Effa recounted the Eagles' inability to put Paige in their lineup, and offhandedly commented (with apparent pride in her voice) that Paige's price for coming to the Eagles was that she would become his girlfriend.

He may have demanded this—Paige was irrepressible in addition to being extremely talented, and a central figure on the Eagles, Monte Irvin, thinks it was true. But although no extracurricular relationship ever developed, the story of one of black baseball's most famous players "propositioning" its beautiful female owner has popped up in many accounts of Effa's career. It has unfortunately served to turn the Paige case into a trivialized footnote to her life in baseball. It was anything but a minor event in Eagle history. The Manleys pursued Paige in the courts, in meetings between the two Negro leagues, and at least once in person. Newspaper reports and letters in the team files indicate that if Effa wanted anything at all from the Paige deal, it was a pitcher and a fair shake.

Paige was the property of Gus Greenlee's Pittsburgh Crawfords in the spring of 1938, even though he had jumped the team in midseason the summer before to play in the Dominican Republic. He had come back to the states, but had also returned his 1938 contract unsigned to Greenlee, who had had enough. Fed up with Paige, Gus made it known that the pitcher could be had for as little as $2,000, although Abe Manley bought his contract for a reported $5,000. But just because the Manleys assumed they had acquired one of the best pitchers in black baseball did not mean Paige saw it that way. He never thought twice about leaving the country again.

"I never did see no contract," he said later, "so when folks say I jumped away from Newark ask them to show you the contract." [22]

Abe and Effa could not have been taken entirely by surprise, since on April 23 the Pittsburgh *Courier* published an interview with Paige. The star was relaxing in New York City while trying to decide whether to play Negro league ball "or succumb to princely offers made him by Argentina, South America interests, whom he said are offering three times the salary he could command in this country."

Succumb he did, and the day before he was to leave, the Manleys obtained a temporary restraining order in a New York City court to keep him in the country. The order required Paige to appear before the judge two days later, but when the case was called that morning, he was not in court, and most likely no longer in the United States.

Effa did not give up. She kept urging Paige to change his mind, and thought she had succeeded. The Newark

Herald reported in a headline on July 30 that "Paige, Badman of the Diamond, Joins Newark Eagles." Effa, "in almost constant communication" with the pitcher, had supposedly persuaded him to report. Satchel was not that easy to persuade, however, and he did not show up. He did get a little closer to Newark, deserting South America for Mexico before the summer was over. He hurt his arm pitching for the Mexico City team, however, probably as the result of pitching too much. The injury was serious, and it appeared for a time his career might be over.

With rest, he rebounded and was ready to give baseball another try in the spring of 1939. Perhaps because he had no certain prospects at that time, he sent Effa a short, enigmatic typewritten note, full of idiosyncratic spellings and capitalization, clearly meant to absolve Satchel Paige from any blame for the previous year's dispute:

> Daer Mrs Manley
> Just a Few Line To Let You Hear From Me I am Well At This Time . . . Listen Mrs Manley I Thought I Heard Some One Say Thet I Belound To You Why Do You Take So Lound To Send For Me I Have Ben Wating And Wating For You To Write Me But It Look Like Something Is Wrong. . . . Listen Mrs. Manley It Look Like To Me When I Make Up My Mine To Do Wright Every Body Want To Do Wrong.

Effa's reply was brief, dry, and businesslike. She would forward his letter to Abe, already in Daytona Beach with the team in spring training, "and will let you know as soon as I hear from him, what he had to say." But 1939 was again to be a year without Satchel. His arm still weak, he signed with J. L. Wilkinson, the white owner of the Kansas City Monarchs. He was made a star attraction of a barnstorming squad Wilkinson ran, which was promptly renamed "Satchel Paige's All Stars." Back in Puerto Rico for winter league ball, he again wrote to Effa in response to a contact she had made through another player in the winter league.

Paige's letter was seductive, in a sense, and is subject to broader interpretations, although since Effa included it in the team's business files, it is clear she thought the promise he was holding out was his presence in an Eagle uniform:

> I was very glad to know that you was still thinking about me . . . don't give up because I am yours for the asking if it can be possible for me to get there . . . I realy want you to be first this year I want to talk to you before I get to Kansas City and you can bring your contract with you . . . I dont think you will wase [waste] any money on me this year that is if you dont give up. listen I want the same thing to go as I say last year. listen Mrs. Manly dont beat around the bush I am a man tell me just wheat you want me to know. and please answer the things I ask you.

Effa thought she had Paige this time, and wrote to Willie Riddick, who helped stage the Eagles' annual swing through the Virginia Tidewater, "I am about sure we will have Satchel Paige with us" when they arrived. But Paige again signed up with Wilkinson. According to newspaper accounts, when he got back to Kansas City, to prepare to come east to Newark, Wilkinson had a new automobile for him, along with a contract to continue playing with the All-Stars.

Losing out again on the pitcher's services was bad enough, but then the Satchel Paige All Stars, which heretofore had toured in the western parts of the U.S. and in Canada, came East to play, and in the Eagles' profitable secondary market in Tidewater Virginia, at that. Paige, ever trying to negotiate a better deal, sent Effa a telegram on May 30 from the Slaughter Hotel in Richmond: "Call me at this hotel Friday at ten o'clock." He may not have expected the result—Effa, Abe and manager Suttles all descended on him the next day. Two days later, Effa unloaded on league presidents Martin and Wilson:

> I was really shocked to find Mr. Wilkinson of the Kansas City Monarchs in Richmond with Satchel and the team. I also learned that The Satchel Paige All Stars, owned by the western booking agent [Wilkinson] and The Brooklyn Royal Giants [an independent team run by Bill Leuschner] have been barnstorming allover the country for the past few weeks playing each other. It is as plain as day that the booking agents have agreed to try and keep Paige away from The Eagles at all cost. . . . I expect each of you to order Wilkinson to send Paige to Newark immediately this week. If organized baseball is not strong enough to do this, it is not strong enough to call itself organized.

At the same time, she invited sportswriters from the major East Coast black papers to Newark on June 7, even offering to pay their expenses, so she could say more. As Randy Dixon reported the meeting, Effa stated flatly that, "the Negro National League as it stands today, will be a thing of the past [if the two black leagues] deny her claim to the services of Satchel Paige, the pitching star." Effa was at her iron-willed best in the news conference. She said that "Paige is my property and I'll get him. . . . Men like Wilkinson, Leuschner and Gottlieb want to keep us disorganized and slip-shod. . . . Most of the owners are either too weak or too something to fight them, but not so with me." [23]

The Manleys threatened to take the Eagles out of the National League if their protest was not honored, and a showdown came at a joint meeting of the National and American Leagues on June 13. The Manleys did not get Paige, but they were awarded ownership of James "Bus" Clarkson, an infielder who became an Eagle regular, and pitcher Clarence "Spoon" Carter, from the roster of the American League's Indianapolis club, which was in the process of going out of business. Given the dismal success record of claims for the return of jumping players, this was a victory. It was brought about in no small part by the Manleys' ability to convince J. B. Martin to ban games between American League teams and Paige's All Stars.

The potential denial of those lucrative games to Wilkinson and Paige made them much more eager to negotiate.

What Effa really wanted, though, was Paige. As star drawing attraction for the Monarchs, to whom he moved from the "All Stars" barnstorming team in 1941, Satchel eventually commanded his own share of gate receipts, payable before the Monarchs and their opponents divided up the remaining cash. In 1945, the Monarchs tried to arrange a game in Newark with the Eagles on those terms, causing Effa to write Kansas City co-owner Tom Baird, "You know of course how I have always felt about Satchel, to pay extra for him to pitch is rubbing it in a little, when he should have been doing all his pitching for us, or I should have been paid something for him."

Even if the other owners did not always listen to the Manleys, there was one other influential group connected with black baseball that thought along their lines. That was the sportswriters for the black weeklies, who expressed many complaints about the way the Negro leagues were run. The most basic problem they had with the leagues was that game results, player statistics, and even the standings of the teams were not always kept up-to-date. In 1944, the Negro National League hired the Elias Baseball Bureau, statisticians for the white National League and other professional leagues. But before that, the National league depended upon teams sending results as promptly as possible to the league secretary, who would compile the standings and averages.

The result was, on the whole, not satisfactory. The lack of accurate player statistics, hampering the ability to prove the worth of the Negro league stars to later generations of baseball fans, is well known. But even the game results and standings were often suspect. Teams might not report promptly to the league, and the weekly standings released as official often did not even accurately reflect the games that had been reported. If a league's results are recorded correctly, the separate sums of all the games won and lost at any point should be equal, since one team's win is someone else's loss. Although touted as "official" standings, the Negro leagues' reports often lacked that balance.

But beyond those complaints, the sportswriters had larger problems with the leagues' credibility. The major black newspapers not only reported what was happening to blacks in their own communities and separate spheres of accomplishment, but also strove to emphasize black accomplishments in the predominant white culture. Any "first" accomplished by a black gaining admittance to a previously white job, for example, was always worth a headline, as were evidence of official discrimination by the white power structure or racially demeaning books, movies, and other entertainment from the mainstream culture.

The sportswriters for these papers looked at the white major leagues, with organization and stability evident from Judge Landis on down. Then they looked at their Negro leagues, and were unhappy with what they saw. They were angered with the evident disorganization, and they disdained the closed-door secrecy in which the owners thrashed out their disputes, instead of having an independent commissioner settle them.

W. Rollo Wilson, writing in the Pittsburgh *Courier* after having ended his short reign as National League commissioner, took the league to task in 1936:

> The club owners are as bewildered men in a large cavern. The escape door is dead ahead of them, outlined by the light from the outside. But, befuddled by the echoes of their thoughts resounding from dim corners, they grope in blind alleys and bump their (unfortunately for them) hard heads against the walls.[24]

Randy Dixon, on the eve of the 1940 National League meeting, criticized the circuit's suspicious record keeping and internal politics with the following question and answers in the *Courier*:

> What is the Negro National League? The Negro National League is much ado about nothing.
>
> Why is there a league? That's another mystery, unless the answer could be that it afford Cum Posey the

> opportunity to grab off pennants for his Homestead Grays.
>
> What is a pennant? In the case of the Negro National League, a pennant can be likened to a marriage between a man, 90, and a teen-age girl. Neither the pennant nor the marriage means anything.
>
> But the league isn't married, is it? Yes, in a sense, the league is married, and that sense is the only sensible item surrounding the league. The league is married to pettiness, lack of foresight and failure to recognize the change in trends.[25]

Oliver Brown, of the New Jersey *Herald-News,* broadly burlesqued the 1944 league meeting. He claimed in a column that he had discovered the results of the "Negro National League's Secret Baseball Society" from various owners by means of bribes that included unlimited elevator trips for one whose secret passion was elevator riding and a plate of hot biscuits for another owner who craved them so much he let slip another piece of information each time he buttered one up.[26]

On a serious note, Brown, a consistent Manley ally, shared their dislike of white involvement in league affairs, and had a constructive solution:

> There is no reason why the owners should not establish a central booking agency and stop paying the booking percentages to white bookers. This money could do much toward providing the funds to pay umpires, a commissioner, publicity men and a statistician.[27]

But the sportswriters did not run the league, and the Manleys became increasingly frustrated with the state of affairs as the prewar years drew to a close. They were not making money, their reform appeals were ignored in league meetings, and early in 1942, they thought of getting out. Coverage of league affairs that February gave little indication of what was going on in Newark. The Manleys were reported to have walked out of the February 19 meeting when they did not succeed in having Joseph

Rainey elected president, and had threatened to quit the league. By the February 28 scheduling meeting, however, they announced they had decided to stay.

But, out of the public eye, they were taking much bigger steps. Gus Greenlee, whose attempt to reenter the National League had been turned down at the first league meeting, wrote them on February 21, declining their offer to sell him the Eagles. "I would rather not be a member if you are going to withdraw," he wrote. "As much as we disagreed, I still admire you for sticking to what you believe to be right. . . . If I was in your place, I would go to the meeting next Saturday [on February 28] [and] get placed in the schedule."

At the same time as the Manleys were making an offer to Greenlee, they were also talking with a group that was supposed to have been among their enemies. They were being courted heavily by Abe Saperstein, the booking agent from Chicago, and were listening closely to his proposal. He wanted to pull the Eagles out of the National League and make them into an independent barnstorming team, which Saperstein would book around the country. From the correspondence that survives in the Eagle files, it appears that Effa was ready to do it, but her husband was holding back.

In response to a pair of Saperstein telegrams, Effa wrote him on February 22 that

> My husband and I are not 100% agreed on this program. However I am sure if he was convinced he could make some money this way he would be inclined to give it a lot of thought. . . . The seven years we have been in the baseball we have consistently fought for organization, but we seem to be more alone each year in this trend of thought. . . . I am sure we would be a lot better off to tie up with some one who knows the ropes.

Saperstein replied two days later. He was very supportive and highly critical of Posey's attempts to control the National League, but was personally tied up in Chicago with promoting his Harlem Globetrotters black basketball team. Instead, he sent Syd Pollock, who lived not far away in North Tarrytown, N. Y., north of New York City. Pollock drove down to Newark on February 27 for a meeting, and followed up the next day with a letter assuring Abe and Effa that "if anytime you feel like pulling out I feel confident Saperstein can line up a real paying schedule for you, as well as provide you with necessary attractions to play at your home park."

Effa informed Saperstein on March 11 that the Eagles weren't interested, and said the decision was Abe's. Lapsing briefly into black vernacular, probably to separate herself another step from the decision, she wrote that "Mr. Manley felt he wanted to take a gamble this year with the 'Ligg.' I certainly hope it is for the best. My attitude hasn't changed one bit, but I have no choice but to go along."

But, in turning him down on principle, she could not resist offering him a parting business deal in terms that he would understand and appreciate. Detroit, which had no Negro league team, but had many black residents and a major league ballpark, was a city with much potential for two visiting black teams. So she proposed

> In going over my schedule, I find the Eagles and the Cubans are booked to play each other Sunday, June 7th. I also see Detroit [in the white American League] is not home that day. Now if you could get Briggs Stadium, and promote this attraction for that day, you would really be doing something. . . . I think the smart thing to do would be keep all arrangements quiet for a while, and make it look like the Eagles secured the park. . . . This affords a swell opportunity to get some satisfaction for both of us.

In dealing with Saperstein, was Effa crossing over to the white world, betraying her "adopted" black life? Probably not, since she remained steadfastly supportive of the Newark black community, black society in general, and even the Negro National League. It is more likely that, faced with continuing deficits that were in part caused by the disfavor she and Abe were in with the league's more powerful members, she disliked the league's internal politics more than the prospect of hooking up with Saperstein and Pollock. After all, they may not have been black entrepreneurs, but they were good ones, and she valued a good business mind.

Just as they decided to stay, conditions in the Negro leagues changed drastically and quickly because of World War II. The Manleys found that after seven years, they had re-enlisted in the National League for what turned out to be its duration. The next seven seasons would include both the best and the worst things to happen to them as baseball owners.

Notes

1. *Courier,* Feb. 12, 1946.
2. Ibid., Oct. 11, 1941.
3. Ibid., March 21, 1936.
4. Ibid., Oct. 3, 1936.
5. Manley and Hardwick, *Negro Baseball,* p. 41.
6. *Courier,* Jan. 16, 1937.
7. Ibid., July 4, 1936.
8. Ibid., Jan. 30, 1943.
9. Manley and Hardwick, *Negro Baseball,* p. 54.
10. Ibid., p. 50.
11. Holway, *Voices,* p. 82.
12. Ibid.
13. *Courier,* March 2, 1935.
14. Holway, *Voices,* p. 321.
15. *Courier,* Feb. 17, 1940.
16. *Age,* Feb. 24, 1940.
17. *Courier,* March 22, 1941.
18. Ibid., March 16, 1935.
19. Ibid., Jan. 16, 1937 and Feb. 5, 1938.
20. Ibid., June 22, 1940.
21. Robert Peterson, *Only the Ball Was White: A History of Legendary Black Players and All-Black Professional Teams* (New York: McGraw-HIll, 1984), p. 95.
22. Leroy "Satchel" Paige, with Hal Lebovitz, *Pitchin' Man* (Cleveland, 1948), p. 56.
23. *Courier,* June 5, 1940.
24. Ibid., Oct. 17, 1936.
25. Ibid., Feb. 3, 1940.

26. *Herald-News,* Jan. 15, 1944.
27. Ibid., July 29, 1938.

Chapter 7
World War II, and Other Battles

The war brought out some of Effa Manley's best qualities, giving her a chance, both in baseball and in the larger wartime world, to display her organizational skills and commitment to her adopted race. Wartime America needed all sorts of volunteer help to make the many home-front government bureaucracies function, and she was willing to contribute to several of them.

"As for me, I am working like a stepchild, wearing the uniform of the Civilian Defense Volunteers," she wrote to her players already in the service in March, 1943. Before the war was over, she would be awarded four annual service stripes for being a local warden for the Newark Defense Council. She also volunteered to serve the Office of Price Administration, and was recognized for 1,387 hours put in on Price Control Board #24-7.1 in Newark, helping make rationing decisions on gasoline, tires, and foodstuffs. She even donated her pet police dog, "Champ," to the war effort. In early 1943, he joined "Dogs for Defense," a program that trained the animals for guard duty.

Effa also gave of the family income. The New Jersey *Herald-News* reported at the beginning of 1943 that she bought the first $100 bond offered by the "Colored Women's Division" of the Jersey City, N. J., War Savings Committee, starting the division toward its goal of $50,000. Among the other wartime certificates kept in her scrapbook was one from the Treasury Department for "distinguished services rendered in behalf of the War Financing Program," so it seems she might have bought other bonds, also.

She also had time to spare for specifically black enterprises, particularly those that filled niches ignored by society in general. For example, men entering the Army in New Jersey were sent to Fort Dix for their induction processing. The fort, located about fifty miles south of Newark, was full of young men from New Jersey who might as well have been on the other side of the world, since they were Army recruits confined to the post. In the summer of 1942, one of Effa's numerous show-business contacts, Maude Mills, the sister of the late Broadway star Florence Mills, organized a group of black entertainers to put on shows for the black soldiers, but she had no reliable means of getting her troupe to the fort, and thought of the Eagles' bus.

It turned out that the thicket of rationing restrictions forbade lending the team bus to the entertainers, but Effa was soon deeply involved in helping the totally volunteer group raise the $29 it cost to rent a bus each Tuesday night for a trip to the fort. The group became officially organized as the Women's Volunteer War Service Committee, and, as so frequently happened with groups in which Effa was involved, she became its secretary and treasurer.

One of her first campaigns for the committee was to canvass Newark's busy defense industry for donations. "If you could see how the soldiers enjoy the show and what it does for their morale, I know you would be enthusiastic about it," was her sales pitch, which included a canny promise that sponsoring companies would be identified to the troops. Other contributions were raised through fund-raising parties, such as the "Cabaret Dance" held in October, 1942, at Skateland, the very popular jitterbug haven in black Newark.

Publicity about the project also brought other donations, including one of $5 from the Young Communist League of New Jersey. American Communists had gone from being strongly against the war to staunchly in favor of it, after Germany invaded Russia in 1941. The Young Communists' New Jersey president, James West, reminded Effa that, "although we have limited funds and are engaged in many patriotic activities ourselves, we nonetheless feel impelled to lend you some support." Support could be lent because the U. S. Communist Party was strongly opposed to segregation, and on this note, West could not resist some propagandizing about white baseball: "Allow me, too, to express our best wishes to you, to the Newark Eagles and to Leon Day and Willy [sic] Wells, both of whom, we are confident, will make good in the majors."

The buses that went down to Fort Dix carried some of the most popular black musicians, singers, and dancers who played the many night spots in Newark. Up to five hundred soldiers would gather at the Negro Recreational Center (the military was still heavily segregated) to hear and see the entertainers. The acts often were recruited from the show that manager Eddie Mosby was currently booking at the Picadilly Club in Newark. The stars included Joe Gregory, a dapper song-and-dance man; Merle Turner, who had sung with the Erskine Hawkins Orchestra and had been a Picadilly regular; and Viola Wells, a Newark native who performed as "Miss Rhapsody" and played the Apollo Theater in Harlem with Hawkins' and Bunny Berigan's bands.

The Newark *Sunday Call* did a photo display on one of the shows, and both the soldiers and the performers seem to be having a high time. Effa often made the trip, too, and her handwritten notes in her scrapbook summed up the effort as "one of my most pleasant experiences and most satisfying accomplishments." For her work, the New Jersey *Afro-American,* a regional edition of the widely circulated Baltimore paper of the same name, included her in its 1944 "New Jersey Afro Honor Roll" for being an organizing force behind the Fort Dix trips. Her Eagles, so often used to promote worthy black causes, were also marshaled to the aid of the black soldier, as when the all-black 372nd Infantry Regiment and the black Free French soldiers were honored on opening days.

But, active or not in support of the war effort, the privations the war caused on the home front hit the Negro leagues hard. In March, 1943, the Office of Defense Transportation, in the name of gasoline conservation, administered a potentially crushing blow by ordering the teams' buses grounded. This, coupled with the rationing of gas for private cars, cut the black clubs' lifelines to their lucrative barnstorming dates. The only alternative was public buses and trains, but both modes were crowded, and neither could hope to meet the frenetic, drive-by-night schedules necessary to squeeze in a 150-game season spread over several states.

The Negro National League had already been aware of potential transportation problems. It had decided on a simplified league schedule, and would have its clubs train "north of the Potomac River," as white major league clubs in the East were doing. Expecting the best, the owners at the league meeting in January produced predictions of a "banner season." [1]

So the decision in early March by ODT Director Joseph B. Eastman to park the baseball buses, along with those for traveling entertainment groups and special charters to race tracks and night spots, hit the owners like a bombshell. "The ban against bus travel would practically seal the doom of the majority of teams in the two Negro leagues" due to the additional expense, the Pittsburgh *Courier* intoned.[2]

An appeal organized by Posey and J. B. Martin emphasized that the five hundred miles each team ordinarily traveled each week during the summer brought baseball, the "National Pastime," to urban blacks and soldiers in Army camps. Posey promised to cut thousands of miles off the National League's spring training travel by keeping the teams in the North (the Eagles would train at Dunn Field, the minor league park in Trenton, N. J.). He also said he and the league's co- secretary, Eddie Gottlieb, could devise a league schedule that would cut travel during the season by more than half. In addition, the club owners agreed to turn their buses over to the government in the off-season.

The defense bureaucracy was unyielding. Eastman's telegram was read at an April 6 league meeting: "Regret to advise special busses cannot be made available for transportation of baseball teams . . . urge your cooperation in utilizing existing transportation services."[3] So the teams squeezed themselves onto trains and rearranged their schedules, until the government finally relented late in the season and allowed the buses to roll again (subject to gasoline and tire rationing, of course). Following the season, Posey estimated each club had spent $3,000 per month more than it ordinarily would have for transportation. But the Negro league owners had not gotten through the Depression and into the 1940s without being adaptable, and they made it work.

The schedule of the Baltimore Elite Giants shows how the familiar pattern of traveling all around the Eastern Seaboard came to a screeching halt for one season. The Giants ordinarily motored back and forth constantly between the Baltimore-Washington area and the Northeast states to get as many games as possible played in both regions of the National League. In 1942, for example, they opened in Philadelphia on May 9, then played at home in Baltimore the next day. On May 30 they played a doubleheader at home and were in New York City to take part in a four-team doubleheader the following afternoon. Over the Fourth of July holiday, they played at home on the third, in New York on the Fourth itself, then were back in Baltimore for a game on the fifth.

In 1943, the situation was entirely different. Except for a doubleheader in New York on May 23, the Elites played all their league games at home through June 27, except for relatively short trips to Washington and Portsmouth, Virginia. Then, beginning with a game in Philadelphia on July 1, they spent most of the rest of the season playing in the Northeast.

The Homestead Grays almost completely abandoned their original Pittsburgh home during the season, at least for league games. Pittsburgh, the westernmost city in the National League, was a little out of the way for the rest of the clubs, and the Grays played there only for a doubleheader on August 21. They arranged the rest of their home games in Griffith Stadium, the major league park in Washington, creating a geographically tidy two-city southern terminus with Baltimore.

The Eagles, whose strong tradition of playing the semipro teams of New York, New Jersey, and Eastern Pennsylvania made them tend to stick around their home region more than other teams, were not as severely affected by the travel ban, but they were hampered by another product of the home front's war readiness.

A coastal blackout, designed to drastically reduce the urban skyline glare which silhouetted offshore vessels for German submarines, required ballpark arc lights to be extinguished an hour after sundown. This put an end to night games in Ruppert Stadium and other parks along the coast. Oliver Brown, celebrating the lifting of the ban in time for the 1944 season, noted that "the Eagles would have cleaned up some nice coin last season if they had been allowed to play night ball."[4]

Although the Office of Defense Transportation had let the buses go back on the road well before 1944 spring training started, the Eagles did not go all the way to Florida that year. They disembarked for training in Norfolk, Virginia, where the Newark team was always welcomed by the Tidewater's black baseball fans. Nevertheless, materiel shortages continued to create unusual situations for the Manleys in fulfilling even routine equipment needs. The Eagle files contain a letter Effa wrote to the Office of Price Administration in April, 1943, seeking its permission to outfit the team with eighteen pairs of baseball shoes. The following winter, she shipped seven dozen baseballs back to Wilson Sporting Goods, to have them recovered before the next season began.

As difficult as it was to manage around the wartime restrictions, the black owners were more than compensated for their extra effort. For the first time in the history of Negro league baseball, even including the Rube Foster years, the whole league could reliably depend upon making money. The 1942 season was declared a "banner year" financially, and Posey claimed that black professional baseball took in more than a million dollars in 1942. Art Carter, in the *Afro-American,* subsequently gave the details about the Grays' success. Attendance in Washington, D. C., had exploded for Posey's team in 1942, as the capital went on a war footing. The Grays might have played to crowds of no more than 3,000 before the war, but in 1942 they drew a total of 125,000 fans to Griffith Stadium and had already topped that mark in July of 1943, with ten scheduled dates to go.[5]

The success was apparently universal. Abe Manley commented in an off-season letter to Jim Semler that in 1943, "the season was successful for everyone, that is, financially" (Semler's Black Yankees, had, as usual, finished in last place). By the beginning of 1945, Pittsburgh sportswriter Ric Roberts could claim that the Negro leagues were a $2 million business; that at $40,000 per year (including all his special appearance fees), Satchel Paige made more than any white major leaguer; and at least one black team (probably the Grays) had grossed over $300,000 and paid better salaries than the Southern League, a white minor league.[6]

In 1944, Ernest Wright reportedly turned down $50,000 for his Cleveland Buckeyes franchise in the Negro American League. That was an amount any black owner would have instantly jumped at five years before, if anyone had been crazy enough to offer it. The growing potential of Negro league ball even brought about two welcome happenings at once in New York, when Alex Pompez made his own deal with the New York Giants to play at the Polo Grounds. In one stroke, Pompez finally found his Cubans a major league home park and also partially broke the white booking agents' grip on big games in the city.

The headaches that the war gave the owners—the travel problems, the ban on night games, and the scramble to find players to replace those who had gone into the military—were just the other side of a wholesale change in black life in America during the war. The changes, as a whole, worked overwhelmingly to Negro baseball's advantage.

The growing numbers of jobs available as American industries began to produce goods for the Allied countries already at war with Germany gave the nation's entire Depression-ridden economy a lift. To the extent that they were ever included in economic gains, blacks improved their lot. But new defense-industry jobs were no more equally distributed across the nation than were industrial jobs in general. Both were overwhelmingly concentrated in the urban areas of the North. Since even a menial job in a factory paid better than sharecropping, a second wave of black migration from the rural South to the urban North took place, just as it had during World War I, only much bigger. Black population in the Northern states increased by 50 percent during the 1940s, and during the war years, there were jobs for nearly everyone.

But while more blacks congregated in their sections of the cities, with the breadwinners of their families making heretofore unimagined amounts of money in the defense plants, the gasoline rationing and ensuing crowding of public transportation left them unable to travel to find entertainment. Black music and shows flourished in the cities, and so did black baseball.

Furthermore, it by no means hurt the Negro leagues' image that they worked at portraying themselves as a patriotic symbol of the American values for which the country's men were fighting. Where black baseball saw itself in the wartime scheme of things was best illustrated by the cover of the 1945 *Negro Baseball Pictorial Year Book,* a magazine full of stories and statistics about 1944 that also promoted the approaching season. Posed in tandem on the cover were Homestead Grays' star "Spoon" Carter, about to throw a baseball, dwarfed by a black infantryman about to lob a hand grenade at the enemy.

Individual Negro league clubs admitted servicemen for free to some of their games and did the sort of local promotions for war bond sales that the Eagles also sponsored. An attempt was made at something much bigger in August, 1942, when the teams from the East-West game staged a repeat performance in Cleveland two days later for the benefit of the Army-Navy Relief Fund. The game raised nearly $8,000 for the fund and was widely hailed as a success in black baseball circles.

Although accounts of the game do not credit her with hatching the idea, the Eagle files do contain a letter written that April by Effa to J. B. Martin, the American

League president, proposing precisely such a contest. Even if she did not think up the 1942 game, in early 1943 both leagues awarded her the job of staging a series of similar games in each Negro league city. The idea died in the planning stages, however, probably as a result of the scheduling complications wrought by the bus ban.

In March, 1943, with the bus problem and night baseball bans added to the other uncertainties the war had brought to the Negro leagues, one of its veteran officials wrote a series of articles for the Pittsburgh *Courier* that precisely predicted what would happen to black baseball during this crucial year.

It was the opinion of John L. Clark, who had been National League secretary when Gus Greenlee was president, and who had handled public relations for both the Crawfords and the Homestead Grays, that despite all their worries, most teams in both black leagues "should have an unprecedented year financially." He reasoned that "the majority will play in nearby boom towns where people spend freely and like sports after a hard day of work in a defense plant. Boom towns will keep Negro baseball going in 1943."

Clark said the need for teams to spend more time around their home cities would force the hands of many owners, who until then had been happy to keep their clubs in nearly constant motion and reap the profits provided by fresh audiences on the barnstorming circuit. Now, some ingenuity would be required to make the product continually appealing to the home area fans.

Clark predicted that this new demand would not cause much hardship for the Newark Eagles, who had already assiduously developed their home area and a couple of other locales, as well. "On the stubborn insistence of Mrs. Manley, the Eagles have played to potential spots year in and year out, right in Jersey. They have played in Albany [N. Y.] several times, also Syracuse." Of their Tidewater region trips, Clark noted that "all of these Virginia towns paid off last year, and it will not be a surprise if these and other spots produced almost double this year."

The Newark area certainly fit Clark's definition of a boom town. Existing industries either stepped up production of their specialties or retooled for defense and went to double or triple shifts. Newark shipped out delicate electronic and surgical instruments, tents, and zippers, among other things. One small firm, Federal Telephone & Radio, expanded its defense work from part of one plant in 1941 to a network of production lines in 44 different locations around Newark by 1944, employing 11,500 people.

A shipbuilding concern in adjacent Kearny got enough Navy business to not only keep its own yards busy, but to justify the immediate rehabilitation by the government of the dilapidated boat works in Port Newark. The Kearny firm, the Federal Shipbuilding and Drydock Company, ran the Newark yards, too, and by October, 1943, had more than 19,000 workers toiling there. Newark Airport was turned over to the military in 1942, and more than 40,000 airplanes landed there, to be shipped to the European Theater through Port Newark. The port, in all, started nearly $13 million tons of cargo on its way to the war. Another enormous support activity was taking place downtown, where the federal Office of Dependency Benefits leased the Prudential Insurance Company's brand new, twenty-story home office building, creating 10,000 new jobs to send allotments from servicemen's salaries home to their families.[7]

The city's black labor force, stifled by both the direct economic and indirect discriminatory effects of the Depression, blossomed during the war. In the summer of 1940, only 7,990 blacks in Newark had jobs, but that had more than tripled by 1945, when there were a reported 27,000 blacks from the city proper and neighboring communities working there. Black families from other areas, particularly the South, came seeking those jobs. Newark, which in 1940 had 45,760 blacks, not quite 11 percent of its population, had more than 75,000 by the 1950 federal census, accounting for more than 17 percent of its citizens.

The black population increase in Newark proper, where most of it occurred, had its negative aspects, too.

Primarily, it exacerbated the existing shortage of clean, safe housing in the black areas, particularly on The Hill. The city's residential vacancy rate dropped to a miniscule .6 percent in 1943. Although housing was scarce all over the city, migrating blacks, arriving with little money, tended to crowd into the most crowded areas with the cheapest rents, further congesting neighborhoods already notorious for substandard housing. A city planning study reported in 1944 that 31 percent of all dwelling units in Newark failed to reach "the generally accepted minimum standards of health and decency" and 5,000 units were "beyond all fitness to live in," although they were being lived in—mostly by blacks.

Black leaders in the city were under no illusions as to why this was so. The New Jersey *Afro-American* reported that June that

> While the overall conditions of Newark houses are bad, on the whole colored citizens, because of economic, social and traditional reasons, are forced to occupy the worst houses of the city . . . because of racial prejudice, colored residents largely are limited to only four of the city's sixteen wards.

But though they may have lived in crowded conditions and were still enduring discrimination, the black community was growing in status by being a productive contributor to the war effort. Even the lower-end, blue-collar jobs available in defense work or clerical positions in the Office of Dependency Benefits provided comparatively large boosts to family incomes.

Thanks to that available extra cash, the Eagles' strong identification with the black people already living in the Newark area, and the good publicity that came from Effa's war work, the team's financial fortunes turned the corner. Solid profitability may still have been elusive in 1942, for Effa later told how a brisk attendance on the road had been needed to counter low home. But 1943 was reported to have been "the year the Eagles hit the black." The Manleys, tapping their own bank account over the seasons to meet cash shortages and chasing down baseballs in the stands to save money, finally were being rewarded.[8]

In fact, the unusual demographic changes that occurred in Northern black communities actually put Negro league franchises on a relatively more profitable footing than their white counterparts during the early years of the war, the only time this ever occurred while the two sides of professonal baseball coexisted. The white major league clubs had finally fought their way out of the Depression by 1939, showing their best profits in ten years, when the uncertainties and added expenses of wartime operation reversed this happy trend. In 1942 and 1943, the white big league teams, as a group, actually lost money, an average of 2.2 percent of gross receipts.[9]

The black teams' success was even more notable when compared to the calamity the war brought to the white minor leagues. The minors were beset by rising expenses and player shortages, just like everyone else in baseball. Except in the Western United States, where major league baseball had not yet penetrated, those leagues did not for the most part have locations in the larger cities, where defense industries were swelling population and payrolls. There were forty-four minor leagues in operation as late as 1940, and only ten in 1944, as several shut down operations for the duration.

Relatively speaking, Negro league players profited even more than the owners. Their salaries kept jumping up while the war was going on, while the pay of the more visible white big leaguers was caught in the general salary freeze imposed by Washington to curb wartime inflation. The $40,000 reportedly earned in 1944 by the indefatigable Satchel Paige, who had special per-game appearance fees and immense self-promotional abilities, was nearly twice the $22,500 earned by the best-paid white, New York Yankee catcher Bill Dickey.

Whereas before the war, a journeyman Negro leaguer could not count on being offered a salary of more than about $150 per month, by the end of the 1945 season, Effa Manley was observing to a North Carolina baseball promoter that most players were making at least $300 per month. She knew whereof she spoke, for by 1946, the average Eagle was making $303 per month (based upon the seventeen player contracts found in the Eagle files in Newark). This was a 110 percent monthly increase from the twenty-two contracts on file from 1941, a 57 percent hike from the fourteen from 1943, and even a 38 percent jump from the eighteen players whose 1944 salaries were recorded.

The players who were able to stay with the Eagles throughout the war made out well. Len Pearson was being paid $170 a month in 1941, but $300 a month in 1946. Outfielder Johnny Davis, who joined the Eagles at $150 a month in 1941, was drawing $350 five years later, and pitcher Len Hooker went from $140 to $300 in the same span. Leon Day was making $300 a month in 1943 when he went into the Army, and got a contract for $450 in 1946, when he returned. Monte Irvin was paid $160 a month in 1941, but commanded $400 in 1946, his first full year back from the military.

Salaries increased in part because profits increased and the players, who could see very well that they were playing to more fans, were able to negotiate for a share of the additional money. But there were two other factors at work to give them leverage. One was the steady stream of talent drained off to the military and fulltime defense plant jobs. At least fifty-four Negro leaguers entered the armed forces during World War II. Others gave up playing ball for defense work, which in many cases provided better pay and certainly better hours than baseball, along with a potential draft deferment.[10]

Possibly because Abe Manley liked to recruit younger players who were likely to be healthier and have fewer dependents, the Eagles were particularly hard hit. Thirteen Newark players, including the prewar dependables Irvin, Day, Max Manning, Charley Parks, and Leon Ruffin, as well as newer faces—Earl Richardson, Charlie Thomas, Wilmore Williams, Jim Brown, Clarence Israel, Jim Elam, Jim Walker, and the newest Eagle star, Larry Doby—were in the service by 1945. This number did not include Oscar Givens, an Eagle prospect whose debut was postponed until 1946 by the war, and Russell Awkard, the team's centerfielder in 1941, who was drafted only two games into the season and never returned to the Negro leagues.

The Manleys bore these losses patriotically, without apparent public complaint, although they naturally longed for their missing talent. Effa's feelings were strong enough on one occasion to cause her to stray from the formal approach she favored in her correspondence. She wrote catcher Raleigh "Biz" Mackey in the spring of 1944 that she had received a letter from Monte Irvin: "He is in England, and wishes he was here for the start of the season. He don't wish it half as hard as I do."

Once, she did intercede on behalf of a player, when Pearson's draft board in East Orange called him up at the very end of the war. Besides pointing out that Pearson had previously been classified 4-F, or unacceptable for service, because of a bad knee, she went on in her letter to argue that his presence on the club was important "because of the big part the baseball team plays in the lives of the Negroes of New Jersey. It is about the only healthy outdoor recreational program they have."

The pressures of the draft forced the club owners to think differently. A 1942 player roster in the Eagle files lists, in addition to the usual age, height, and weight data for the men, each one's draft board and classification. In March of 1944, the usually choosy Grays, their roster riddled by call-ups, placed an application blank in the sports pages of the Pittsburgh *Courier* to recruit players. "Promising young ball players, yearning for a chance in organized Negro baseball, will have an opportunity to make their dreams come true when the Homestead Grays, world's sepia champions, launch their spring drills," ran an accompanying story that read like a sales pitch.

Effa had a solution to the draft problem. She may have derived it from a proposal by John Clark, who suggested in his 1943 articles how the Negro leagues could cope with the war: players deferred to work in defense plants could be allowed to play baseball a couple of weekends a month, to replace those who had been drafted. She advanced substantially the same idea a few weeks later in a telegram to Paul V. McNutt, the federal war manpower commissioner. McNutt was mildly receptive, allowing that the proposal was "acceptable." But he was clearly in no mood to make it high-level policy, adding unencouragingly that "requests for the occupational deferment of necessary men must be considered on an individual basis by local Selective Service boards even though a registrant is engaged in war production."

A draft of her request to McNutt shows that Effa was not merely concerned with keeping black players from crossing the Atlantic and Pacific oceans. She also wanted to keep them north of the Rio Grande River. "For the past few years, they have gone to Mexico to play ball, even though American Negroes invested heavily to build the business [of the Negro leagues]," she complained. Latin American baseball entrepreneurs, frequently assisted by their governments, had been raiding the Negro leagues since the mid-1930s. They capitalized on the players' liking for winter league play by offering them salaries that were eye-popping by Negro league standards to play there in the summer, also.

Effa said more than once while the war was on that she considered the Latin American threat, at that point primarily coming from the Mexican League, to be the worst peril facing black baseball during the war. There was no question that the opportunity to play in Mexico worked along with the general wartime player shortage to cause the upward spiral in salaries.

The first wholesale defection from the Negro leagues had occurred in 1937, when Dominican Republic dictator Rafael Trujillo came shopping in America for some top-flight ball players to improve his personal team in the Dominican league. Baseball in his country was almost as important as life itself, and a strong political rival had fielded a team that challenged Trujillo's squad, and thus his political hegemony. There was an election coming up, and he was losing face badly. Trujillo wanted Satchel Paige, and found him that spring in training with the Pittsburgh Crawfords in New Orleans. Paige, the ever restless, was persuaded to jump. By the time he had passed the word around, ten other Crawfords, including the slugging catcher Josh Gibson, had gone south, wrecking Greenlee's powerhouse Pittsburgh team.

Mexican and Venezuelan interests made successful overtures to several regular players in 1939, and thereafter the danger of a key player leaving for southern climes was always on the minds of the Negro league owners. Many other Negro league stars besides Paige and Gibson left their teams at one time or another to play in Latin America. The speedy outfielder James "Cool Papa" Bell, catchers Roy Campanella and Quincy Trouppe, pitcher Chet Brewer and Ray Dandridge, Willie Wells, Monte Irvin, and Leon Day from the Eagles all opted to play at least one season there.

But although players had been leaving since 1937, the wartime threat from Mexico was considered the most serious, both for appearance during a time of general crisis and for its apparent strength. The chief "villain," from the stateside owners' point of view, was Jorge Pasquel, who had founded the Mexican League. Pasquel wanted to inject United States' talent into his league's ranks to raise the caliber of play and make it more popular with Mexican fans.

Many of the players, who could not have missed the cavalier attitude some Negro league owners took toward the sanctity of player contracts, were not impressed by pleas to preserve the integrity of the Negro leagues, and could see no reason not to take advantage of this fine opportunity. The reasons they went boiled down to basically two, one of which, of course, was money.

In 1937, Josh Gibson got $2,200 from the Trujillo team to play just seven weeks in the Dominican league, which was more than a good player could count on making in an entire summer in the Negro leagues. Two years later, Gibson went again, for $6,000 for an entire season, a sum no Negro league owner could come close to matching. In addition to a better monthly salary, the Mexican League season was longer because of more good baseball weather, which also increased a player's season's pay. In many cases, a housing allowance was furnished on top of the salary, a particular benefit to players who brought their families with them.

In 1943, Terris McDuffie, the sometime Eagle pitcher, gave a reporter the players' side of the story, as far as money was concerned:

> Sure, we'd like to stay in the United States and play ball. Nobody wants to be forced to go outside his native land to earn a living for what he thinks he is rightfully due. But what are we going to do when we aren't given a chance to make the money? [11]

Willie Wells, interviewed by Wendell Smith of the Pittsburgh *Courier* while getting a shave in a Mexico City barbershop in 1944, expounded on some of the other reasons for leaving the states:

> I've found freedom and democracy here, something I never found in the United States. I was branded a Negro in the States and had to act accordingly. Every thing I did, including playing ball, was regulated by my color. Well, here in Mexico I am a man. I can go as far in baseball as I am capable of going. I can live where I please and will encounter no restrictions of any kind because of my race.

The vastly more favorable racial situation in Mexico made the blacks from the U.S. both wanted by Mexican baseball and willing to go. Quincy Gilmore, the business manager of the Kansas City Monarchs, saw the difference in a flash, simply standing in front of his Mexico City hotel: "I saw a young colored lady coming down the street on the arm of a young Mexican student. This same student was just as white as any white student in the States and this young woman was about the color of myself." [12]

Mexico, Venezuela, the Dominican Republic, and the other baseball countries of Latin America were not home, however. Few Negro leaguers failed to return to the United

States, often after a single season, albeit with a nice nest egg they would not have earned playing Negro league ball.

Members of the black baseball power structure understandably were unhappy with these defections, although there was a general understanding that even with salaries going up during the early 1940s, no Negro league owner had a chance of winning a bidding war with someone as wealthy as Jorge Pasquel. Dick Powell, who was business manager of the Baltimore Elite Giants when Campanella went to Mexico, said of the jumpers, "We didn't relish it too much, but if we couldn't pay a man $500 or $600 [a month], and he could get it there, we wouldn't stand in his way."

A tougher stance was set forth by Sam Lacy, the baseball writer for the *Afro-American* newspapers. Lacy addressed Willie Wells' defection in 1944 at about the same time Wendell Smith was interviewing Wells about the feeling of freedom that came with playing in Mexico. Wells had returned from there after the 1943 season and had signed a contract with the Manleys in March of 1944, stating that playing in the United States was the "patriotic thing" to do during the war. But before he could report to the Eagles' spring training, he jumped again, to manage and play for the Vera Cruz team in the Mexican League.

While Smith may have interviewed Wells between strokes of a barber's razor, Lacy's point of view was considerably more cutting. "It stands to reason that any man will go to whatever job offers him the most money, especially in times like these," Lacy observed, "but it is neither understandable nor excusable for a ball player to agree to join a team and then wilfully and deliberately run out on that agreement."[13]

The Latin American leagues had very helpful allies, when it came to recruiting in the United States. Their national governments would frequently prove to be much more helpful in getting players out of the U.S. than the American government was in keeping them in, or once gone, getting them back. It was not unusual for the Latin American consuls in the U.S. to actively recruit players—both the Dominican and Mexican governments did so.

Mexico even sent its state tourism agent in New York over to talk to a Newark draft board during the war about obtaining permission for Wells and Dandridge to leave.

Getting ball players out of the country would have seemed a difficult feat during the war, since all of them were under jurisdiction of local draft boards, either in the cities where they played or in their home towns. But this was not the case if a player was going to Mexico. They were often able to initially procur a tourist visa to cross the Rio Grande, and the visa was then magically extended to cover the length of the baseball season.

Prior to the war, the Negro leagues could count to some extent on the U.S. State Department for help if a Latin American country raided their rosters. But once the Latin nations and the U.S. were allies in World War II, needs prevailed to satisfy higher purposes than protection of a baseball team's roster. Wendell Smith attributed this to the U.S. "Goodwill" program in Latin America. He predicted protests to Washington about the Mexican League would come to nothing, because "we aren't going to do anything in Mexico but spread goodwill. And if there is anything that will get under the Senors' skins, it's snatching back the Negro players that they snatched."[14]

Quincy Trouppe, the catcher who spent the war years playing in Mexico, later explained how that country dealt with the U.S. to clear the way for the players it wanted. When the 1943 season rolled around, Trouppe was working as an inspector in an aircraft plant, and would have become immediately draft eligible if he had given up the job. So, he says, he wrote Jorge Pasquel, whom he knew personally. "Pasquel got in touch with my draft board and the Curtis Wright Aircraft Company," and Trouppe was soon free to go.

In the spring of 1944, Trouppe's draft board again blocked him from leaving for the Mexican season, and again he contacted his benefactor in Mexico City. A short time later, the Mexican government contacted Trouppe at his home in St. Louis to tell him Mexico "had loaned the United States 80,000 workers to fill the manpower shortage caused by the war" and that his freedom to travel

South another year was one of the concessions given in exchange by the United States.[15]

The Negro leagues might have had more credibility with both the U.S. and Mexican governments, and with the players, if they had taken strong measures against the jumpers for violating their American contracts. But, as so often happened in organized black baseball, short-term expediency undercut the long-term gain that might have resulted from slapping meaningful suspensions on the jumpers. Losing a player to Mexico, Venezuela, or the Dominican Republic was bad enough, but forcing him to sit on the sidelines under suspension when he came back, instead of helping your club win and draw fans, was perhaps even more intolerable.

When Paige led the exodus to Trujillo and the Dominican Republic in 1937, the Negro National League owners rose up in their righteous wrath and voted to suspend the jumpers indefinitely. "But later," Chester Washington of the *Courier* noted, "they realized that this action might result in irreparable loss to individual clubs," so when the players returned for 1938, their only penalty was a fine of one week's salary. Much the same thing happened in 1941, when those returning from a 1940 sojourn south were readmitted for the price of a $100 fine. This led to typical scorn on the part of black sportswriters. They said the owners were at fault themselves for not enforcing the bans, which just encouraged the Mexican clubs to get the better of them.

In addition to calling on Washington to help them out, the Negro league owners sometimes defended themselves in ways far less subtle. Not surprisingly, the most outrageous moves happened in Pittsburgh, home of many of the best ball players and some of the most dedicated owners. In 1937, when the Dominican Republic was the threat, a Dominican consular employee from New York, Luis Mendez, and Frederico Nina, a lawyer and sports enthusiast from the republic, were arrested at Greenlee Field, during a May 8 Crawfords-Grays game, at the instigation of Crawfords' owner Gus Greenlee and Rufus Jackson, the co-owner of the Grays.

The Dominicans' presence in the city, and suspicion they were going to contact players from the two teams, had been noted by people close to both clubs. They were profoundly nervous, since Paige, catcher Bill Perkins, and outfielder Thad Christopher of the Crawfords had already deserted. A newspaper photographer caught the two Dominicans chatting at the game with John Clark, of the Crawfords' front office, who was said to have been conversationally prying their mission out of them. Mendez and Nina were released shortly thereafter, the thwarting of their mission having done little to stop the wholesale abandonment of the Crawfords and the defection of Gibson of the Grays.

Jackson was on the receiving end of a court complaint six years later, when he personally ejected a Mexican consulate employee from Forbes Field in Pittsburgh. Jackson was standing in a runway leading to the playing field when the man from the consulate, A. J. Guina, asked him where he could find Grays' infielders Sam Bankhead and Howard Easterling. According to Wendell Smith:

> Jackson detected Guina's Latin accent and became suspicious. He asked the diplomat if he were Mexican, and when he found his suspicions were correct, proceeded to escort Guina out of the park . . . After a heated argument outside the park, the Mexican called the police and Jackson was taken to the station.

Charges were soon dropped, and Jackson boldly declared, "I don't care if they send Pancho Villa, they're not going to get my ball players."[16]

Dating back to their attempt to keep Satchel Paige in the country after they had purchased his contract in 1938, the Manleys' position on players who wanted to jump to Latin America was clear. In 1939, Abe went on record with a Newark newspaper as favoring a five-year ban on jumpers, and Effa was described as "even more bitter on the subject."

"There is a big race issue involved," she said. "For the past five years colored owners have been sinking thousands of dollars into Negro baseball and the fans are rallying in a splendid manner. The players owe something to these loyal fans who have made it possible for them to earn a living."[17] While publicly championing the Negro leagues' fans, she was not disregarding the threat to her own interests, either. She wrote league presidents Wilson and Martin in 1940 that "for the large amount of money I have invested, all I really have for that money is the ball players," and made it clear she was tired of seeing talent she had developed run off to play elsewhere.

The Eagles were hurt substantially by losses to Latin America. Except for part of the 1942 season, Dandridge was gone from 1939 through 1943; Wells was in Mexico in 1940, 1941, 1943, and 1944; Day went there in 1940, 1947, and 1948, and Irvin went in 1942. In a later interview, Effa adopted what has become the commonly accepted reaction of the black owners to the Latin American threat: She didn't like it, but was not about to start a bidding war (citing $1,000 a month that Jorge Pasquel had given Ray Dandridge), so she decided not to compete.

While it may have been true that she would not part with the money (as far as Irvin is concerned, she was willing to have her best teams broken up to save the cash that would have gone into a salary war), this does not mean she sat idly by while players boarded planes and boats for the south. Irvin recalls that in 1942, while the Eagles were working their way north from spring training at Virginia Union College in Richmond, he found a telegram from Pasquel waiting for him at the team's Washington hotel. The Mexican owner was offering Irvin, currently making $150 a month, $500 a month, plus $200 for expenses, with a month's pay in advance. Irvin told Effa of the offer, but said he would stay for a $25 monthly raise. "She said she couldn't do it, because she had to pay the stars. I said, 'What am I, chopped liver,' and I left the team in Washington.'" Irvin went home to his parents' house in Orange, N. J., to get ready to depart for Mexico, but "I woke up the next day and there she is, in my living room. She was talking to my mother, saying 'Don't let him go.'"

While Effa confined her attempts to stop Irvin to mere persuasion, she got lawyers, congressmen, the state department and the selective service system involved in other plots to keep her players under control. In 1940, when word reached the Eagles that Len Pearson was joining the exodus to Mexico, she engaged Harlem attorney Richard E. Carey, who had been active with her in the Blumstein's picket six years before, to act on the team's behalf.

Carey's efforts were impressive. On May 8, he fired off a telegram in Abe's name to the state department, seeking a hold on issuance of a passport to Pearson, on the grounds that he had "defrauded his employer." On the same day, an explanatory letter followed, noting that not only was Pearson under contract to the Eagles, but had already been advanced part of his salary. "If a passport is issued to Pearson . . . my client would be defrauded not only of his money but would suffer irreparable loss," Carey claimed.

Whether the federal government threat was what kept Pearson in the United States is not known, but it is true that he did not go south. Nor did he leave when he was allegedly contemplating doing so in 1942. That time, Effa appealed to his draft board in East Orange.

Her attempts to bring official power to bear on the jumpers came almost annually during the war. In 1942, she arranged for a prominent Jersey City, N. J., lawyer, Robert S. Hartgrove, to represent the Negro leagues before the state department and to contact Senator William H. Smathers on their behalf. In 1945, she hired a Newark lawyer, James A. Curtis, to go to Washington on the same sort of mission.

Before the 1943 season, she tried to bring the considerable power of selective service to bear on Dandridge and Wells, by having their draft status changed because they had left the country. She even offered her plot to J. B. Martin on behalf of all the Negro league clubs with players likely to go to Mexico that year. She wrote Cumberland Posey, "I have gone to the head of Selective Service in New Jersey" and was optimistic. She did note ruefully, however, that if she were successful, she would have to trade the infielders, since "they will be too mad and evil to play a nickle's worth of baseball for the Eagles."

Her plot failed, however. Major P. E. Schwehm, from the state capital in Trenton, replied that, since Wells and Dandridge each had draft deferments on account of the sizes of their families, "no action can be taken under present law to make them stay in essential industry." Schwehm also warned that the draft was not about to be discriminatory:

> There is a further angle, in that minor and major league baseball has not been prohibited in this country . . . consequently, any attempt to prevent these persons from playing ball in Mexico might be definitely misconstrued, particularly because of their color.

So, with the exception of Pearson, Effa Manley's attempts to keep the Eagles away from both the armed services and foreign governments were unsuccessful, as a more detached appraisal of her chances might have told her in the first place. It was her nature, though, to give it a try.

The Eagles' extensive loss of players to the armed forces, defense plants, and the Mexican League caused the team to drop a bit from its usual position of chief pursuer of the perennial National League champion Homestead Grays. Between 1939 and 1941, the Manleys' team had jelled. It finished second in a full season schedule in 1939, second in both halves of the 1941 split season, and a respectable third in the 1940 full season, winning nearly 60 percent of its games.

But in 1942, the first war year, the Eagles' third-place finish was much less remarkable—they barely won more than they lost. Although 1943 and 1944 each produced second-place finishes in one-half of a split season (they nearly won the first half in 1944, denied only by losing the makeup game that resulted from the Roy Partlow incident), they finished in fourth and fifth places in the other two halves. In 1945, a split season produced fourth- and third-place finishes.

The squad that Abe Manley had so painstakingly assembled by the late 1930s came apart rapidly after 1941. Irvin went to Mexico in 1942 and was drafted before the 1943 season began, to be lost until the very end of the 1945 season. Max Manning was also in the army by 1943, as was infielder Clarence "Pint" Israel. Fran Matthews had returned to Boston to work in a defense industry. Leon Day had been inducted by 1944, along with outfielder-pitcher James Brown.

Willie Wells was at his usual shortstop position in 1942 and also managed the Eagles, but was gone to Mexico in 1943 and 1944. He returned in 1945 as the team's playing manager, but Abe traded him to the Black Yankees early in the season after the two had their falling-out over pitcher Terris McDuffie. Dandridge, who had gone south in 1939, returned for part of the 1942 season, but then went again to Mexico in 1943, before coming back to play second base regularly in 1944.

Of the remaining regulars from the prewar era, Ed Stone remained an outfield fixture until traded to the Philadelphia Stars in 1944 with pitcher Fred Hobgood. Jimmie Hill, the little lefthanded pitcher whose off-season problems vexed Effa so, was conversely a reliable member of the pitching staff throughout the war. Although his ability had declined due to injuries, he still pitched a no-hitter in 1943. Pitcher Len Hooker defected to Mexico at the beginning of the 1945 season but returned in a matter of weeks, the only time during the war he was not a starting pitcher for the Eagles. Probably the most dependable of the veterans, though, was Len Pearson. From an early career that featured an ability to play a number of positions, he settled in as the regular first baseman when Matthews left after the 1941 season. Only once did Pearson fail to hit more than .300, when he hit .295.

The Manleys filled the gaps in their team by bringing in veteran players, some for repeat performances as Eagles. McDuffie returned in 1944 in a three-team trade that saw Stone and Hobgood leave the Eagles. He won five league games and lost six in 1944, and on opening day at Ruppert Stadium in 1945 he was fabulous, shutting out the New York Cubans and hitting two home runs. But McDuffie failed to complete the first inning in his second league start, and won only two league games that year. His relations with Abe had not been good since Manley, overruling manager Wells, had ordered Terris, though out of condition, to pitch in spring training, and in August McDuffie defected to the Mexican League.

Mule Suttles, still occasionally dangerous as a home run hitter, although past forty years old, rejoined the Eagles in 1942 and stayed through 1944, serving a second stint as manager in his last two years. The even more venerable Biz Mackey returned in 1945. He turned forty-eight in the middle of the season and had put on a little weight (he wore a size 50 uniform shirt), but caught nearly all of the league games and hit .307. He also became the manager when Wells was traded.

Abe Manley went out and found the other players who were needed, exercising his ability to spot promising youngsters and put them in Eagle uniforms. Of course, young players were often highly draft eligible, and some who had put on Eagle baseball suits in the early years of the war were in very different uniforms by the time it ended. A local youngster, Earl Richardson, was recruited from the Montclair High School team in 1943 to replace Wells at shortstop, but was in the military after that one year. Israel, signed in 1941 to play the infield, was in the service by August, 1942.

As always, local New Jersey talent was highly sought after, and in 1942 Abe's scouting brought the Eagles one of the best players, black or white, to ever grace Ruppert Stadium. Larry Doby, later to become the second black to integrate the white major leagues and the first in the American League, began playing for Newark in May, 1942, even before graduating from high school in nearby Paterson. A lefthanded hitter with obvious talent, even at seventeen, Doby was in the lineup at all the infield positions except first base, although he became the regular second baseman after Dandridge left in the middle of the season for Mexico.

Doby had six hits, one of a them a home run, in a single game in early June, and available statistics show him hitting .391 in twenty-six league games. As an Eagle, he would have been trumpeted as the pride of Paterson's blacks, except that it was not common knowledge that he was starring for a Negro League team. Doby, a basketball as well as a baseball star, was enrolling in college the coming fall, and his professional athletic status during the summer would have ended his amateur eligibility, so, for the 1942 season, he was billed as "Larry Walker, from Los Angeles."

This was at least the second time the Manleys played a local star under an assumed name. Monte Irvin had broken in with them as "Jimmie Nelson" while still enrolled in Lincoln University in Philadelphia, but he had only played in out-of-town games. Doby, alias Walker, played his first game for the Eagles in a four-team doubleheader before 17,000 fans in Yankee Stadium, and was even in the lineup for home games at Ruppert. Brazen as the deception was, it worked. Doby played college basketball the following winter and, his being drafted into the military imminent, returned to the Eagles to play under his own name until July, 1943, when he went into the Navy.

Another local athlete, pitcher Don Newcombe from Elizabeth, also showed promise. Recommended by an Eagles' fan, Newcombe presented himself at the Manleys' house the day before the team members living in the New Jersey area were to head south for 1944 spring training. Effa, who was at home, sized up the seventeen-year-old, and told Abe, "he is a big, strapping fellow, and might be of some help."

It turned out he was not really ready for Negro league competition yet—he was winless, and generally not too impressive, in eleven league games that year. The situation was quite different in 1945, however. On a team that had a shortage of good pitching, Newcombe won eight and lost three in league competition. Having developed the fast ball that later made him a star in the integrated major leagues, he struck out fourteen men in a game twice in 1945.

Recruiting Newcombe and Doby was easy; getting Johnny Davis to Newark was hard. Davis was actually a native of the city, but he had been long gone from there when Abe heard of him. Davis was playing outfield and hitting the ball hard for a well-known upper New York State independent team, the Mohawk Colored Giants of Schenectady. The Giants' white owner, Henry Bozzi, was more than willing to sell the Manleys the rights to Davis. There was only one problem holding up the transaction, but it was a big one. Davis was on parole to the State of New York for an offense committed while a youth, and was not permitted to move from the state.

Beginning the summer of 1940, Abe and Effa carried on a determined campaign against the bureaucracies of the two states involved to get Davis to Newark. At various times they enlisted the aid of the Rev. Charles C. Weathers, a black protestant clergyman in Newark who was also a parole officer; the Rev. John H. Johnson of St. Martin's Episcopal Church in Harlem, who with Effa had organized the Citizens for Fair Play in 1934; and state assemblyman Danny Burrows from Harlem.

Effa later credited the successful transfer of Davis's parole to the influence of the "biggest Negro politician in New Jersey," whom she declined to name. At any rate, by the middle of 1941, Davis was a member of the Eagles.[18] He became a fixture in the team's outfield for the rest of its years in Newark, and beginning in 1944, also filled in as a pitcher.

Maryland, part of the region that was the Eagles' "second home," yielded two other important members of the team. Murray Watkins, an infielder from Baltimore, joined in August, 1942, as Israel's replacement when he was drafted. Although never a powerful hitter, Watkins batted consistently in the middle .200s and was a good fielder who could play anywhere in the infield. He became the regular shortstop in 1943 when Wells left the team, and then was the regular third baseman the following two years. The Newark fans especially liked him. A 1945 Boys

Club poll to pick the most popular Eagle selected him with 1,245 votes, while his nearest competitors, Hill and Matthews, trailed far behind with about 300 each.

One night in 1943, Bob Harvey was playing for a semi-professional team sponsored by his employer, the Phillips Packing Co. in Cambridge, Maryland, when he caught the notice of Webster McDonald, a former Negro league pitcher who was managing the independent black team opposing Phillips. McDonald was an old acquaintance of Abe's and one of Manley's network of scouts. Word was passed back to Newark, and shortly afterwards Harvey was invited north for a tryout.

"Originally, I was a catcher, but when I got to the team the catcher [probably Ruffin] told me they didn't need any more catchers, so they decided to put me in the outfield," he recalled. Harvey hit .307 in 1944 and .389 in 1945, which was second best among regular players, and joined Davis as a regular in the outfield for the rest of the Newark Eagles' existence.

But despite these finds, the Eagles' wartime lineups never had enough quality players. Winning a championship was going to have to wait until the veterans in the service could come home to join the caretakers such as Pearson and Hooker and the newcomers like Harvey and Davis.

Notes

1. *Afro-American,* Jan. 30, 1943.
2. *Courier,* March 13, 1943.
3. *Afro-American,* April 10, 1943.
4. *Herald-News,* Nov. 13, 1943.
5. *Courier,* March 27, 1943; *Afro-American,* July 24, 1943.
6. Ric Roberts, Negro Big League Baseball a Two-Million Dollar Business, *Negro Baseball Pictorial Year Book,* 1945, p. 5.
7. Cunningham, *Newark,* pp. 293-96.
8. Manley and Hardwick, *Negro Baseball,* p. 59; "Newark Eagles," unsigned article, *Our World,* August, 1947.
9. David Quentin Voigt, *American Baseball,* Vol. 2 (Norman, OK: University of Oklahoma Press, 1970), p. 269.

10. Art Carter, "Negro Baseball Players Star for Uncle Sam," *Negro Baseball Pictorial Year Book,* 1945, p. 22.

11. *Afro-American,* Sept. 25, 1943.

12. Dixon and Hannigan, *Negro Baseball Leagues*, p. 162.

13. *Afro-American,* April 29, 1944.

14. *Courier*, Feb. 20, 1943.

15. Quincy Trouppe, *20 Years Too Soon* (Los Angeles: S and S Enterprises, 1977), pp. 139-44.

16. *Courier,* July 17, 1943, and July 31, 1943.

17. *Herald-News*, May 20, 1939.

18. Richardson, "Retrospective Look," pp. 176-77.

Chapter 8
The Championship Season

Leon Day pitched a no-hitter against the Philadelphia Stars on opening day at Ruppert Stadium on May 5, 1946. The Eagles scored their first run in the sixth inning, when Clarence Israel tripled and Larry Doby drove him home with a single. Doby was then barely called safe at home after a daring dash from second on an infield ground out, and Bill Cash, the Stars' catcher, was so enraged at the umpire's decision that he began waving his arms angrily and hit him.

The question in the minds of the 8,500 fans leaving the stadium onto Wilson Avenue that cloudy day could reasonably have been, "What can the Eagles do for an encore?"

Quite a bit, as it turned out, for 1946 was the year the Manleys and the Eagles won all the honors black baseball had to give. They took the National League pennant without even having to take part in a playoff, running away with first place in both halves of the split season. Then they won the Negro World Series from the American League's champions, the Kansas City Monarchs.

The black sporting press had predicted Newark a favorite to win the National League pennant before the season began, as the writers appraised the strong core of the team that had treaded water through the final years of World War II, then added the great value of the players returning from the armed forces. Not only were opening day heroes Day, Doby, and Israel back from the service, so were Monte Irvin, Max Manning, and the two catchers, Leon Ruffin and Charlie Parks. Just adding Doby and Irvin's hitting to that of Pearson, Harvey, and Davis would have produced a formidable offense, but the Manleys went one step further, making a controversial trade of the fans' favorite, Murray Watkins, to Philadelphia for third baseman Pat Patterson.

The trading of Watkins, voted the most popular Eagle in a fan poll the previous season, subjected the Manleys to a great deal of criticism from the fans at Ruppert Stadium, much of which was directed at Effa when she showed up at the park. Later, she recalled how, this time, she had questioned her husband's baseball judgment:

"Abe, the fans seem awfully upset about Watkins's being traded. Do you think you are making a mistake?" she asked him.

"Effa, don't ever speak of Watkins and Patterson in the same breath," he replied. "The only reason I can get Patterson is because he's not getting along with the manager. He is one of those outstanding players that Philly wouldn't think of giving up otherwise."

Patterson was all Abe had said he was—soon after he became an Eagle, the same fans shouted at her, "Girl! The trade's okay!" [1]

As a consequence, the Eagles had an explosive batting order. Reminiscent of the league's disorganization of earlier years, final batting and pitching averages were never published, even though they were being kept by the reputable Elias Bureau. But a surviving Elias press release just before the end of the season gives a good idea how well the Eagles performed.

In 59 official league games, in all but the last four that Newark played, the entire team hit .301 and cracked 46 home runs. Both were league highs at that point by substantial margins, and produced an average of 6.8 runs per game. This was more than a run better than the next highest scorers, the Homestead Grays, who had three future Hall of Fame members, Josh Gibson, Buck Leonard, and James "Cool Papa" Bell, in their lineup.

Five Newark regulars were hitting more than .300 (Irvin topped the regular lineup at .394, Doby hit .342, Davis .338, Patterson .337, and Pearson .322). When Leon Day was pitching or filling in at a field position, the Eagles had a .431 hitter in the lineup, which was a better percentage than any regular in the National League. Harvey batted a highly respectable .282, Ruffin belied his general reputation as a weak hitter by finishing at .276 while doing most of the catching, and Jim Wilkes, playing his first full season for the Eagles, hit .264. Davis's nine home runs in official games were only two behind league leader Josh Gibson, and Irvin, Doby, and Pearson had eight each.

With this sort of batting support, it would not have been hard for any decent group of pitchers to prosper. But the Eagle mound staff outdid itself. Max Manning had won eleven league games and lost only one when the nearly complete statistics were compiled. A further indicator of his excellence was that he allowed only slightly more than one base runner per inning pitched, a surefire prescription for keeping the opposition's scoring down. Day's won-lost record was 11 and 4, and his 105 strikeouts led all National League pitchers. The third ace of the staff was a new Abe Manley find, righthander Rufus Lewis, who won nine and lost only two in his first year with the Eagles.

When the big three were not pitching, the rest of the staff kept the opposition sufficiently at bay. Hooker had a 5 and 5 record as the fourth starter, and the next winningest pitcher was a player with a name right out of a "Great Books" literature course, a second-year man named Warren Peace. He won three league games and lost none.

The Eagles' eventual success was not too apparent as the season began. After winning the opening day game and the next two league contests, the team went into a slump. The pitchers were pitching pretty well, but the hitters were not scoring runs, leading to four straight losses through May 25, two to the Baltimore Elite Giants and one each to the Stars and the lowly New York Black Yankees. At the end of the month, Newark split a doubleheader with the Stars on Decoration Day (the old name for Memorial Day), and on Sunday, June 2, the team was in third place, with 5 wins and 5 losses.

It was from this point that Abe Manley and Biz Mackey, the manager, began to make changes. Patterson, whose salary disagreement with Philadelphia management had kept him out of league play altogether, came to the Eagles the first week in June, to replace Israel as the regular third baseman. Ruffin took over most of the catching from Parks, who was not hitting well, and Wilkes became the regular center fielder. Then, later in the month, another significant lineup shuffle took place.

Shortstop had been a problem position for Newark since opening day, when Bill Felder, a light hitter, made two errors. Oscar Givens, a native of Linden, N.J., took over the position briefly when his semester at Morgan State College ended in June, but Manley and Mackey soon made another switch there, designed to maximize Newark's offense. Irvin was brought in from the outfield to play short, where he stayed through the rest of the season. This freed up a spot in right field for Harvey, who had not been in the lineup consistently, and gave Mackey the comforting opportunity to write out a lineup for nearly every game that had eight (or nine, when Day was pitching) good-to-outstanding hitters in it.

This gave the Eagles all the resources they needed to make their anticipated move on the first-half pennant. But they didn't so much as move up, actually, as take off like a rocket. On Sunday, June 9, they beat the New York Cubans decisively in a doubleheader, to tie Philadelphia for first place. In the first game Day pitched a four-hitter and got three hits of his own for a 7-1 victory, and Lewis allowed the Cubans only 7 hits in the second game, as Newark won 6-2.

Then the Eagles beat the Elites, 7-4, in a "home game" played in Trenton, N.J., June 14. Two days later, they swept a three-team doubleheader (where one team would play a different opponent each game) at Ruppert Stadium. Lewis and Manning each pitched four-hitters as they beat Baltimore again, 5-2, and the Black Yankees, 2-1. The week's work put the Eagles in first place by themselves.

Sunday, June 23, Newark won another doubleheader from the Cubans, 6-1 and 5-1, and had a record of 18 wins and 8 losses. The Philadelphia Stars were 15 and 8, and were close behind, but the Eagles were in the midst of a powerful winning streak. Up through the last day in June, they won 14 of 15 games, roaring past all opposition. The final two wins, over the now-distant second place Stars in a July 30 doubleheader in Newark, really defined their level of success. Day and Lewis each pitched shutouts.

But a set of games leading up to that Sunday doubleheader must have been very satisfying to the Manleys and anyone else on the team who remembered chasing the Homestead Grays all those years. Within the space of four days, the Eagles and the Grays played four games, in which both teams unlimbered their sizable batting arsenals, and Newark won three of the matches. The Eagles beat the Grays 12-8 in Newark on Tuesday, June 25, and again 8-4 in Trenton on Wednesday. The Grays won a slugfest, 13-11, down in Washington on Thursday, but after a nighttime trip back up to Ruppert Stadium, the Eagles prevailed on Friday, 11-10.

For the season's first half, Newark won 25 games and lost 9, for a winning percentage of .735. The second-place Stars were far in the rear, with a .586 percentage. Wendell Smith, of the Pittsburgh *Courier,* celebrated Newark's accomplishment with understandable caution, since the season was only at the halfway mark:

> It has taken Abe Manley and his ever-loving wife, Effa, something like eleven years to weld themselves a championship ball club . . . But the pleasure of owning a championship club was never realized until this year, and even now you might say they only have half of a championship team . . . it's a long rocky trail from now until Labor Day. . . . However, the way the team is going now, winning every series it plays and blasting the seamed tomato all over the lot, it difficult to see how they can lose the second half.[2]

The Eagles continued hitting and pitching the "seamed tomato," winning the first five games of the second half. They beat the Grays, who now were easy pickings for them, twice on July 8, and won two from the Black Yankees and one from the Cubans in the next few days. Then they stumbled a little, losing a July 14 doubleheader in their home park to Philadelphia.

This put them temporarily in second place behind Baltimore, which had won one less game but which also had one less loss. But Newark was back in first place by July 21, even without playing any league games for a week, when the Elites won only one of two league contests, giving both clubs identical 5-2 records. This week spent playing nonleague games was preparatory to another Eagle surge, as they won three of four games up to and including a win over Philadelphia on July 27, to move back alone into first place.

They stayed a little bit ahead of the Cubans, who had moved into second place on the strength of four straight wins that week, and ran their record to 9 wins, 3 losses, by August 4, with a win over Baltimore. Another double-header win over the Grays August 11 that included more Leon Day heroics (he pitched all fifteen innings of the opening game and hit a last inning home run to finally win it) gave the Eagles a little breathing room. They now had a 12 and 3 record, and the Cubans were 10 and 4.

By August 25, they were still in first, and the Cubans, although theoretically within winning distance, had fallen farther off the pace. Each team won three games the following week and lost none, but Newark now had a 17 and 3 record, and time had about run out for any challengers.

The rest of the "pennant race" changed nothing, and for the Manleys' team the second half of the season was as successful as the first. The Eagles won 22, lost only 7, and had a winning percentage of .759 that was more than 100 points ahead of the second-place Cubans. The Eagles' 1946 team photograph shows nineteen men and a boy, the players, manager Mackey, and the batboy, radiating feelings of confidence and relaxation. If they were not already league champions when it was taken, they seemed to know that in due time they would be.

Abe and Effa were also reveling in their success. While their team was outscoring the rest of the National League, it had drawn a year's home attendance of 120,292 that, for the Newark club at least, was the best season ever. Effa's account of this attendance figure does not say how many games it took to draw this many people, although the figure did include the three Negro World Series games played in Ruppert Stadium. Even if the six league games scheduled by the Manleys in Trenton's Dunn Field are counted, the number represents not more than about 20 playing dates, and a healthy average of 6,000 per game. In later interviews, Effa recalled drawing "capacity crowds" at Ruppert in the team's best years. Most, if not all, of these sellouts must have come during the championship season, since existing financial and attendance information for the periods before and after the immediate postwar years make such attendance marks very unlikely during those seasons.

Unfortunately, no attendance or financial records survive from the championship season, but Wendell Smith reported in the *Courier* that, including World Series income, the Manleys had netted $25,000 for the season, their best year ever. Although he did not name his source, it probably was Effa, who was friendly with Smith and wrote or talked with him often.[3]

The Eagles' World Series opponents were the Kansas City Monarchs, who had also won both halves of the American League split season. The Monarchs, who were owned by J. L. Wilkinson, the white man who had made a career out of Negro league baseball in the Midwest, and managed by former catching star Frank Duncan, had handled the other members of their league with about as little trouble as the Eagles had experienced in winning the National League pennant.

Among its stars, the team had four men who would eventually play in the integrated major leagues, outfielder Willard Brown, infielder Hank Thompson, pitcher Connie Johnson—and Satchel Paige. The Monarchs had come to Ruppert Stadium August 6 on a barnstorming tour, and the Eagles, with Day and Peace pitching, had beaten Paige 7-4 before a large crowd of 10,000 fans. That had been an exhibition game, which did not count in either league's standings, but the next meetings between the long, tall, star and the Eagles he had once spurned would be crucial.

Othello "Chico" Renfroe, who as a youth had hustled around in Jacksonville playing batboy to the original Brooklyn Eagles in spring training in 1935, was now playing shortstop for the Monarchs. Later, he remembered the 1946 Negro World Series as "the last of the great ones," which it was. When white professional baseball began to recruit Negro leaguers, it naturally went for the best players. But, in this first year of integration, only five men had been signed. The most able black players were still available to the black leagues, and many were represented on the Eagle and Monarch rosters.

Effa prepared for the games in Newark as if they did indeed represent a great occasion. She outfitted the Eagles in new white home team uniforms for the Ruppert Stadium games, at a total cost of $700. And she persuaded Joe Louis, the heavyweight boxing champion so admired by her, all of black America, and many of the country's whites, to throw out the ceremonial first ball at the opening game in Newark on September 19.

This first pitch ceremony was more than just the usual celebrity appearance, since the ball that Louis tossed from his front-row box seat was no ordinary baseball. It was a silver ball, the trophy awarded the first fulltime professional black team, the Cuban Giants, for winning a tournament in 1888 that stood at that time for the championship of black baseball. The ball was owned by Benjamin Holmes of nearby Orange, N.J., who had been a member of that Giants team and was a frequenter of Eagles' games. With a sweep of his right arm, Louis, the greatest black athlete of his day, symbolically linked the earliest era of Negro baseball with its most recent high point.

At the time of the champ's toss, however, the Eagles were already one game down to the Monarchs in the race to be the first to win four Series games. Operating under the same theory that allowed games to be scheduled in neutral cities all over the East and Midwest to bring the Negro leagues to more fans, the World Series also included contests played in neither team's home park. The first game had been September 17 in the Polo Grounds, the

New York Giants' home park in New York City. There, 19,423 fans were counted, and Kansas City beat Newark, 2-1.

Leon Day and Hilton Smith, the Monarch starting pitcher, were each stiffling the other team's bats early in the game. Kansas City scored a run in the first inning on an error, the only run scored until the bottom half of the sixth inning. Smith walked Larry Doby to start the inning, and Monarch manager Duncan took him out of the game, relieving him with none other than Paige. Satchel nearly got out of the inning without being scored on, but Johnny Davis drove in Doby, who had stolen second, with a two-out single.

Rufus Lewis relieved Day in the sixth inning, and in the seventh Paige, never known as a great hitter, redeemed his failure to hold the lead. He bounced a sharp grounder back to Lewis that deflected off the pitcher's glove for a hit, and then proceeded to second base when Doby made a wild throw to first in a vain attempt to get him out. Herb Souell, the Monarch's third baseman, followed with a single, and as Sam Lacy, of the *Afro-American* newspapers put it, "Paige Satchel-footed in across the pan."[4]

That might have been just the tying, not the winning, run, except for one of those occurrences that turn managers' hair even greyer than it already might be. In the second inning, Newark had Pearson on second and Davis on first, with only one out, when Mackey set them running on a hit-and-run play. The maneuver looked successful, as Ruffin bounced a ground ball past the pitcher that ordinarily would have gone into center field and scored Pearson. However, the apparent double steal, the very smokescreen strategy meant to pull the infielders out of position, had drawn the Monarch shortstop over to cover second base. The ball bounced right to him, and he started a double play that killed the Eagle rally.

It did not look as if the first game in Newark two nights later was going to go the Eagles' way, either. Willard Brown, the Monarchs' centerfielder and clean-up hitter, homered with two men on base in the top half of the sixth inning, to break up a tied pitcher's duel and give Kansas City a 4-1 lead. But the Eagles, who made a season-long practice of putting together big-scoring innings, did so again in the seventh. Doby hit a two-run homer, and the Monarch pitching, which included an ineffective relief performance by Paige (he gave up four hits, including the home run), was shelled for six runs. That was all the scoring, and Newark tied the series with the 7-4 win. Nearly 10,000 fans were at Ruppert for the occasion.

Kansas City won the third game in its home park on September 23, scoring six runs off Hooker in the first four innings, then treating his relief, Bill "Cotton" Williams, even worse. Williams gave up nine runs (seven in the eighth inning) and eleven hits in less than five innings. The Monarchs got twenty-one hits and fifteen runs in all, the effort dwarfing the five runs Newark could score off Jim "Lefty" LaMarque.

As often happens when two teams play each other in consecutive games, the next evening bore no resemblance to the previous bloodbath. Rufus Lewis pitched a four-hitter, and the Eagle offense generated fourteen hits, a combination that could be expected to produce something resembling the actual outcome, an 8-1 Newark victory.

But things rapidly got worse for the Eagles. The next game was in Chicago's Comiskey Park, site of the annual Negro leagues' East-West All-Star game. Kansas City won, 5-1, Hilton Smith outpitching Manning. This left the Eagles in the unenviable position of having to win both of the remaining games to become Series champions. Working to their advantage was that they would be at home in Ruppert Stadium for both contests on Friday, September 27, and the following Sunday.

There was enough scoring in the first inning of the sixth game of the Series to satisfy any fan bored by pitchers' duels. Willard Brown hit a three-run homer in the top of the inning, and Kansas City scored four runs before three men had been retired. The Eagles then scored four in their half of the inning, Pearson and Ruffin getting crucial singles after a handful of walks. And Newark didn't stop scoring. Irvin hit a two-run homer in the second, his first of two for the day, and Pearson did the same thing in the fourth. Hooker, in early relief of Leon Day, was much more effective than he had been in Kansas City, and the Eagles insured a seventh game showdown with a 9-7 victory.

The last game was everything a championship game ought to be. Newark scored a single run in the bottom of the first inning when Patterson was safe on an error, Doby moved him along to second by drawing a walk, and Irvin singled him home. John "Buck" O'Neil, the Kansas City first baseman, tied the game with a home run in the top of the sixth, but Newark went ahead, 3-1, in the bottom of the inning. Doby and Irvin both walked, and Johnny Davis scored them both with a line drive that eluded left fielder John Scott's attempt at an ankle-high catch. The Monarchs had not gotten to this critical afternoon by being pushovers, of course, and they scored a run in the top of the next inning by bunching up three of their eight hits off Rufus Lewis.

All was quiet until the top of the ninth inning, when the Monarchs gave it one more try. With one out, Mickey Taborn, the catcher, singled, but Wilkes threw him out at second when he tried to make the hit a double. But then, with Kansas City all but disposed of, pitcher Ford Smith singled and Chico Renfroe drew a walk. Souell, who had damaged the Eagles' chances many times during this series, was at bat.

Effa Manley was among those in the stadium that day who would vividly remember this game. Years later her ghost writer, Leon Hardwick, recorded her dramatic play-by-play of Souell's at bat:

> My eyes are riveted to the playing field . . . Souell fouls off one pitch . . . the suffocating tension is mounting steadily . . . Next, a ball . . . I lower my head . . . How much can the nervous system take?
>
> Then, as if from another world, I hear the sickening, cracking sound of bat striking ball . . . I'm almost afraid to look up . . . Has Souell homered?

> From somewhere I muster enough courage to raise my eyes—just in time to see our huge first sacker, Lenny Pearson, fondly squeezing that little old round white ball . . . Souell has popped up!
>
> THE GAME IS OVER . . . The Newark Eagles are World Champs! I recline in my seat, thoroughly drained . . . too numbed to move.[5]

So, at last, the Eagles were the princes of the kingdom of black baseball, and Abe and Effa Manley its king and queen. But, although no one realized it that September, they were presiding over a crumbling domain. There had been clues to this impending demise, but no one as yet knew how to read them. For example, one of the keys to the long-term meaning of the last great black World Series was not who was on the Monarch and Eagle rosters, but who was not. In 1945, the Kansas City shortstop had not been Chico Renfroe, it had been Jackie Robinson. Now he had the tremendous honor of being the first black man in modern white baseball, playing one step below the major leagues for the Montreal Royals in the Brooklyn Dodgers farm system. And the acquisition of Rufus Lewis was so critical to the Eagles because Don Newcombe, who would otherwise have filled out the threesome of dependable Newark starting pitchers, had also left to play minor league ball for the Dodgers.

Robinson and Newcombe, as well as Baltimore catcher Roy Campanella and pitchers John Wright of the Homestead Grays and Roy Partlow of the Philadelphia Stars, were the players that black sportswriters and fans really had their eyes on during the summer of 1946. From the beginning of spring training, Robinson dominated the sports sections of the black weeklies. In the May 11 New Jersey *Afro-American,* for instance, Leon Day's opening day no-hitter merited a banner headline across all eight columns of page 18. Robinson's play with the Royals earned an equal headline on the facing page.

As the season went on, that equal treatment would diminish. The Pittsburgh *Courier* made room every Saturday for the playing statistics of the five blacks in the white minors, and as Robinson, Newcombe, and Campanella showed they could keep up with their white counterparts, they got even more coverage. Even before baseball integration, the black sports news would be dominated by Joe Louis every time he made a statement for his race by successfully defending his heavyweight crown. In June, 1946, he knocked out a major contender, Billy Conn, and between his fight and the new interest in integrated baseball, the Negro leagues almost disappeared from the sports pages.

There were some who thought Negro league baseball, buoyed by the population shifts, income growth, and the black pride brought about by World War II, would get a further boost from baseball integration. Ric Roberts of the Pittsburgh *Courier* predicted a sort of well-heeled minor league status for the Negro leagues in the 1946 *Negro Baseball Yearbook:*

> The beckoning of the majors—the fortunes of Jackie Robinson, John Wright, Roy Campanella and Don Newcombe in a white situation—will point up new interest, fetch new followers, new fans and better players. The game will go on—it will improve and soon, perhaps, the prosperous owners of Negro franchises, mindful of the nebulous promise of selling ace colored stars to the multi-millionaire major league market, will hire ex-major leaguers to coach and train their athletes.[6]

This never happened, couldn't happen, in fact, because no matter how farsighted the black owners might have been (and many of them were not), a lasting liaison with major league baseball could only occur if the white owners wanted to cooperate, and none of them did. Whether black newspapers took their cues from the black baseball fans or whether it worked the other way around was immaterial. The attention of both focused on the wonderful young black men who had crossed the unspoken but long-existing color line in baseball. Their progress got the newspaper ink and blacks' attendance dollars at the expense of the all-black teams which had gotten used to having the biggest shares of both.

The Negro leagues, instead of continuing to prosper in the newly integrated world of professional baseball, were doomed, both by the events that had shaped them and by things that were going to happen in the near future. A very apt metaphor for them in 1946 was the state of the Eagles' home city, Newark itself.

John T. Cunningham, a historian of the city, points out that after the economic euphoria of the wartime defense industry ended, Newark was forced to face the facts—its aged industrial sections were losing tenants and jobs to areas outside its crowded urban setting, slum housing was still prevalent for the lower classes, and the city's tax base, from which could come the money to cure some of these ills, had shrunk drastically.

This had been going on since before the war, only it had been ignored. "In the 1930s, Newark prided itself on the Golden Age," Cunningham says, "and yet, the traces of rot were there."

Notes

1. Richardson, "Retrospective Look," p. 171.
2. *Courier,* July 13, 1946.
3. Ibid., Dec. 21, 1946.
4. *Afro-American*, Sept. 21, 1946.
5. Manley and Hardwick, *Negro Baseball,* p. 37.
6. Ric Roberts, "The Game Goes On . . . " *Negro Baseball Year Book*, 1946, p.5.

Chapter 9
Good-bye to the Queen

In 1933, Al Monroe, a black Chicago sportswriter and sometime Negro league official, wrote "The Big League," an article for the black magazine *Abbott's Monthly,* in which he asserted, "there are Race players we would like to see in the big leagues and would bet the family purse that they would stick." His nominees for membership in the white majors included pitcher Willie Foster, the late Rube Foster's half-brother and a star in his own right, and the great Oscar Charleston.

The next year W. Rollo Wilson, Monroe's Eastern counterpart as a dean of sportswriters who had also lent his services to Negro baseball as an official, wrote his own magazine piece, "They Could Make the Big Leagues." He named Charleston and Foster, as well as Satchel Paige, outfielder James "Cool Papa" Bell, and several others, insisting that "most of these lads, if given the chance—and if prejudice were not the powerful agent we know it to be—would be valuable decorations in any American or National league ballyard." His argument was given additional credibility by being published in *The Crisis,* the official organ of the NAACP.

Other blacks had even greater hopes for their side of professional baseball. Mabry "Doc" Kountz, sports editor of the Boston *Chronicle,* proposed in 1934 that the Negro National League become a minor league in white organized ball, with the white majors underwriting expenses in return for the right to draft players off the black rosters.[1]

Far ahead of eventual integration, these writers were secure in their knowledge of what should also have been obvious to all baseball people: skill observed no racial dividing line. Dave Malarcher, a Negro league player and Rube Foster's successor as manager of Chicago's team in the mid-1920s, recalled that, even then,

> I used to have Negroes occasionally tell me, "Do you think Negroes can play in the major leagues?" And do you know what I would say to them? "Do you think so and so here, who is a barber, can cut hair like a white man? Do you think Doctor so-and-so, who is teaching in a medical school, can teach a white professor?" [They would reply] "Well, certainly." And I would say, "What's baseball that I can't play it like a white?" [2]

The voices urging integration were mostly, but not always, black. Several prominent white sportswriters, including Heywood Broun and Westbrook Pegler (who wondered why it was thought that Negroes would besmirch a sport that had already suffered the Chicago "Black Sox" betting scandal) had also made the argument.

There was evidence to prove that black players could measure up to the level of major league play, since after the regular baseball season, black teams often played barnstorming "all star" squads that included white big leaguers, and Negro leaguers and their white counterparts often competed against each other in the Latin American winter leagues.

These encounters helped keep pressure on white baseball, with integration advocates making their points as publicly as they could. In 1937, Chester Washington, the Pittsburgh *Courier* sports editor, sent a telegram to Pittsburgh Pirate manager Harold "Pie" Traynor at the major league winter meetings in Chicago, and made sure the wire also was published in the *Courier.*

> KNOW YOUR CLUB NEEDS PLAYERS [STOP] HAVE ANSWER TO YOUR PRAYERS RIGHT HERE IN PITTSBURGH [STOP] JOSH GIBSON CATCHER BUCK LEONARD FIRST BASEMAN AND RAY BROWN PITCHER OF HOMESTEAD GRAYS AND SATCHELL PAIGE PITCHER AND COOL PAPA BELL

> OUTFIELDER OF PITTSBURGH CRAWFORDS ALL AVAILABLE AT REASONABLE FIGURES [STOP] WOULD MAKE PIRATES FORMIDABLE PENNANT CONTENDERS [STOP] WHAT IS YOUR ATTITUDE?[3]

The Pirates made no official answer to the offer, of course. But Wendell Smith of the *Courier* collected many unofficial favorable responses two years later, during the 1939 baseball season, when he traveled from one major league city to another, interviewing players and managers on their views about integration. It was unlikely that Smith, a black man working for a Negro newspaper, would have gotten any quotes in favor of segregation, but forty players and eight field managers were willing to go on the record with positive views of black players' abilities, and Smith's long interview series that summer added to the growing body of opinion that favored letting blacks into the big leagues.

In addition to gathering favorable views from whites in baseball, Smith also was adept at exposing the white baseball power structure's continuing hypocrisy on the integration issue. Typically, he reported an interview in February, 1939, with Ford Frick, then National League president, who asserted that "major league baseball is willing to accept Negro ball players today." The problem, Frick told Smith, was that "the general public has not been educated to the point where they will accept them on the same standard as they do the white player." That left baseball in a position in which "we cannot do anything we want to until public opinion is ready for it." [4]

Smith held his fire for a few weeks, but then observed in his regular sports-page column that Frick had been unable to explain

> how it is that these same Americans will pay as high as $100 to see Joe Louis, a black man, knock a white man out in quicker time than you can say the white man's name. He can't seem to explain how it is that they can't stand to see a Negro hit a ball thrown by a white pitcher,

but delight in seeing a Negro hit a jaw owned by a white boxer.[5]

The war, which gave black Americans a greatly increased role in filling the country's needs, provided both moral and practical backdrop for further advances. Baseball's moral predicament was summed up succinctly by a member of the white press, Atlantic City, N. J., *Press-Union* sports columnist Whitey Gruhler: "And what are we fighting for? Freedom and democracy. But some of us seem to have forgotten that freedom and democracy are the human rights for which we fought the Civil War."

As more and more major leaguers entered the armed forces and the quality of the remaining talent noticeably thinned, it became more difficult to justify not recruiting good black players who weren't in the war. As Wendell Smith pointed out, if the St. Louis Browns could actually use Pete Gray, a one-armed outfielder, as they did in 1945, it only proved that "the big leagues will stop at only one point—where Negroes are concerned—to make money. [6]

Smith and other journalists also forced the issue during the war by maneuvering "tryouts" for black players with white major league clubs. The first target was the Pittsburgh Pirates, since team owner William Benswanger had been quoted sympathetically regarding integration. But Benswanger could never seem to actually get black players into the Pirates' Forbes Field to watch them play.

In April, 1945, Smith worked with a Boston City Councilor, Isadore Muchnick, to get black players a tryout with the Red Sox. There was no ducking the issue as the Pirates had done, for Muchnick threatened to make trouble with the issuance of the team's permits to play Sunday baseball if they did not take a look at black players. Smith came to Boston with Jackie Robinson, outfielder Sam Jethroe of the Negro American League's Cleveland Buckeyes, and Marvin Williams, an infielder with the Philadelphia Stars. Red Sox management watched them work out, but ended the session with a "don't call us, we'll call you" message, and then never called.

This audition came shortly after the most famous of these confrontations. On April 6, Joe Bostic, sportswriter for *People's Voice* newspaper in New York City's Harlem, showed up at the Dodgers' spring training site at the Bear Mountain resort area north of the city with two Negro league veterans, Newark Eagle Terris McDuffie and New York Cubans first baseman Dave "Showboat" Thomas. Bostic demanded the Brooklyn team give them a tryout.

Dodger President Branch Rickey, who was well along in his secret plan to break the big league color line and had no use for an incident staged by a black newsman with two aging Negro league stars in tow, was "reported to have sputtered, gone into seclusion, come out of it, and held a conference." He took Bostic and his entourage to lunch and gave McDuffie and Thomas a tryout the next day. It turned out the Dodgers had no interest in McDuffie and Thomas, although Rickey, of course, was to be heard from again before too long.

Just before World War II, the American labor movement picked up the crusade to integrate baseball. In the summer of 1940, the New York Trade Union Athletic Association demonstrated against "Jim Crow" attitudes in the sport at the New York World's Fair, after having announced in the spring that it would launch a million-signature petition drive.

Labor intensified its drive for blacks in the big leagues in 1942, when the Congress of Industrial Organizations formed a "Citizens Committee to End Jim Crow in Baseball." The Communist newspaper the *Daily Worker,* which was vigorously pursuing the baseball integration issue, predicted in August that because of the committee's work, "the ump will soon be calling Jim Crow in baseball out on strikes." Just after the World Series ended in October, the committee, recruiting a roster of more than seventy members, including prominent blacks, labor leaders, politicians, and well-known literary figures, announced it would launch a campaign to have black players signed by major league clubs in time for the 1943 season.

Effa Manley's name was on the committee's imposing list of members—she had been present for the citizens' committee's founding a few months earlier, and was the lone person involved who was connected with Negro league baseball, other than several black sportswriters. Predictably, she lent not only her name to the endeavor, but also gladly supplied her opinions. At a committee strategy meeting, she advised caution in selecting the black players to be put forth as candidates for the white majors. "'If we don't send up our very best, and the ones we actually do send prove disappointing,' I reminded the audience, 'then the Big League officials can turn them down with a 'Well, there you are. We gave you your chance and you couldn't cut it.'" Her strategy, to present the major leagues with just one prospective big leaguer, "the finest player we have," who could meet "the toughest of big league standards," was in fact the path followed three years later by the man who would become her arch enemy, Brooklyn Dodger President Branch Rickey.[7]

Before the deleterious effects of integration on the Negro leagues' health became obvious, the Effa Manley of the old Blumstein Department Store days was totally committed to breaking down the color line in baseball. When Monte Irvin was contemplating leaving the Eagles again to play in Mexico in 1946, she wrote him and urged him to stay, not only for the team's sake, but for his own. Play in the United States and be seen by major league scouts, she advised, because if Rickey's experiment with Jackie Robinson works, "all the teams will be ready to take you."

She could say that, because at that point she apparently had no fear that the Negro leagues themselves would not somehow become partners in integration. Interviewed by the *Daily Worker* to publicize the organization of the citizens committee, she contended integration would help the Negro leagues. "If our men made good in the majors, fans all over the country would want to see the teams that they came from. Just as Joe Louis made other Negro fighters popular, so would Negro big league stars increase interest in other Negro players." [8]

But when integration came, Effa was as indignant as the black owners who had heretofore remained silent on the topic. In recruiting Jackie Robinson to play for the Dodgers' minor league club in Montreal in 1946, Rickey had conducted a painstaking search for the best candidate, although he was looking for more than athletic skills. Robinson had been a college athlete and an army lieutenant during the war, both of which had given him a great deal of experience in dealing with whites.

He clearly was also a superb athlete, although Rickey had his baseball ability evaluated much more accurately than Negro leaguers who knew him. Robinson had played a single season in 1945 for the Kansas City Monarchs at shortstop, which was not his best position, and few black baseball men thought he was capable of the success he later enjoyed as a major league player.

So when Robinson signed a contract to play minor league ball for the Dodgers in October, 1945, Effa Manley's requirements for an integration effort benefitting both black and white baseball would have seemed to have been met, except for one important difference. When Rickey signed up Robinson, he treated him as if he were a free agent, with no existing contractual obligations to the team for which he had finished playing the month before. Rickey neither consulted the Kansas City Monarchs ownership nor offered them any money for the right to sign Robinson. Under these terms, if integration succeeded and more Negro league players crossed over, the black teams would be systematically bled of their best talent. This would mean almost certain doom for their popularity and economic viability.

The immediate reaction of J. L. Wilkinson, the primary owner of the Monarchs, and his partner, Tom Baird, was to protest, claiming thievery. But Robinson was quoted as saying he had no contract with the Monarchs at the time he signed with the Dodgers, only a handshake agreement for the coming 1946 season. At any rate, it soon became apparent that it would be extremely impolitic for Wilkinson and Baird to complain in any way about the opportunity Robinson represented for American blacks, and they shortly subsided.

But Rickey was not through. He signed four more players from the Negro leagues before the 1946 season was over, putting them all on Dodger minor league teams. The short-lived furor over Robinson's contractual status apparently made Rickey careful, if not generous. Pitcher Roy Partlow had a written contract with the Philadelphia Stars, so Rickey paid Ed Bolden $1,000 for the rights to Partlow. But John Wright, a pitcher who started the season at Montreal mostly to function as Robinson's roommate and one-man black support group, came from the Homestead Grays for no compensation, as did future Hall of Fame catcher Roy Campanella, from the Baltimore Elite Giants. Rickey also paid nothing for the rights to his fifth signing that year, which guaranteed him the everlasting enmity of that player's previous employer. The player was pitcher Don Newcombe, who had last worn the uniform of Effa Manley's Newark Eagles.

Effa's public comments were fairly restrained when Robinson and Newcombe were signed. She showed her satisfaction that blacks would play in the previously white leagues, while making it clear that she thought Negro league baseball had been wronged in the process. "Rickey is to be commended for his democratic pioneering," she said after Robinson's signing was announced, "but I am surprised at the method employed in the assignment. I never knew that it was good business for the owner of one team to negotiate solely with a player of another club without his manager." [9]

Newcombe's signing, coming just before the 1946 Negro National League season was to open, and after the Eagles had figured him into their pitching plans for the year, nevertheless drew an expression of "elation" from her over the advancement of another black player. But she again made the point that Rickey had made his deal with the player, not the player's team, and this time voiced the black owners' underlying fear of this method of integration. "What will become of colored baseball leagues if players are picked out by major league owners without consulting the team management?" [10]

Privately, she was much less diplomatic, and clearly angry with the precedent Rickey was setting. Years later, she would characterize his treatment of the Negro leagues in unmistakably unforgiving fashion: "He raped us."

Fortuitously, she got the chance in the middle of the 1946 season to let Rickey know how she felt. On July 4, Rickey showed up unannounced at Yankee Stadium, although his own Dodgers were at the moment playing directly across New York's East River before a large holiday crowd in the New York Giants' Polo Grounds. What made his appearance even more curious was that the Yankee Stadium game was another league's Fourth of July gala—the Newark Eagles were playing the New York Black Yankees.

By then, the Dodgers had but one reputation among Negro league owners—when the team's scouts showed up at a black game, it was a portent that another star player might soon be leaving for white baseball. And here was the Brooklyn president himself, torn away from his own team's important day. Only the sudden appearance of President Truman himself might have more startled the Negro league officials present.

Effa was there with the Eagles, and when she learned Rickey was in the stadium, she went to see him, although not to pay a social call. Dan Parker, the New York *Daily Mirror* sports columnist, described her pointed greeting:

> "Mr. Rickey, I hope you're not going to grab any more of our players," she cooed, as the Deacon turned purple. "You know that the contracts we have with our players would stand up better in court than those you have with the majors. You know, Mr. Rickey, we could make trouble for you on the Newcombe transaction if we wanted to," continued Mrs. Manley, enjoying the Deacon's discomfiture.

This confrontation was by no means their first meeting. Rickey had been carefully working on his plan to integrate the Dodgers since 1943, when he first broached to the club's directors the idea of signing "a Negro player or two" as part of a program to revitalize the team with new, young talent. Having obtained the directors' secret permission to proceed, Rickey began to have his scouting staff look for black, as well as white, prospective major leaguers. But sending white major league scouts to Negro league games would eventually make their mission obvious, so Rickey joined forces with one of the legendary figures of Negro league baseball to create what, for the Dodgers, would be the perfect cover.

William "Gus" Greenlee's famous Pittsburgh Crawfords had gone out of business in 1939, taking their owner with them as far as Negro league baseball was concerned. Gus had made several attempts to get back in, but neither the Negro National nor American leagues were interested in having him return, for reasons that easily had as much to do with internal politics as finances. The powerful Cumberland Posey, for example, was not likely to want renewed competition for Pittsburgh's black baseball dollars.

Then, in January, 1945, Greenlee announced the formation of a new Negro league, the United States League. The Crawfords would be in it, along with teams in five other Eastern and Midwestern cities. In May, even more surprising news emerged—Branch Rickey announced that the Dodgers' Ebbets Field would be available to the U.S. League as the home park for a Brooklyn team. Rickey stated that his interests were to increase revenue from the park, but also to see Negro baseball run on a more "organized basis," a clear slap at the existing Negro leagues.

But while Rickey had no apparent use for the Negro leagues, he did invite a single one of its officials to the press conference at which he announced the Dodgers' involvement. As Effa Manley later remembered, one day she got a telephone call from Branch Rickey's secretary, who said, "Mr. Rickey would like to know if you would be available for a meeting in his office one day next week?"

"So it came to pass," she continued, "that the following week I found myself sitting in on one of the strangest press conferences I have attended in all of my life." Rickey, presiding in his Dodger executive office, sat at his desk, surrounded by a semicircle of U. S. League officials and New York area journalists from both black and white publications. Effa sat quietly and listened as he set out the league's advantages "in a droning sort of way" until he came to the promise that he, personally, would try to have the new league become affiliated with white baseball.

"Ah," she recalled, "I was beginning to see the light."

Then Rickey threw the meeting open for questions, and Effa unwittingly played into his hands. She asked why, if Rickey and the rest of the league's organizers wanted to get into black baseball, had they not contacted the two existing leagues. Rickey turned the question over to John G. Shackleford, a lawyer from Cleveland and former Negro League player who was the U. S. League president. Shackleford said he had written to both of the other presidents. J. B. Martin had replied that the American League was not interested in an affiliation, and Tom Wilson (who was notorious for ignoring correspondence) had not answered at all.

Prior to that day, Rickey had made another, even more confounding, overture to Effa. That time his secretary had called to invite Effa to join him in his private box for a Dodgers' game, and she had accepted. They must have made a strange pair, the 63-year-old Rickey, favoring conservative three-piece suits and with a dedication to stiff morality that had earned him religiously inspired nicknames such as "Deacon" and "The Mahatma," and the sharply dressed Effa, gliding gracefully into middle age, known for her keen and ready tongue and, above all, a light-skinned black woman, so far as the public knew.

The only things they had in common were a love of baseball and the ability to run their teams with high standards. But although they met at a ballpark, this was not enough common ground. Effa said that after she was escorted to Rickey's box, "only awkward silence" resulted. "I was sure he wanted to talk about something," but the topic never arose. [11]

Why Rickey reached out to Effa remains a mystery, but he may well have regarded her as his one potential ally in the Negro leagues. She already was on record as favoring baseball integration, had a favorable relationship with Gus Greenlee, and had a reputation as a progressive owner. So far as Effa was concerned, once it was clear Rickey was doing the Negro leagues no favors, it only meant that he was opportunistic: "He thought he saw a chance to get my cooperation, but I was in my husband's corner 100 percent. I never tried to persuade Abe to go along with him."

When Effa told the other Negro National League owners about Rickey's United States League press conference, their attitude was one of indifference. Except for Ebbets Field, where the Eagles had begun playing again on occasion since 1942, none of the other ballparks leased by Negro league teams belonged to the Dodger organization. Hence, they reasoned, if they still had control over their good venues, they would otherwise be unharmed by the upstart league.

After a shaky first year in 1945, the U. S. League did, in fact, expire after the next season. But by then Robinson, Campanella, and Newcombe had each had outstanding minor league seasons, Robinson was expected to move up to the Dodgers' major league roster the next year, and doubts about black men playing on the white side of baseball had pretty much been expelled. In the end, Effa noted, Rickey "outmaneuvered us completely."[12]

She added that as a byproduct of the integration set in force by the Dodger president, black owners "were draped over the well-known barrel," squeezed between wanting to be seen anxious for integration to succeed, and coping with white baseball owners who more and more seemed to have a need for their players, but not for them.

There was no question what America's black communities thought of the Robinson signing and his elevation to the major leagues after a single season of minor league play. An editorial cartoon in the April 19, 1947, *Afro-American* newspapers the Saturday of Jackie's first week in Brooklyn, told it all. In it Robinson, in uniform with a baseball bat slung over his shoulder, is shaking hands with Rickey, who is standing in a doorway. The door, which is ajar, is labeled "Brooklyn Dodgers."

"Rickey Opens the Door," the caption read.

Shortly after Robinson signed his contract, J. B. Martin made a point of publicly applauding the new minor leaguer. "I feel I speak the sentiments of Negroes in America, who are with you 100 percent," he announced. But at the same time, he, Tom Wilson, and the owners in both leagues were putting several events in motion to try to strengthen the Negro leagues' position.

A November 9, 1945, joint meeting of the two black leagues produced a letter to white baseball's commissioner, Albert B. Chandler. The letter was apparently written with Effa Manley's help, since a draft of it found in the Eagle files bears corrections in her handwriting. Released to the press November 13, it laid out the Negro league case succinctly: The black leagues had constitutions and player contracts, just as did the white leagues. The Negro league contract had passed a court test in 1941, when the Grays won a $10,000 judgment in Pittsburgh against Josh Gibson for contract jumping. "We feel that the clubs of Organized Negro Baseball who have gone to so much expense to develop players and establish teams and leagues should be approached, and deals made with clubs involved."

Release of the letter was accompanied by a press release from Martin, again stating that the Negro leagues had no objection to black players advancing to the major leagues, "however, we feel that Mr. Rickey is too big not to compensate the Kansas City Monarchs for Jackie Robinson." Martin had conceded in a private letter to Effa, written just before the joint meeting, that getting adequate compensation for Robinson was probably a lost cause, for no action would be taken that might jeopardize his chance to break down the color line. "If they say $500.00 or $5,000.00, all well and good, we will accept it. . . . BUT when they get other players, if they get them, we will place a reasonable price on them and demand it."

The owners also hustled to transform their leagues into more organized businesses. At a joint meeting of the two leagues in Chicago December 13, they voted to adopt the white major leagues' form of player contract, which included the "reserve clause" that protected clubs against being outbid for their players between seasons, and the constitutions of the white American and National leagues.

At the same time, they tried to convince white organized baseball of the advantages of having the Negro leagues as partners in developing talent. This approach is what led Effa to make her fruitless trip to Washington, and what brought her, New York Cuban owner Alex Pompez, and Curtis Leak, an official with the New York Black Yankees and the Negro National League secretary, to the Manhattan office of attorney Louis F. Carroll.

The three met with Carroll, who had the white National League, the New York Yankees, and the Dodgers among his clients, on September 26, 1946, to discuss Negro league recognition and protection of its players. Carroll listened noncommittally, then pointed out a number of problems with the merger, primarily the question of straightening out territorial rights conflicts caused by the overlay of the black leagues onto the white organizational structure. He did allow as how that might not be a problem, though, since Negro league attendance was 98 percent black, and he apparently presumed it would stay that way. Carroll said he would take their case to Chandler and report back, but this effort also produced no results.

However, the meeting that really defined the unlikeliness of the Negro leagues becoming part of the major and minor league system took place in January, 1946, between Commissioner Chandler and presidents Martin and Wilson. The two blacks had requested the meeting, but Chandler's version of what transpired was the first made public. He said he told the Negro leaguers to "get your house in order" before formally asking to join white organized baseball. Chandler's prescription for order included better scheduling, better umpires, and the expunging of gambling from Negro league games (he presumably meant betting by fans in the stands, which was also an unwelcome occurrence at white professional games, since there are no recorded instances of "fixed" Negro league games, where bribery determined a contest's outcome).

The commissioner also claimed that "the Negro leagues favor keeping their own boys and with the leagues on a sound basis . . . they want those boys to stay in their own class."[13] The black press was a little taken aback by the segregationist overtones of this last statement. The minor leagues were, and are, organized into "classes" based on the abilities of their players, and this may have been all Chandler meant. On the other hand, he was at an appearance in Dallas, Texas, when he spoke, and—as an experienced Near South politician from Kentucky—may have been taking pains to assuage Southern baseball people. Otherwise, the black sportswriters were receptive to the commissioner's statement, and proceeded to roundly criticize the Negro league presidents. This left Martin and Wilson with the need to do some explaining, and they leaped to do so. Martin promptly issued a news release denying that there had been any discussion at all either of the Negro leagues' retaining the rights to players who had a chance to advance, or of the black owners' expectations of Negroes staying "in their own class" (he was a little taken aback by that phrase, also).

The minutes of the Negro National League's meeting in New York on February 20 record Wilson as asserting Chandler's response had been much more positive.

> He would be glad to help us and he wanted to do something helpful for Negro Baseball. . . . He suggested that we get the lawyer of the National League to draw up a petition and present it to him and that it would be considered to have us recognized by organized baseball.

Wilson claimed Chandler even wanted to know what minor league class they sought, and that they had told the commissioner, "we were not major leaguers; but that we were better than the International League [a top-rated minor league]."

Martin addressed the meeting the next day and also claimed that Chandler had not accurately represented them to the press. He also added that Chandler had said that, in addition to the other conditions the black leagues needed to meet to become acceptable, "the Negro Leagues needed their own parks in order to accomplish anything."

This last requirement, almost impossible to fulfill for all twelve black teams, showed as well as anything the insurmountable hurdles facing the Negro leagues in their quest for acceptance. White organized baseball in those days was an intensely conservative, unchanging institution—there had not been a new addition to the sixteen major league teams, nor had an existing franchise moved between cities, since 1903. The reserve clause, upheld by a 1922 Supreme Court decision, served to eliminate any sort of free market for valuable players and made the white leagues even more stable. Although segregation was no longer an unspoken standard in the majors, old habits die hard in such organizations.

Also, recently this bad habit had received tacit support from the highest baseball authority. In December, 1943, the Negro Newspaper Publishers Association was allowed to address the white owners on the subject of integration. The publishers chose as their keynote speaker Paul Robeson, the famous actor and former college football star. Kenesaw Mountain Landis, the strong-willed baseball commissioner who had served since 1920, opened the session at which Robeson and the publishers were present with a ringing statement uttered for their consumption:

> I want it clearly understood, that there is no rule, nor to my knowledge, has there ever been, formal or informal, any understanding, written or unwritten, subterranean or sub-anything, against the hiring of Negroes in the major leagues.[14]

But before the blacks had come into the meeting room, Landis had told the owners that they would listen to the presentation but engage in no discussion afterwards. They obeyed—there were no questions. When one owner objected to this straitjacket the commissioner had placed over the issue, Landis simply said, "the gentlemen asked for an opportunity to address the joint meeting. They were given the opportunity. What's next on the agenda?"[15]

After the color line was broken on the field, two sets of reasons emerged for restraining relations between the white and black leagues. Both rationales could be heard often in New York City. One argument, for which Branch Rickey was the chief proponent, held that there was room for the better Negro league players, but that the existing Negro leagues were too corrupt to do business with. The day after evading the confrontation Bostic had set up by bringing McDuffie and Thomas to Bear Mountain, Rickey held a press conference. To keep from being put on the defensive, he went on the offensive, instead. He blasted the Negro leagues as "a front for a monopolistic game-booking business, controlled by booking agents in Chicago, Philadelphia and New York" (undoubtedly he meant Abe Saperstein, Eddie Gottlieb, and Bill Leuschner). When the Monarchs complained about the signing of Jackie Robinson, Rickey denounced the leagues as "the poorest excuse for the word 'league'... I failed to find a single player under contract, and learned that players of all teams become free agents at the end of each season." In a comment that must have stung the black owners who were or had been numbers bankers, but who had kept their illegal business separate from their baseball teams, Rickey described the Negro leagues as "in the zone of a racket."

When Rickey likened the leagues to rackets, he may have been referring to the booking agents, but it was nonetheless a fighting term that disturbed the black owners. When he claimed there were no standard contracts and no reserve clause binding players to their teams from year to year, he was on shaky ground and apparently knew it, because he made a point of paying the Philadelphia Stars for Roy Partlow's services less than a year later.

Whatever the status of the agreement between Robinson and the Monarchs, uniform written contracts did exist, and by reference, incorporated the major league reserve clause. The Eagle office files contain dozens of Negro National League preprinted contracts, which the Manleys were clearly sticklers on getting signed each spring. The ones in use through the 1945 season contain eight clauses pertaining to salary for the player and several specific league rules, and then state, "with the exception of the above articles, the rules of Major Minor League [although slightly misworded, the term for the overall agreement governing white professional ball] shall be in effect."

By the start of the 1946 season, the leagues had adopted a much more detailed three-page contract with specific language reserving a player's services to the signing team and providing for automatic renewal of the agreement the following spring, in case the player and club could not come to terms again. But by this time, it was too late. The perception was that Negro league contracts were no good, and black teams' owners would have faced ostracism for retarding integration if they had tried to go to court to prove otherwise.

The other point of view, voiced by New York Yankee President Lawrence MacPhail, held that white baseball should have no formal ties with black baseball at all. When the integration pot was bubbling in the spring of 1945, but Rickey had not yet brought it to a boil, MacPhail wrote Chandler that "we can't stick our heads in the sand and ignore the problem [of blacks in baseball]. If we do, we will have colored players in the minor leagues in 1945 and in the major leagues thereafter." [16]

In 1945, New York City Mayor Fiorello La Guardia created a Mayor's Committee on Unity to foster better racial and religious relations in the city. One of its tasks was to look into baseball integration, and its director, Dan W. Dodson, called on the presidents of the major league teams in the city for help. Rickey took Dodson into his confidence and arranged for the committee to put no pressure on baseball to sign blacks until he had carried out his own integration plan.

Dodson's interview with MacPhail was very different: "When I called on him, in his inimitable way he said: 'You damned professional doogooders know nothing about baseball.'" MacPhail pointed out that not only did the Negro league clubs have a substantial investment in their players, but white clubs made money renting parks to them. "I will not jeopardize my income nor their investment until some way can be worked out whereby it will not hurt the Negro Leagues for the major leagues to take an occasional player of theirs," he told Dodson. However, as Dodson noted, "he had no suggestion as to how this could be done." [17]

The next year, MacPhail was chairman of a major league "steering committee" developing new approaches to several off-the-field aspects of the game. The committee submitted a comprehensive draft report in August, 1946, that included a potentially controversial section on the "Race Question" that was eventually dropped from the final document. A copy of the original draft survived in Commissioner Chandler's private papers, however. The draft makes it clear that while baseball should recognize that "the Negro fan and the Negro player are part and parcel of the game," the enormous growth in black attendance for International League games in which Jackie Robinson had played in 1946 meant "a situation might be presented, if Negroes participate in Major League games, in which the preponderance of Negro attendance in parks such as the Yankee Stadium, the Polo Grounds and Comiskey Park could conceivably threaten the value of the Major League franchises owned by these clubs."

Later in the "race question" section came mention of another important economic consideration which also showed MacPhail's influence over the entire issue, since it also used the Yankees as an example:

> The Negro leagues rent their parks in many cities from clubs in Organized Baseball. Many major and minor league clubs derive substantial revenue from these rentals. (The Yankee Organization, for instance, nets nearly $100,000 a year from rentals and concessions in connection with Negro league games at the Yankee Stadium in New York—and in Newark, Kansas City and Norfolk). Club owners in the major leagues are reluctant to give up revenues amounting to hundreds of thousands of dollars every year. They naturally want the Negro leagues to continue.[18]

Adding to white baseball's stonewalling of the Negro leagues was the inability of the leagues themselves to get a reform agenda underway. Allen Johnson of Mounds, Illinois, an investor in Negro league teams in the past, wrote Abe Manley in January, 1946, that he was going into the United States League because he saw the prospects were dim for the existing organization. The Negro National and American leagues will not be able to protect their players from raiding, he predicted, since "the argument to Chandler in 1945 [sic] was met with a 'clean your house' . . . but they are not doing so . . . hence they do not intend doing so." Cum Posey wrote Effa disgustedly that same month, asking, "do you realize we have not made one single change for the better since Negro baseball was called a 'racket'?"

Continued missteps were pounced upon by the black press. J. B. Martin was criticized twice, once when he protested to Chandler in 1947 over the signing of one of his Chicago players who was supposedly under contract, but then could not produce a copy of the document, and again when the owner of the Asheville, N.C., Blues in the newly formed Negro American Association accused him of signing away one of the Blues' players, who had a contract with Asheville.

In addition, it was hard to convince people of the black power structure's willingness to let the Negro league players cross over when someone such as black promotor John R. Williams of Detroit was quoted as saying that since Negro league salaries were about equal to those in the white minor leagues, the black player "is not particularly concerned whether or not he is admitted to white organized base ball where restrictions and formalities might prevent him from performing in his own inimitable and carefree fashion."[19]

Consequently, there was no middle ground available for the Negro league owners. Any lack of support for integration was treated as a form of heresy by the black sports press, and the owners, whenever they tried to defend their investments, were subjected to criticism for all the changes—more dependable scheduling, less influence from the booking agents, independent league presidents and a commissioner, strict adherence to other teams' player and territorial rights, and better umpiring—that they had never gotten around to making.

As black players finally attained the major league level beginning in 1947 and financial conditions began to get seriously worse for the Negro leagues, the black writers softened, much as one might show sympathy for a long-time adversary who had become seriously ill. Wendell Smith wrote that fans should continue to support the leagues, since "owners of Negro teams deserve consideration too. After all, they have made big investments and are risking a good bag full of dough each season." The leagues deserved support, Chester Washington of the *Courier* wrote the following year, because they had given blacks a chance when the majors were closed to them.[20]

But when the issue was in the balance, the sportswriters had scant sympathy. Sam Lacy of the *Afro-American* papers characterized Chandler's attitude at the January, 1946, meeting with Wilson and Martin as "arrogance," but said that the leagues had it coming because, since Robinson's signing,

> colored baseball has been acting after the fashion of a mongrel puppy licking at the heels of a prospective master. The years that were spent by friends of the sport [the writers] in an effort to straighten out colored baseball went for naught until Branch Rickey reached into the ranks and took out one of its young stars. When that happened, but not until then, colored baseball operators began to see the implications.[21]

That same day, Wendell Smith of the *Courier* damned the histories of both houses, white and black:

> Organized baseball has practiced a vicious policy of discrimination against Negro players, and in so doing made it possible for the segregated Negro leagues to flourish and prosper. While wallowing in the mire of segregation and discrimination, the owners of Negro

> baseball were the benefactors of that vicious system, and they benefited greatly. So much so, that the gold blinded them and they are now firmly caught in their own trap.[22]

Since the perception existed that one must either be enthusiastically in favor of baseball integration the way it was happening or be classifed as some sort of enemy of progress, Effa Manley, the civil rights advocate, often found herself grouped with the enemies. True to her usual behavior in the midst of controversy, she was unhappy about her treatment, but unrepentant about her opinions.

As far as integration went, she had made it clear as early as 1942 that if an Eagle were given an opportunity, "we will not only not stand in his way, but we will give him all the help he needs to get a trial in the majors."[23] On the other hand, both Manleys had made it clear that they wanted the Negro leagues to have a future in integration, too. When, in 1943, *Afro-American* sports editor E. B. Rea queried black baseball officials on their integration views, the Eagle response (signed by Abe, to whom the letter was addressed, but drafted by Effa) pointed out that a key issue was whether or not white baseball forged "farm team" ties with the Negro leagues or went out and developed its own talent. "Almost all the capital invested in Negro Baseball has been invested by Negroes," they told Rea. "It has been an uphill struggle to build it up to the status it now enjoys. Needless to say its future is important to most of the race."

Thirty-seven years later, she still held the same opinion, telling an interviewer, "Mr. Rickey's program was very unfair. After all, he took Jackie Robinson and Don Newcombe and Roy Campanella without even saying thank you, let alone answering our letters." She also restated a complaint from the late 1940s that had gotten her into as much trouble then as had her opposition to uncompensated signings. The black fans, she said, "deserted us."[24] The years had mellowed her slightly on this subject, since in November, 1948, when it was originally announced that the Eagles would disband, she was much harsher, blaming Rickey and "the gullibility and stupidity of Negro baseball fans themselves in believing that he has been interested in anything more than the clicking of the turnstiles."

In addition to wasting no opportunities to condemn Branch Rickey, in 1948 Effa also leveled a blast at Robinson, baseball integration's other hero. Jackie actually had started the fight with an article in the June, 1948, edition of *Ebony* magazine. "What's Wrong with Negro Baseball" concluded that nearly everything was. Robinson thoroughly debunked the black leagues and said they need a top to bottom "housecleaning." Among other things, he criticized the teams' insistence on playing so many games at the expense of players' conditioning, the quality of the umpiring, low salaries, lack of formal contracts for the players, and the favoritism caused by having team officials double as league officials.

Effa would probably have agreed with Robinson on this last indictment, but as for the rest, she was angry, and fired back promptly. In a clipping kept in her scrapbook, she said Robinson had turned against the institution that gave him his start, and

> frankly, no greater outrage could have been perpetrated. No greater invasion of the good sense of the American people could have been attempted. No greater ingratitude was ever displayed. I charge Jackie Robinson with being ungrateful and more likely stupid. How could a child nurtured by its mother turn on her within a year after he leaves her modest home for glamour, success and good fortune?

Her salvo earned her some commendations from the black press, and at least one owner, Ernest Wright, president of the Cleveland Buckeyes in the Negro American League, wrote her that "my hat is off to you for undertaking the job [answering Robinson] that we all felt it was our duty to do." It was notable that in calling Robinson ungrateful, and even stupid, Effa was going public with the kind of language and direct confrontational tactics that she had previously reserved for closed-door debates. Now the whole baseball world could get a glimpse of the vitriol that had so enraged Cum Posey at the 1940 league meeting.

Perhaps she had just had enough of the Dodgers, but she may also have been moved to this public outburst by what she correctly perceived as an increasingly desperate situation for the Negro leagues. In its August edition, an *Ebony* competitor, *Our World* magazine, published an article signed by Effa in which she rebutted Robinson's criticisms point for point and called for black fans to come to the rescue of black ball, "otherwise 400 young men [the Negro league players] and their families will be dumped among the unemployed." [25]

The piece was titled, "Negro Baseball Isn't Dead!" but a copy of the article that she later provided to the Baseball Hall of Fame's library in Cooperstown, N.Y., contained a clue to her real state of mind at the time. Next to the title she had penned in longhand, "But it is pretty sick".

Just the presence of Jackie Robinson on baseball fields that had previously been reserved for white players caused attendance increases in the parks where he played, and his immediate success as a player brought even more fans out. The Montreal Royals, Robinson's minor league team in 1946, set a home attendance record of 412,744 paid admissions, and drew 399,047 fans in their opponents' parks, three times as many as had come to see them play in road games in 1945.

The powerful Royals won two sets of International League playoff games after the regular season ended, to become league champions. They then beat the Louisville Colonels of the American Association in the "Little World Series" between the champions of those two top-rated minor leagues. By the time the series with Louisville had ended, more than a million fans had come out to see Robinson and the Royals in 1946. When Robinson was promoted to the Dodgers in the spring of 1947, the team played four exhibition games just prior to the opening of the regular season and drew a total of 95,000 fans, a large number for games that did not count in the standings.

While Branch Rickey's integration experiment no doubt brought many white fans out to see Robinson, the burgeoning attendance was also swelled by blacks eager to view this new hero of their race. Given a choice of seeing Robinson play or attending a Negro league game, many of them opted to pay to see Jackie. Effa Manley recalled that "after Robinson signed, our fans would go as far as Baltimore [then an International League city, 200 miles from Newark] to see the team play with him on it." By the 1948 season, four blacks—Robinson and Roy Campanella, with the Dodgers and Larry Doby and Satchel Paige, with the Cleveland Indians—were established major league players, several other former Negro league stars were in the minor leagues, and the black leagues were running out of fans. Jack Saunders of the Pittsburgh *Courier* interviewed a league official in late August during a four-team doubleheader in Philadelphia's Shibe Park, which once would have drawn several thousand fans. Saunders estimated the turnout that day was only about 1,700, and asked the official if attendance was as poor elsewhere. "It's just awful," the unnamed official answered. "The Grays played in Washington last Sunday. Nine hundred. The Eagles played in Newark one day last week. Twelve hundred. The Elites played in Baltimore Saturday. Seven hundred."

When attendance plummeted, the Negro leagues' team owners were caught in one particularly serious economic bind that was difficult to solve. The surge in fan interest in the black game during World War II, coupled with the scarcity of good players, had driven salaries up tremendously. The trend continued in the immediate postwar years, as the teams continued to make money and reward their players accordingly. When attendance, and thus income, fell precipitously, the clubs were still stuck with high payrolls. This made making a profit nearly out of the question.

Wendell Smith pointed out in the *Courier* that the Homestead Grays, playing to mostly black patrons in Pittsburgh and Washington with a potential market of about 300,000 people, had a higher team payroll in 1947 than the Montreal Royals of the International League, a multiracial team with a multiracial base of twice as many people. Smith's solution to the dilemma was to cut player salaries, but he quoted one owner as saying this was too hard to do: "The players won't stand for it, I've got to pay them big salaries or they'll quit." [26] Before play began in 1948, both leagues had imposed team payroll caps of $6,000 per month after a season in which only three teams—Memphis, Chicago, and Indianapolis—in the Negro American League, made money.

The letdown for the Negro World Champion Newark Eagles was abrupt and unmistakable. Through spring training in the South and in the first part of the season, the team drew fans in numbers befitting its status. But, as Effa recounted, "as we got deeper into the schedule, it became increasingly more apparent that something extremely peculiar was taking place. Our crowds got smaller and smaller." Fans were now more interested in Robinson and the Dodgers, and the Eagles were as vulnerable as anyone. Although, since he had graduated to the parent Brooklyn team Jackie would play no more games in the minor league city of Newark, black fans could see him as many as 77 times in Dodger home games in Brooklyn, plus 11 more each in the New York Giants' Polo Grounds and the Philadelphia Phillies' Shibe Park. The Eagles were surrounded by the new phenomenum, and proximity took its toll.

Attendance fell more than 50 percent, from 120,092 in 1946 to 57,119 in 1947, and 1946's profit turned into a $22,000 loss. In July, the Manleys made a decision that clearly showed they realized they belonged to an organization that was losing status. They sold one of their star players, Larry Doby, to the previously all-white American League. Effa said that one day Abe walked into their office, "with a peculiar look on his face" and matter-of-factly announced, "Bill Veeck is going to call you."

"What's it all about?" she remembered asking her husband.

"It's about Larry Doby. Veeck's interested in buying him," Abe replied. [27]

Veeck, president of the Cleveland Indians, had wanted to integrate major league baseball for years. In 1942, when Eddie Gottlieb received the distinct impression that Jewish ownership of the Philadelphia Phillies was not desirable, Veeck had gotten the same message when he tried to acquire the Phillies and stock the club at least partially with Negro league stars.

Veeck's preparations to integrate the American League in Cleveland were much less elaborate than Branch Rickey's had been. For one thing, he had doubts about Cleveland being the ideal city in which to break the color line, whereas he considered the richly ethnic New York City much more suitable. Nonetheless, going into the 1947 season he had made some plans, which included hiring Louis Jones, a black public relations man, to take the American League's first black player under his wing. Indian scouts had been searching Negro league games for prospects, and "the player whose name kept floating to the top was Larry Doby." Veeck then had a scout watch the Eagles, without telling him specifically that Doby was the target, and finally took in a game at Ruppert Stadium to see for himself. [28]

His next step was to call Effa with his proposition—purchase of Doby's contract for $10,000. Once the offer was made, there was no question the deal would be consumated, just as there was no question, at least from the Negro league point of view, that the price was far too low. Effa was fully aware of both factors. She acquiesced immediately to Veeck's request, and when Abe, down in Washington with the team, objected that "we can't let Doby go for that small amount of money," she pointed out, "we're in no position to be dickering. Everybody would start claiming that we were denying him his greatest break. Actually, don't you see we have little choice?" [29]

But this pragmatic approach did not prevent her from needling Veeck about his offering price and successfully driving it up.

> Mr. Veeck, you know if Larry Doby were white and a free agent, you'd give him $100,000 to sign with you merely as a bonus. . . . However, I realize I'm in no position to be bargaining with you. If you feel you're being fair by offering us $10,000, I suppose we should accept.[30]

Her tactic of "injecting the racial injustice angle" succeeded in getting Veeck to offer an extra $5,000 if Doby stayed on the Cleveland roster a minimum of 30 days. This was likely to happen, since Veeck intended to start Doby right out at the major league level and was not likely to give up his integration experiment that soon, even if it did not go well.

The deal for Larry Doby has been pointed to as a precedent in which a white major league owner paid a Negro league owner for a player's contract, and to some extent allowed the black owner to set the price. It was not quite all that, since Rickey had paid the Philadelphia Stars $1,000 for the rights to Roy Partlow the year before. But Veeck deserves a great deal of credit for realizing that, since the Manleys had no choice but to agree to lose Doby, he should compensate them. "For anyone to take advantage of that situation, particularly while talking about equal rights, was terribly unfair," he later said.[31]

Given the limb he was going out on by adding only the second black player to major league baseball, the $15,000 price may not have been so little. While it was clear that Doby had the physical attributes needed for major league play, it was by no means a sure thing that he could stand up to the less-tangible demands of play at that level—the added pressure of performing before the largest crowds in baseball and the special need to set an example for his race. No one knew at that time that Doby was just starting a very successful thirteen-year major league career.

But if Effa drove the best bargain she could for Larry Doby, she is reported to have proposed another transaction with Veeck that, at least on its face, made her look much less astute. According to Veeck's 1962 ghostwritten autobiography, she also wanted to sell him Monte Irvin's contract for only $1,000. Veeck turned the offer down, much to his later regret, for Irvin also proved to be of major league caliber.

Veeck was determined to initially bring only one black to Cleveland. This would allow him to extricate himself as easily as possible if integration did not work out. Unlike Rickey, who could lodge Robinson at his minor league team in racially tolerant Montreal, the top two Cleveland farm clubs were in Baltimore and Oklahoma City, much less receptive places for breaking the color line.

If Veeck's recollections are correct (the story about Irvin appears nowhere else), it may have meant that Effa was already reading the handwriting about Negro baseball on the ballpark wall, and was trying to get as much cash as she could for her players before her business collapsed. She may also have had a related goal of cutting her 1947 payroll. Doby was making $4,000 for the summer, and Irvin $5,000, and replacing them with lower-paid players would have produced some immediate savings.

In 1948, though, Effa said that the $15,000 purchase price "wasn't enough to counteract the red ink Doby's loss entailed." [32] The Eagles were leading the league again when the Doby deal occurred, but lost ground thereafter. Doby hit his fourteenth home run in a July 4 doubleheader, his last games with the Eagles, and departed with a stellar .414 batting average, so there was no question his offensive effort would be hard to replace. As Bob Harvey, the outfielder on the team, said, "Doby was the backbone, he was the run producer."

Effa thought the transaction also created a morale problem, just as her husband had warned when Veeck first called. Many of the players may have thought what Harvey expressed years later: "You always want to see somebody make it, and I don't regret any of them going up there [to the major leagues]. But, you say, why not me?"

The team's decline was not all that pronounced, but it cost the Eagles a second straight league championship. In first place with a 27 and 15 record on July 4, the Eagles were gradually overtaken by their nearest pursuers, the New York Cubans, who finally passed them in the standings for good on September 19 by beating them in both games of a doubleheader. Even though they lost the pennant, the Eagles by no means had a bad season. They led the league with seventy home runs, and Irvin was the individual homer champion with sixteen, and runs-batted-in leader with sixty-nine. Pearson led the league in doubles with eighteen, and Manning in pitching wins with sixteen. If more people had come to see them play, it would have been a perfectly creditable year.

But the Eagles continued to fall in the standings the following season, even fewer fans came to see them play, and more money was lost. The team finished third in 1948, which was nothing to be ashamed of, but only about 35,000 fans came out, and even with a reduced payroll, the Manleys lost another $25,000.

Effa was publicly speculating that the Eagles would go out of business even before the season had ended. The final 1948 home game, she announced, "will be the last for this year and probably the last one for the Newark Eagles forever." The writer to whom she spoke, Jack Saunders of the Pittsburgh *Courier,* drew a generally pessimistic future for the Negro leagues based upon Newark's problems, because

> when a team like the Newark Eagles, with plenty of money behind it, is the first to cry "quits," it looks bad—very bad. For if the Eagles cannot stand the gaff of empty seats, what is to happen to the New York Cubans, Baltimore Elites, New York Black Yankees and Homestead Grays?[33]

As soon as the season was over, the Manleys announced that they would, in fact, disband the Eagles. According to Effa, she had been in favor of getting out back in 1947, but "Abe, a born gambler, wouldn't quit." But after the 1948 losses brought the Manleys' total deficit to $100,000 since 1935, the man who seemed happiest barnstorming with his team and presiding from the owner's box seats at Ruppert Stadium finally agreed to get out of baseball.

It turned out that despite the Manleys' announcement that September, the Eagles weren't dead yet, although their Negro National League was. By December, the Black Yankees and the Grays, two of the other teams Jack Saunders had speculated about in September, had also dropped out of the league. At a meeting of the surviving clubs in Chicago, it was decided to merge the three remaining National league squads into the six-team Negro American League. The league turned out to have ten teams, however, when the Manleys were able to sell their franchise to some Memphis interests, who relocated the Eagles to Houston.

The owner of record was a Memphis dentist, Dr. W. H. Young, but it appears that a brother of American League President J. B. Martin, Dr. B. B. Martin of Memphis, was also a partner. Abe and Effa sold all their baseball assets, primarily their player contracts and team bus, for $15,000. That was less than the reported profit margin of their single best year, the glorious 1946 season, but it was something, and they would lose no more money on Negro league baseball.

As they were leaving baseball, they were presented with one last business opportunity which offered not only a modest monetary profit, but a chance for sweet revenge. Shortly after Doctor Young and his partners agreed to buy their team, but before the deal could be closed (literally while Effa was flying back from the Chicago meeting at which the sale agreement had been struck), the Brooklyn Dodgers signed the Eagles' most valuable single asset, Monte Irvin, to play in 1949 for their minor league St. Paul team.

Branch Rickey's scouts had noticed Irvin (it was hard not to, if they had been watching the Negro National League play at all). *Afro-American* sportswriter Sam Lacy had tried to confirm a rumor in the spring of 1946 that Rickey was interested in signing him even then, and reported the Dodger president's cautious reply: "I'm definitely interested in that chap, I'd like to see more of him." Irvin, playing in Cuba during the winter of 1948-49, knew nothing about the sale of the Newark franchise. Acting on the last information he had heard, that the Eagles had gone out of business, he had assumed he was a free agent who could sign where he wished. Effa had no argument with Irvin, but she was not going to take another flouting of the Negro league player contract by Branch Rickey, even if she had all but made her exit.

She hired Newark attorney Jerome Kessler, who had been a part-time publicist for the team while working his way through college and law school, to press the case. She and Abe decided that while they had no desire to hinder Irvin's advancement, their contractual obligation to turn all their assets over to Young, plus their painful remembrance of Don Newcombe's loss, led them to "the mutual conclusion that the time had arrived when we could no longer go along with Rickey's obvious attitude of playing our Negro Baseball business interests so cheaply."[34]

They instructed Kessler to write Rickey and protest, and Effa also officially complained to baseball Commissioner Chandler, National League President Ford Frick, minor league commissioner George Trautmann, and Bruce Dudley, the president of the American Association, the league in which Irvin would play if with St. Paul.

Rickey, who with his signings of Newcombe, Robinson, and Campanella had elevated the question of the validity of black baseball's reserve clause from a subject of infighting in Negro league meetings to a peripheral issue in the whole matter of baseball integration, was now honoring contracts, even for teams that might no longer exist. "It was our understanding from published newspaper reports quoting Mrs. Manley that her club was disbanding," he said in a statement, adding that if Irvin was indeed under contract to the Eagles, he would be released.[35]

Not long after that statement, the Dodgers informed Irvin that he had been released from his Dodger contract. An *Afro-American* correspondent who tracked him down in Cuba reported that Irvin was upset and had stated, "I don't know what I'm going to do next summer." But having chased off Rickey, Effa was not going to abandon one of her star players. She had Kessler contact the New York Yankees, who were not interested, and the New York Giants, who were. A deal was struck to sell Irvin's contract for $5,000—more than Effa was reportedly ready to take from Bill Veeck in 1947, but clearly less than Irvin's services were worth. Sent to the Giants' top minor league club in Jersey City, N. J., he hit .373 and soon proved he belonged in the major leagues, to which he was promoted before the season was out.

The weeks in between the Dodgers' loss of interest and Irvin's signing with the Giants saw Effa reviled by the black sportswriters for depriving a deserving black player of his chance to play integrated ball. In their eyes, she had compounded this serious offense by not even being able to guarantee him further Negro league employment (the Eagles at that moment were regarded by the black press as defunct, just as Rickey had assumed, because the sale of the team and the disposition of its players had not yet been finalized). Irvin was described as being tied to Effa's apron strings, which were "around Monty's neck so tight he may never realize his dream of playing in the big leagues." [36]

Furthermore, once divided among all the parties involved, the $5,000 did not go far. Kessler got half of it as his contingency fee, and, according to the agreement between the Manleys and Young, they split the other $2,500 equally. There no longer being any baseball-related use for the Manleys' $1,250, with Abe's permission, Effa invested it in one of her other passions. She bought a mink stole, which she wore for years and which, given the story attached to it, became part of her baseball memorabilia. "It serves to remind me of yet another bit of baseball history in which I have been privileged to play a small role." [37]

She left the Negro leagues well dressed, but with mixed emotions that included resentment. On the one hand, she was proud that black players, particularly Doby, had become successes in the integrated major leagues. But she clearly felt she and the other black owners had been sacrificed, both unnecessarily and dishonestly, to make this happen. Interviewed by the *Sporting News* in October, 1948, she cast aspersions on unnamed major league owners (Rickey, that is) for stealing players, the black sporting press for not publicizing the Negro leagues sufficiently once integration had occurred, and the black fans for deserting their old interests. "Negro leagues were born of prejudice," she said. "Now, the whole matter is so involved, with prejudices inside prejudices, and in some places a total lack of sincerity."

After the sale of the Eagles, she proclaimed herself a freelance ambassador for Negro baseball and continued to advocate its survival. One of her arguments was that if the Negro leagues did not survive, the flow of black players to the major leagues would end. This ignored the possibility, so obvious in retrospect, that major league clubs would simply develop young blacks in their own minor league systems. But in the late 1940s, with minor leagues in the South still closed off to black players and only small numbers of blacks at any professional level yet, this evolutionary process may have seemed far less likely than it does now.

She made this argument before the Negro Newspaper Publishers Association in the summer of 1949, exhorting them again to use their sports pages to boost the Negro leagues. But the sportswriters themselves, covering baseball integration, the biggest story of their lives, were unsympathetic. To these writers, who once had substantially enhanced Effa's reputation in their columns when she was fighting for the organizational reforms they always favored, but who were now tired of her criticisms of their work, her failure to wholeheartedly endorse what was happening in baseball made her a reactionary—a sharp-tongued one at that.

Sam Lacy, who had devoted a large portion of a favorable 1947 column to her peculiar place in a nearly all-male business, wrote in the aftermath of her speech to the Negro publishers that "the applause [for her departure] was premature . . . baseball still has Mrs. Effa Manley" who "still blames everyone but those who are really responsible [the black owners] for the present plight of Negro baseball." Wendell Smith, who had praised her aggressiveness and reform agenda during World War II, now wondered if her new role as black baseball ambassador was sincere, or just the action of a "publicity hound." [38]

Smith's September 18, 1948, column, "Baseball's Glamour Girl Bows Out . . . ", was a graceful and perceptive valedictory to Effa's career and to the Negro league era in which she had thrived. He noted that, despite her differences with the black writers, "there are many of us, however, who will miss the 'Queen of Newark' because despite the fact that she tried to tell us how and what to write, she was always good copy."

Smith claimed that, when thwarted at league meetings, Effa would frequently use tears as a weapon.

> Her weepings always gave those meetings an atmosphere of moistness, whereas before her arrival on the baseball scene it was always dry as an African desert. . . . She didn't always win using this feminine attack, but the flowers on the table over which she stood did.

He forgave her latter-day attacks on the black press.

> It was just that times were changing and so was the entire structure of Negro baseball. Mrs. Manley knew it but refused to believe it. She was trying to fight off the inevitable and cling to the great days . . . She refused to recognize that nothing was killing Negro baseball but Democracy . . . When men like Rickey and Veeck decided to put some Democracy in baseball, it meant that the lush days for owners of Negro teams were over.
>
> The old days have gone. So has gracious, charming, eccentric Effa Manley. The boys in the press box are gonna' miss her—tears and all![39]

Notes

1. *Courier,* Sept. 8, 1934.
2. Holway, *Voices,* p. 56.
3. *Courier,* Dec. 11, 1937.
4. Ibid., Feb. 25, 1939.
5. Ibid., March 11, 1939.
6. Ibid., Jan. 27, 1945.
7. Manley and Hardwick, *Negro Baseball,* p. 62.
8. New York *Daily Worker,* Aug. 13, 1942.
9. *Afro-American,* Nov. 3, 1945.
10. Ibid., April 20, 1946.

11. Rogoson, *Invisible Men,* pp. 212-13.
12. Holway, *Voices,* p. 324.
13. *Courier,* Jan. 26, 1946.
14. Ibid., Dec. 11, 1943.
15. Murray Polner, *Branch Rickey, a Biography* (New York: Athenaeum, 1982), p. 148; Tygiel, *Baseball's Great Experiment,* p. 31.
16. Polner, *Branch Rickey,* p. 187.
17. Dan W. Dodson, "The Integration of Negroes in Baseball," *The Journal of Educational Sociology,* October, 1954.
18. "Report for Submission to National and American Leagues on 27 August, 1946," in Albert B. "Happy" Chandler papers, University of Kentucky, pp. 19-20.
19. Detroit *News,* May 8, 1945.
20. *Courier,* May 3, 1947, and March 20, 1948.
21. *Afro-American*, Jan. 26, 1946.
22. *Courier,* Jan. 26, 1946.
23. *Daily Worker,* Aug. 13, 1942.
24. *There Was Always Sun Shining Someplace,* Refocus Productions, Westport, CT.
25. Effa Manley, "Negro Baseball Isn't Dead," *Our World,* August, 1948, p. 27.
26. *Courier,* Sept. 20, 1947.
27. Manley and Hardwick, *Negro Baseball,* p. 74.
28. Bill Veeck, with Ed Linn, *Veeck—As in Wreck, the Autobiography of Bill Veeck* (New York: G. P. Putnam's Sons, 1962), p. 175.
29. Manley and Hardwick, *Negro Baseball,* pp. 74-76.
30. Ibid., p. 75.
31. Veeck, *Veeck—As in Wreck,* p. 176.
32. Newark *Evening News,* May 1, 1948.
33. *Courier,* Sept. 10, 1948.
34. Manley and Hardwick, *Negro Baseball,* pp. 89-90.
35. *Afro-American,* Jan. 22, 1949.
36. *Courier,* Jan. 22, 1949.
37. Manley and Hardwick, *Negro Baseball,* p. 92.
38. *Afro-American,* June 25, 1949; *Courier,* Nov. 26, 1948.
39. *Courier,* Sept. 18, 1948.

Chapter 10
Still Fighting

Abe died late in 1952. He had not been well for several years, suffering from prostate trouble and diagnosed with uremia. That fall his condition became so serious that he needed surgery, although after it he actually seemed to be recovering. But he also had heart disease and was literally wasting away, and this last illness had taken a toll that years in the hard business of the Negro leagues had never cost. He was clearly no longer his old confident self. The change showed when Effa's sister Ruth, a nurse, had come over from Philadelphia to visit in mid-November while Abe was recuperating at 71 Crawford St. When she got ready to leave, he broke down and cried.

Abe had no family in the North other than Effa, so her family looked after him. Effa recalled that after his breakdown upon Ruth's leaving, "my mother said, 'bring him to Philadelphia,' so the next day I drove him and Ruth there." He stayed in Philadelphia for almost a month, but when "I came back to Newark to get more clothes, the next day [Dec. 9] his heart gave out."

Years later Effa surmised that if having to sell the Eagles hadn't led directly to her husband's death, the disappointment could have been a contributing factor. By then she was steadfastly portraying him as the founder of the Negro National League and an all-around savior of black baseball during the Depression, so his pining away after losing his team made a fitting conclusion to the story. More likely, his history of poor conditioning made him respond weakly to a serious health threat for any 67-year-old man.

He was buried out of a Catholic church in the Germantown section of Philadelphia, where Effa's mother and her second husband lived. Monte Irvin and Larry Doby, the two young men whose talents he had spotted on the ball fields of New Jersey who had gone from his Eagles to stardom in the integrated major leagues, were the lead pallbearers carrying him out of the church. The hearse took him back again to Newark, this time to a plot in Fairmount Cemetery he and Effa had purchased for themselves in 1949.

Although the black sportswriters had not been on the best of terms with the Negro league owners when the Manleys had left baseball, they eulogized Abe as befitted his significant contributions to the sport. Jack Saunders of the Pittsburgh *Courier* wrote that while

> there have been men who were better known as baseball powers . . . none of these men did more than Manley to pave the way for Negroes in major league baseball. [He] invested more than $100,000 of his personal fortune in baseball, Negro baseball, and because he did spend so freely of his money, Doby, [Don] Newcombe, Irvin and [Ray] Dandridge were given a chance to develop into the superlative stars that they are.[1]

Abe's death came at the end of a period during which the black sportswriters had acquired a great deal of practice in seeing off the members of the Negro leagues' late power structure. A large part of the Negro National League owners' group—Cumberland Posey, Rufus Jackson, Tom Wilson, Gus Greenlee, and Abe, passed away between the spring of 1946, when Posey succumbed to lung cancer, and Abe's demise at the end of 1952.

Newark now had no hold on Effa. In 1955 she sold the house at 71 Crawford St. and several of their possessions, including the jewelry Abe had given her so long ago when they first met, and moved to be near her family in Philadelphia. Although the sale of the Eagles in 1948 had not meant she had faded from the public eye (she was featured prominently in a 1949 *Ebony* article on "How to Stay Young after 40" which noted that "she admits she's nearly 50 although she looks nowhere near that age," her ties with baseball had been severed.

Her return home to Philadelphia was not to be her last move. She had visited Southern California on a trip after the 1946 championship season, and had friends in Los Angeles. Some visits eventually persuaded her to move there. She bought a four-unit bungalow colony at 451 North Occidental Boulevard, in hopes that some members of her family would move there from Philadelphia. None did, but the rent from the other three units covered her mortgage and other expenses, allowing her to live "rent free," as she called it, in sunny California.

Her life of retirement, however, did not include retirement from men. The woman who had met her first husband while he was angling for another female's attention on the beach at Atlantic City, who met her second at a World Series game in Yankee Stadium, and was so attractive that the great Satchel Paige would make a public joke about making her his extramarital girlfriend, was still attracted to men. This time she married an old boyfriend, a musician named Charles Alexander.

The marriage to Alexander, a singer and piano player, lasted about a year. In an interview at age eighty, she readily admitted that it had been a mistake, but noted that she had always had a weakness for musicians. It seemed that a relationship with a musician—the show business culture she enjoyed in addition to baseball—was something she just had to try. Later she ruefully recounted a joshing she took over her failed marriage to Alexander from a visiting friend from Philadelphia, who asked: "Effa, are you ready to settle for records yet?"

At the bottom of this all was an apparent desire for male companionship. Her scrapbook, filled almost entirely with memories of the Eagles, her volunteer efforts in Newark and Harlem, and her civil rights work, also contains a few telling personal items. She saved a 1939 letter from an actor admirer who had sent her a love poem he had written, and a typewritten copy of another poem, "Most Every Woman's Rhyme."

This is most every woman's rhyme,
and will be 'till the end of time.
I'm looking for a man who weaves Black Magic
That's what most every woman really seeks
He doesn't have to look so hot, just as long as he has got
The charm to make me give my heart complete
The thing in life that really is most precious
Is the one you love, and know's your very own
Life is really mighty bare, theres just nothing really there
Unless that man is living in a home with you
Unless the guy is truly all our own-true blue.

A number of Effa's acquaintances, both from baseball and show business, had settled down in the Los Angeles area, so she was able to keep up several friendships. Andy Razaf, the Broadway lyricist and fervent Newark Eagles baseball fan from Englewood, N.J., had moved there, and his oft-times partner, pianist Eubie Blake, also came west from New York. Francis Matthews, the former Eagle first baseman, settled in Los Angeles after a career with the U.S. Army, and was an occasional visitor at Effa's apartment.

Chet Brewer, a leading Negro league pitcher whom Abe had tried to acquire for the Brooklyn Eagles in 1935, was running a boys' baseball program at a city-owned park, and Effa lent her influence to help get the field named after him. The successful campaign eventually brought in yet another old baseball contact. Danny Goodman, who had run the ballpark concession business for the white Newark Bears at Ruppert Stadium in the 1940s, now handled promotions for the major league Los Angeles Dodgers, and was happy to donate $250 for a sign to mark "Chet Brewer Field".

The Dodgers of Los Angeles were the direct descendants of the team from Brooklyn that had been first the benefactor, and then the nemesis, of the Manleys' Eagles. In 1957, long after Branch Rickey had left the club, the Dodger ownership, along with that of the archrival New

York Giants from Manhattan, had pulled up stakes and moved west, becoming the first two of what are now six major league clubs on the Pacific Coast.

Although Effa still held a grudge against the old Dodgers and confided once that so far as she was concerned, Branch Rickey's mistreatment of the Negro leagues was responsible for any of the teams' subsequent failures, her relations with the club in a new place and time had considerably mellowed. She carried on an extensive correspondence with Fred Claire, the Dodgers' publicity director, which was aimed at getting Negro leaguers recognition at Dodger games. When she died in 1981, Claire, who is now the club's executive vice president, represented the Dodgers at her funeral.

In the 1970s, it had at last become possible to get recognition for the Negro leaguers, because black baseball was being rediscovered. The black major league player had become an accepted figure in the sport, although fewer than are now concerned seemed worried that there were nearly no black field managers or baseball executives. However, this acceptance alone did not directly connect their present-day success with black ballplayers' roots in the Negro leagues. Even though many of the best blacks, including future Hall of Famers Willie Mays, Hank Aaron, and Ernie Banks, had started their careers in the Negro leagues, few remembered them for those early accomplishments, because they had subsequently fulfilled the bigger promise of the black player as a dominating major league player.

The average major league baseball fan, ill acquainted with the Negro leagues at any time, had no particular reason to remember them after their demise. Yet, as baseball became more and more popular, the interest it generated broadened to elevate less-well-known aspects of the game into the baseball public's consciousness. This trend coincided nicely with a growing awareness of American black history in general.

The gates to the old black ballparks were unlocked in 1970 by publication of the first comprehensive Negro league history, *Only the Ball Was White,* by New Jersey writer Robert Peterson. Five years later came John Holway's *Voices from the Great Black Baseball Leagues,* the first of several compilations of oral histories he had collected from former participants. In 1983, a second general history of the black leagues, *Invisible Men,* was written by Donn Rogosin, who had gathered part of his material by attending the first reunion of Negro leaguers in Ashland, Kentucky, in 1979. By the time the mid-1980s had come around, there was a sizable written body of knowledge on the Negro leagues, and there were some well-produced documentary films, as well.

Holway and Rogosin had interviewed Effa for their books, two of several sessions she granted to writers, filmmakers, academics, and television newsmen as it became known that one of the few remaining ties to the Negro league owners, with memory fresh and opinions unabated, was alive and well in Los Angeles.

She was also interviewed extensively by William Marshall, curator of former baseball Commissioner Albert "Happy" Chandler's papers at the University of Kentucky; Craig Davidson for his film, *The Sun Was Always Shining Somewhere,* and Allen Richardson, for a master's thesis at San Jose (CA) State University.

Several Los Angeles television stations included her in black baseball pieces, and newspaper columnists sought her out. She was particularly proud that Jim Murray, the Los Angeles *Times*' award-winning sports columnist, had come to her house for an interview. Murray had been lured by Effa's own contribution to the Negro league revival, the 1976 book *Negro Baseball. . . . Before Integration.* She had been inspired to produce the book when she learned that younger blacks, including some news reporters who had grown up since the end of the Negro leagues, knew nothing about them. This would never do, as far as she was concerned—it left her "heartbroken." After all, it was her personal history, too, that was being lost.

Her collaborator, Leon H. Hardwick, was a former sportswriter and editor for the black weekly newspapers who was then working in Los Angeles as a freelance writer. She sought him out, and after some reluctance to participate (among other problems, he thought women were "too bossy" to work for), he was recruited. Hardwick's bigger problem was that he did not believe he had the time to do the research necessary to recreate the history of the Negro leagues. Then Effa showed him her voluminous scrapbook (and probably impressed him with her sharp memory, too) and he agreed to be her writer.

Hardwick provided an opening chapter in which he picked a mythical "Black Baseball Hall of Fame," plus an epilogue on major league records set by black players. These provided a framework of perspective for the book's core, nine chapters drawn from Effa's memory and scrapbook that detail the story of the Brooklyn and Newark Eagles. Except for her tendencies to give Abe credit that he did not deserve for founding the Negro National League (which had been in existence for two years before the Eagles were created) and to play down her tempestuous clashes with the other owners over booking agents and the league's general style of doing business, the book's account of life with the Eagles is highly accurate, when compared against the Eagle team files archived in Newark and the memories of others involved with the team.

Effa and Hardwick were unable to find a publisher for the book, a circumstance she blamed on white reaction to Hardwick's laudatory section on black record breakers. Undeterred, they undertook to publish it themselves. She took out advertisements in the *Sporting News,* the weekly newspaper that advertised itself as "The Bible of Baseball," and the black weekly newspapers. She also enlisted old friends to sell copies. The former Eagle third baseman Pat Patterson, by then an educator in Houston, sold 200 books for her. She and Hardwick sold out a first printing of 500 copies, but judged by the book's current scarcity, sales did not thrive. This may have disturbed Hardwick, who made his living writing, but it never seemed to have bothered Effa. She had participated mainly to ensure a place in posterity for the Negro leagues, as well as for herself and Abe.

She also spent her last years not just successfully helping revive the history of black baseball, but in a failed attempt to get its best players the credit she thought they deserved in the Baseball Hall of Fame. Since the first group of baseball stars had been inducted in 1936, membership in the Hall had been based upon achievements in organized baseball's major leagues. Exclusion from the segregated majors, then, had also meant automatic exclusion from Hall of Fame consideration, even for such recognized Negro league greats as Satchel Paige and Josh Gibson.

But the new interest in the black leagues resulted in a plan to honor their best with selection to the Hall. In 1971, the Hall's Special Committee on the Negro Leagues was formed. Monte Irvin, the former Eagles star who was by now a special assistant to the commissioner of baseball, was a member of the group. So were two Negro National League owners, Eddie Gottlieb of Philadelphia and Alex Pompez, who had run the New York Cubans.

The committee's first pick that year was Satchel Paige, who might have been, but never was, a Newark Eagle. Before the panel was finished, it had also admitted Josh Gibson, the home-run hitting nemesis who helped thwart for so long Effa's hopes to wrest the league championship from his Homestead Grays, as well as Irvin himself. In 1977, the committee disbanded, after picking nine Negro leaguers, leaving further selections to the standing Veterans Committee, which with the Baseball Writers Association of America is responsible for the regular annual selections. To date, the Veterans Committee has picked only two more men, Negro leagues' founder Andrew "Rube" Foster and Ray Dandridge, the Eagle third baseman.

The disbanding of the Negro leagues committee made Effa, always sensitive during her career to perceived unfairness against the Eagles, angry on behalf of all black baseball. In her opinion, the end of the special selection process left many deserving former players outside the Hall, just as they had been denied the opportunity to play major league baseball during their careers.

She had fewer issues to be passionate about in her old age, but this subject was capable of summoning the blunt-spoken Effa Manley, restoring to her voice the unmistakable edge that Cumberland Posey, Ed Gottlieb, and Tom Wilson would have recognized instantly from long-ago days in the Negro National League's boardroom. "Why in hell did the Hall of Fame set that committee up, if they were going to do the lousy job they did?" she demanded of Donn Rogosin when she was eighty.

She began a letter-writing campaign, targeting the Hall of Fame, baseball Commissioner Bowie Kuhn, and C. C. Johnson Spink, editor and publisher of the *Sporting News.* Her goal was to have another committee review Negro league candidates, selecting the best to have their names inscribed on a single special plaque (the prevailing practice is for each Hall of Fame inductee to have his own plaque).

Her position was, "I would settle for 30 players, but I could name 100." She listed for Spink her top twenty candidates. Not surprisingly they included seven former Eagles: first baseman Mule Suttles, shortstops Willie Wells and Dick Lundy, third basemen Dandridge and Patterson, catcher Biz Mackey, and outfielder Clarence "Fats" Jenkins. [2]

The goal of a special plaque honoring dozens of Negro leaguers was probably not attainable, since it would have needed a major policy change from the Hall of Fame, an institution generally as conservative as organized baseball, itself. In addition, mass recognition of Negro leaguers would have undercut what had become the main thrust of the effort to better include minorities in baseball, which was to have them admitted to the game's various levels, both of stardom and everyday workmanship, on their individual merits.

However, the kind of plaque she was seeking would have certainly addressed her fear that Negro league baseball would fade away and be forgotten by succeeding generations, including black ones. Although unsuccessful, her efforts won her some attention. The *Sporting News* had been lukewarm to integration in the 1940s, but Spink was receptive to her crusade. He devoted his entire June 20, 1977, column to her quest and referred to her as a "furious woman." She liked that, and saved the clipping.

Although she suffered from a loss of equilibrium that kept her from going to too many public places including Dodger games to which the club had invited her, she was alert, aggressive, and friendly as late as the spring of 1980, when Rogosin interviewed her at her home. But her health deteriorated soon afterwards. By the end of the year, she could no longer live in her apartment, and she moved into a rest home run by another former Negro leaguer, Quincy Trouppe.

According to Trouppe, one day in the spring of 1981 "she said she didn't feel too good, and we called the ambulance." The medical attendants did not believe her to be seriously ill, and left the decision of hospitalization up to Effa. She told Trouppe and his wife, Bessie, that "she would go and have the hospital test her out, but she never did get well enough to come back home."

The medical problem which took her to Queen of Angels Hospital was cancer of the colon, but matters got worse. She developed peritonitis after surgery on April 8. As had been the case with Abe after trying to resist his illness in 1952, she suffered a heart attack and died a little after 6:00 P.M. on April 16. Her death followed by only four days the heart attack death of her old sports idol, boxing champion Joe Louis. He had been the individual personification of the importance of black athletes in the 1930s and 1940s, just as Effa's Negro leagues had been its institutional embodiment.

Although the other half of the double burial plot was waiting for her beside Abe's grave in Newark, she was buried in Culver City, near Los Angeles. The Trouppes, her last caretakers, became executors of her estate, although she had already bequeathed her best keepsakes—the Baccardi trophy and her voluminous scrapbook—to the Baseball Hall of Fame in Cooperstown, N. Y., and the new Negro Baseball Hall of History in Ashland, Kentucky. Her richest heritage (other than her own recollections), the Newark Eagle business files, were beginning yet another decade sitting forgotten in the cellar of 71 Crawford Street, where they would remain untouched until a new owner found them during renovation work in 1989 and they were donated to the Newark Public Library.

The house at 71 Crawford today is the only surviving structure of those which figured prominently in the history of Effa and Abe Manley and their Eagles. A combination of urban renewal and official indifference sealed the fate of the other buildings. Both of the Eagles' ballparks are long gone. Ebbets Field in Brooklyn, a major league park without a team after the Dodgers moved away, was leveled in 1960 to make way for a housing project.

The Newark Bears survived only one year longer than their Negro league counterparts. The team, once arguably the best franchise in the minor leagues, was no longer prospering, and the parent New York Yankees pulled out after the 1949 season. The Yankees eventually sold Ruppert Stadium to the City of Newark, which used the park at times but put little maintenance effort into it. Ruppert declined steadily and, finally all but abandoned, was torn down in 1967, the land sold as an industrial site.

The Grand Hotel fell victim to expansion of the nearby Essex County courthouse complex. The building at 101 Montgomery St., where the Eagles' offices were located, is now part of a large vacant lot, everything there having been knocked down, but nothing having gone up to replace it. And 1090 Fulton St., the Brooklyn address of the Eagles' offices during their first year, is now only a gap in an otherwise unbroken line of typical older Brooklyn granite-faced low-rise buildings.

Of course, the Negro leagues were not unique in baseball in losing their landmarks. Ebbets Field is by no means the only historic major league ballpark no longer in existence. But the disappearance of the tangible remains of the Newark Eagles leads to reflections on what happened to the black leagues' intangible infrastructure, the team owners and their staffs.

While there is a lack of evidence that the white baseball owners overtly conspired to keep Effa and her black colleagues out of the integrated game after 1946, the whites were clearly recalcitrant, and the results tend to speak for themselves. The best Negro league players were sought after with increasing interest after the success of Jackie Robinson, Larry Doby and the rest of the first handful of black players to reach the previously white majors. But no invitation was ever extended to the Negro league owners.

To this day, organized baseball bears the significant stigma of calling itself the National Pastime while providing few executive opportunities for members of minorities. Since such situations are not remedied overnight (major league baseball vowed in 1987 to improve its minority hiring record, but only increased such hires from 15 to 17 percent by early 1993), it is fascinating to think what might have happened had the white owners and Commissioner Chandler allowed the Negro leagues into the minor league structure in 1946.

One result, of course, would still have been the end of the Negro leagues. Major league clubs committed to integrating their playing rosters would have had no interest in exposing their young players to segregated minor league playing conditions. The Negro leagues would themselves have become integrated or, more likely, have broken up, and their teams been absorbed into other minor leagues.

But as they passed on, they would have left behind a core of black owners, team officials, and field managers who would have become ingrained in professional baseball's management structure. The most able and, in the case of the owners, the most well-heeled financially, would have advanced in integrated baseball as surely as Jackie Robinson and the other pioneer players. They, in turn, would have hired other blacks to be team executives or managers, beginning a network of minority representation in baseball's dugout and executive offices.

Given the chance, some of the Negro league owners could have thrived in integrated baseball. Imagine, for example, Cum Posey having a retinue of assistants to put his decades of baseball wisdom to work for a big league franchise. Imagine Alex Pompez scouting Latin America for its best talent, and then being able to keep it on his team.

And imagine Effa Manley, with a deed to her own ballpark in her pocket, along with "raiding-proof" contracts for the services of a crop of good ball players, sitting down across a table to negotiate with some male owners, who might not be inclined at first to take her seriously.

Imagine that.

Notes

1. *Courier,* Dec., 27, 1952.
2. *The Sporting News,* June 20, 1977.

Appendix A
Effa's Competition—The Other Owners of Black Teams

The black big leagues had teetered on the edge of extinction in 1932, since the death of Rube Foster's National League at the end of 1931 wiped out the strong competition that had existed between the Midwest and East Coast. The Eastern Colored League had gone out of business in 1928, and a replacement, the American Negro League, lasted only one year (although the name was to be revived in 1937 for a stronger league that outlasted all the other circuits.)

To fill the void in 1932, the Negro Southern League added teams in Chicago and Indianapolis and enjoyed a brief elevation from its otherwise consistent minor-league status. An attempt was also made to start an East-West League stretching from Baltimore to Cleveland, but it lasted only a few months.

The second Negro National League began play in 1933, and, as is often the case with any new professional sports league, picked up and dropped franchises and owners from year to year until it had weeded out those not likely to succeed over the long haul.

By 1936, the league had settled down with a dependable core of two teams in Pittsburgh, one in Philadelphia, one in the Baltimore-Washington, D. C., area, and one in New York City, in addition to the Eagles. The loss of one of the Pittsburgh teams in 1939, to be replaced by another team in New York City, was the only significant change in this list until the league went out of business in 1948.

The existence of a highly developed amateur and semiprofessional sports culture in Pittsburgh, coupled with the organizing skills of two particular men, made that city the leading one in the National League's first years. William A. "Gus" Greenlee, the founding father of the second Negro National, didn't work his way up through baseball, as Rube Foster had. He bought in, and entered as close to the top as possible. In 1930, Greenlee purchased the Crawfords, an excellent semipro team. In 1932, he built his own stadium, a rarity for black teams, and put together a squad that, playing as an independent, won 99 games and lost only 36. Greenlee needed a bigger forum, however, and "no longer satisfied with barnstorming against the best available opponents . . . he resurrected the Negro National League in 1933." [1]

Gus was aggressive, had big plans, and possessed a lot of money for a black man in a society in which whites controlled most of the business capital. He might have established a lasting reputation in black baseball circles at a level near Foster's, if circumstances had been kinder to him, but they weren't. Greenlee overreached himself as a sportsman and was undercut by his ambitions and his source of wealth, the numbers gambling business.

He had come to Pittsburgh in 1916, when he was nineteen. He drove a taxi and did odd jobs until adding bootlegging to his repertoire, illegal liquor becoming an additional passenger in his taxi. From there he opened and ran several clubs, the most famous being the Crawford Grill, a classy restaurant and night spot in Pittsburgh's black "Hill District."

Greenlee was only one of several numbers operators in black Pittsburgh, but his professional credibility soared one day in 1930 when, for a change, the odds caught up with the operators, not the bettors. On August 5 an excessive amount of money bet on a particular number far exceeded the means of most numbers bankers to pay off when it became that day's winner. Numbers operations folded all over the city, and some of the men running them left town for awhile. But Greenlee and his partner, William "Woogie" Harris, mortgaged their homes and a number of other assets and paid off all their winning bettors. Their reward, of course, was the allegiance and wagering business of many who had been burned by those who had welched on payoffs, and Greenlee and Harris were on their way to much bigger success.[2]

Greenlee developed a reputation as a city political force and as someone who would use his wealth to help the many blacks in the city who had been disadvantaged by the Depression. But he was best known as a sportsman. Besides owning the Crawfords he was an original organizer of the annual East-West All-Star game, and sponsored a stable of boxers, including light-heavyweight champion John Henry Lewis.

But the financial tide began to turn against Greenlee as his sizable sports investments failed to make a profit. Greenlee Field, a laudable black sports enterprise, closed and was torn down in 1938, the site of Greenlee's $100,000 investment becoming a housing project. Deprived of his park, Greenlee soon found himself without a team, as the Crawfords were sold and moved to Toledo, Ohio, for the 1939 season. By then he had also resigned as league president.

Although out of the National League, Greenlee was not out of baseball for several more years. He reorganized the Crawfords in Pittsburgh as a barnstorming semipro team and made efforts in the early 1940s to have them readmitted to the league. He never was allowed to rejoin. Despite claims of his friends that his failure to get back in was merely revenge by his remaining enemies in the league's leadership structure, there seem to have been reasons related to his own financial problems.

Cumberland Posey, an owner of the other Pittsburgh black team, the Homestead Grays, confided to the Manleys in a letter that league president Thomas T. Wilson "is not anxious for Gus to come back into the league. He says he would want him back if Gus had a chance to make some money . . . but he is afraid the gates [attendance profits] will be attached where ever Gus goes."

One example of what worried Wilson was a lawsuit against the league which had been caused by Greenlee. In

1939, the Phoenix Indemnity Co. sued for nonpayment of a $173 rain insurance policy covering a playing date at the Polo Grounds, the major league park in New York, because Greenlee, the president when the policy was bought, had defaulted on its payment. Abe Manley, as league treasurer, was one of the defendants in the case. The league settled the suit in 1940 for $100, but if Wilson was correct in surmising that more such claims existed from the Greenlee years, intertwining Gus with the league's finances again could indeed have been precarious.

The black major leagues were not finished with Greenlee yet, nor he with them. In 1945 he was the driving force behind a competing organization, the United States League, with a Pittsburgh Crawford team in it. The other main organizer was Branch Rickey, president of the Brooklyn Dodgers in the white majors. Rickey was apparently using the USL as a way to get closer to the black baseball community in preparation for his historic recruitment of Jackie Robinson, who in 1946 became the first black player in organized baseball since the 1890s, and the first in the major leagues since 1883.

The United States League only lasted through the 1946 season and was never the threat to the established Negro leagues that the major leagues would soon become. Greenlee spent most of his time successfully running the Crawford Grill, until it burned down shortly before his death in 1952. William Nunn, managing editor of the Pittsburgh *Courier,* was only guilty of a slight overstatement when he wrote in Greenlee's obituary that "Gus was the guy who put Negro baseball on big time."

Greenlee's fall from power left the field in Pittsburgh open to Posey, his chief rival and, in many ways, his antithesis. Posey was from an old-line black Pittsburgh family (his father had been one of the most prosperous black businessmen in the Pittsburgh area, and a civic leader). He himself had been a prominent athlete both in college and in his hometown of Homestead, a steel mill community next to Pittsburgh. There is no question he had a drive to succeed. Black sportswriter Sam Lacy described Posey after his death in 1946 as "one of those cussing, fighting, rootin' tootin' hombres who cared little about what he did to you and less about whether you liked it."

Posey's deep involvement with local amateur sports, both as a player and coach, led to his playing outfield for a well-known local semipro club, the Homestead Grays, when he got out of college in 1911. Gradually Posey became involved in operating the team, and by the early 1920s, he owned it. The Grays under Posey became a powerhouse, despite not belonging to any league. They played independently and won often. Posey acted just as independently, raiding league clubs for better players and controlling much of black baseball scheduling in the Western Pennsylvania-Eastern Ohio area for a percentage of the profits. He knew, as had Rube Foster, that the real power and money in baseball lay not just in winning, but in using the drawing power of a winner to command the best possible financial terms for games.

If Posey was affronted by Greenlee's ascendancy with the Crawfords, he was even less happy when Gus began winning with the Grays' players. The old raider was himself raided by Greenlee, who proceeded to skim off the cream of the Grays, including two men now in the Hall of Fame, catcher Josh Gibson and outfielder Oscar Charleston.

The Grays joined Greenlee's new National League in 1935. They finished well below the Crawfords in the standings that year and the next, but then the tide began to turn Posey's way again. He, of course, capitalized on Greenlee's financial woes by luring Gibson back to Homestead to join a powerful squad that proceeded to dominate the Negro National League for the twelve more seasons of its existence.

While on the surface Posey's eventual victory over Greenlee appears to have been a satisfying one of a traditional baseball man over a usurper with a large bankroll, the Grays themselves were only able to reach their dominant heights with an infusion of gambling money. The Depression had hit Posey's operation hard, too, and his commitment to the failed East-West League as one of its organizers in 1932 didn't help matters. So in 1935 he turned to one Rufus "Sonnyman" Jackson, who owned a nightclub and a jukebox distributorship, as well as a slice of Pittsburgh's black gambling business. Jackson had a distinction unknown to any other major league baseball owner, black or white. As the target of an extortion attempt in 1935, he had become the bait in a trap laid by law enforcement officers trying to catch the extortionists, and narrowly missed being involved in a shootout in which the thieves eluded federal agents.

Posey, rescued by Jackson's money, became a leading figure in black baseball throughout the late 1930s and 1940s. Never flashy like Greenlee, he was a family man and a member of the Homestead school board, as well as an official of the black wing of the Elks. His domestic side never dulled his combativeness—he was rarely without an opinion on how black baseball could be run better. He had a soapbox none of his fellow owners possessed, a regular column on the sports pages of the *Courier,* which he often used to expound on how black baseball could be improved. Although he was often critical of his peers in the league and elsewhere in the sport, a reading of his columns leads to the conclusion that if Cum Posey ever made a mistake in baseball, he kept it to himself.

John R. Williams, a black baseball promoter in Detroit, may have been right on target when he irately wrote Posey that "Unfortunately . . . you are a gentlemen who wants his own way about everything at all times. If you can't have everything as you want it, everything is wrong and everyone unable to do your bidding is a rascal." It is hardly surprising that Posey often clashed with Effa Manley in the early 1940s, as their strong personalities collided in league meetings. The relationship mellowed, however, and he became a regular correspondent with her and Abe about the intense politics that underlay the league's operations.

By the 1940s, Posey had become a powerful man in black baseball, Pittsburgh politics, and social organizations, writing the Manleys at various times on the letterheads of the Grays, the National League, the Borough of Homestead, and the Benevolent and Protective Order of the Elks. Yet he does not seem to have derived much personal wealth from it all, and maintained some habits that may have been born in the penny-pinching Depression-era days. For example, despite presumably having access to ample secretarial services among all those organizations he represented, he usually wrote his personal letters in longhand, with a pencil, on the back of stationery from one of his offices.

Despite their various disagreements, there was one subject that united Posey with his rival Greenlee and with Abe and Effa Manley, the relative newcomers. All of them believed that the profits from Negro league baseball ought to accrue to the black people who ran the leagues, not to outsiders. It only made matters worse that some of those outsiders were white.

Baseball that made money could only be played in stadiums which could seat large numbers of paying customers. But since the lack of investment capital in the black business community also applied to its baseball entrepreneurs, most were beholden to white teams or to local governments which owned parks. Most often, the black owners would have to deal with professional booking agents. The agents owned no real estate, but had ironclad deals with stadium owners to keep their parks active and profitable. The vast majority of Negro league games were played under these arrangements, with the booking agents getting a percentage of the gate receipts for their efforts.

Opposition by blacks to the booking agents' presence in their league affairs echoes the complaint Langston Hughes made about the Harlem Renaissance running on white publishers' money. In Negro league baseball, the business setup often meant that behind the solid phalanx of black players performing to a mostly black crowd were white deal makers who, because of their monopolies, were indispensable to success.

Which did not mean they were not resented. One reason given for the construction of Greenlee Field in Pittsburgh was that Gus Greenlee "wouldn't use a white man's field if he didn't have to." [3] The Pittsburgh *Courier* described Greenlee's re-election as league president in

1937 as "the opening gong on a 'finish fight' with the Eastern bookmakers."

Posey, who appreciated the advantages of a regional scheduling monopoly, often made pointed comments about whites who had those monopolies elsewhere. For example, in 1941, he referred to Abe Saperstein, a Chicago sports agent active in both baseball and basketball (he founded the Harlem Globetrotters) as "a symbol of those who are attempting to edge into professional Negro athletics and to eventually control them." [4]

Posey's opposition to whites controlling the scheduling of Negro league games even extended to J. L. Wilkinson, the white owner of the Kansas City Monarchs, a leading Midwestern black team since the 1920s. Posey threw Wilkinson in with the other whites, even though the career of the Missourian, who had assiduously built up his squad over a period of years, survived financially brutal Depression seasons, and used the Monarchs' popularity to gain control of playing dates in the plains states, closely resembled Posey's own success story.

Despite some black owners' dissatisfaction with the white booking agents, the National League clique included in its midst not one, but both, of the most powerful sports bookers in the East. Edward Gottlieb, who ,like Saperstein, has come down through sports history as more of a basketball than a baseball figure, was a part owner of the Philadelphia Stars. William J. Leuschner of New York, had a share in that city's Black Yankees team. Leuschner operated Nat C. Strong Baseball Enterprises, named after its late founder, one of the earliest and most powerful of the agents. In the early decades of the 1900s, Nat Strong controlled the booking of games for the black clubs with the hundreds of semiprofessional clubs that covered the East, and prevented teams that refused to do business with him from getting lucractive playing dates in the best parks. The formation of the Eastern Colored League in 1923, which included the Strong-owned Brooklyn Royal Giants, was a direct challenge to Rube Foster's Midwestern National league, which itself was in part an attempt to keep Strong from extending his influence to the Midwest.

Gus Greenlee, whose theories of who should control black baseball naturally were at odds with Strong's, generously wrote shortly after Strong's death in early 1935 that the agent's opposition to black league baseball was understandable, since it threatened his livelihood, but also noted that "he fought the idea . . . with every weapon at his command." [5] Much more critical was old-timer Sol White, who had his own run-ins with Strong when he tried to launch a black-run team just after the turn of the century. As far as White was concerned, "there is not a man in the country who has made as much money from colored ballplaying as Nat Strong, and yet he is the least interested in its welfare." [6]

Leuschner presided in Strong's headquarters in the World Building in Manhattan. From downtown Philadelphia, Gottlieb ran Ed. Gottlieb Sporting Enterprises, which was, according to its letterhead, "associated with Nat C. Strong." Between them, they divided up Nat Strong's old territory along the East Coast from Long Island through New Jersey, down to Eastern Pennsylvania.

Neither made any pretense of hiding his membership in the Negro National League's power structure. League meeting coverage in the black newspapers was often illustrated with photos of the owners clustered around a desk or relaxing at a banquet table. The round faces of Gottlieb and Leuschner could usually be found mixed in with a dozen or so black and brown ones. Gottlieb also served for several years as league recording secretary.

Gottlieb's partner in running the Philadelphia Stars, Edward Bolden, was the most senior black among the owners. Bolden, a 42-year civil servant with the post office, was a postal clerk in 1910 when he organized his first team, the Hilldale Club that Abe Manley liked so much. He had seen it grow into a powerful member of the Eastern Colored League in the 1920s, and had been the president of that league. Bolden, as had other owners, reached out for fresh capital during the hard early days of the National

League. He turned to Gottlieb, who was already well known in Eastern sports circles for his Philadelphia Sphas basketball team.

As Richard Powell, an official with the Baltimore Elite Giants, recalls, "The Philadelphia Stars were virtually Gottlieb's team. When things got pretty bad and Bolden had a problem making his payroll he perhaps might say to Eddie, 'I need $500 or $600.' " The loans became Gottlieb's increasing stake in the team.

The Black Yankees, despite being namesakes of what was then the greatest team in baseball, the New York Yankees of the white American League, did not play many of their games in Yankee Stadium, the mammoth seating capacity of which was reserved for special occasions, as far as the Negro leagues were concerned. Nor, in fact, were the Black Yanks a very good team. They never finished in first place during their thirteen years in the National League, and were more frequently found down toward last place. The chief black official of the club was James "Soldier Boy" Semler, another entrepreneur with numbers gambling ties. Semler seemed to specialize in fielding teams of older, but well-known players, possibly on the theory that if his aggregation was not good enough to win pennants, it could at least exert box office drawing power through its collective reputation.

In 1944, when the military draft was making it as difficult for the Negro league teams to field competitive squads as it was for their white counterparts, Semler boasted that he was putting together a team that was "draft proof" by virtue of its players being either too old to be drafted or 4-F due to physical problems. Veteran observers of the Negro National League might well have wondered how the 1944 Black Yanks differed from Semler's past squads, and indeed, they didn't. They finished in last place in the first half of the season, and next to last in the second half.

The Black Yankees began in 1931 as an independent team, and were partially owned by the famous black dancer, Bill "Bojangles" Robinson. During the period from 1932-34, the team relatively thrived, while the black baseball league structure was weak. It was able to pick up players who were dissatisfied with their low pay on struggling teams by offering them payment on the "co-plan" system. This meant they shared in the gate receipts of each game, instead of drawing a regular paycheck. The usual agreement was for the winning team to take 60 percent of the gate, and a former player, Othello "Chico" Renfroe, recalls that when the Yankees played on those terms, "the man would be sliding home with the winning run, and Semler would be out there at home plate sliding with him."[7] The Yankees also acquired Nat Strong's financial backing, since they were a good draw in New York City, and Leuschner became a regular member of the team's small official retinue.

But when Greenlee and the others got the National League going again in 1933, Semler's advantages made the other black owners uneasy. Although Strong was soon dead, Leuschner's hold over the Yankees remained, and people such as Greenlee, Posey, and the Manleys did not like it. Membership in the league began to work in their favor when the comparative security of playing in a successful league caused a reverse flow of players from the co-plan Yankees to the other clubs. Semler's reaction was to try to sue the Manleys' Brooklyn Eagles and the New York Cubans before the 1936 season to recover some of his players.

As the other teams got stronger financially and were able to honor their salary commitments to their players, Semler's Black Yankees acquired just the opposite reputation, as a team which did not always pay on time. In a 1941 letter to a Jacksonville, Florida, promoter, the Manleys noted that the other owners "all seemed to feel they wanted to give Semler a chance to get going. However the first time he does not pay the players, they will be declared free agents."

By the late 1930s, the Black Yankees seemed to have only one advantage over their fellow league clubs — they could always get booked in a profitable location in New York or New Jersey by Bill Leuschner at the Nat Strong Baseball Co. That was all they needed.

The owner of the third metropolitan New York team, Allesandro Pompez, could have been the most successful of all the owners. Although soft-spoken, he had a noticeable presence and a lot of friends and acquaintances. He possessed both baseball acumen and numbers gambling money to back it up. He also had a connection available to none of the other owners—as a native of Havana, he had a pipeline to the best baseball players in Cuba, a country in which baseball was as much a mania as in the United States. While some Cubans with pure Spanish backgrounds had already made it to the major leagues, the Cuban Blacks were, of course, barred, and were always available to Pompez.

Alex, however, was not always available to them. At the height of his ownership career, he spent the 1937 baseball season in a Mexico City jail, fighting extradition proceedings brought by New York City authorities bent on breaking up the Harlem numbers business and the political corruption that went with it. The demise of his baseball empire was the price Pompez paid for getting mixed up with the true bad guys of 1930s crime, the white bootleggers, when they moved in on black numbers operators to expand their control of the illegal business. Pompez's particular nemesis is probably known to more people today than the great Josh Gibson. He was mobster Dutch Schultz.

Pompez ran a team called the Cuban Stars, which had played independently in the early 1920s. The Stars had joined the Eastern Colored League in 1923 and stayed in league baseball until the Eastern league folded before the 1928 season. Although he never had a pennant winner, Pompez did North American baseball the great favor of introducing it to Martin Dihigo, a Cuban who starred both as a pitcher and hitter, and who was eventually named to the Hall of Fame. Pompez was also a member of the group that set up the first Black World Series in 1924, between Bolden's Hilldale team and J. L. Wilkinson's Kansas City Monarchs.

Pompez came back to the Negro leagues in 1935, with the New York Cubans. The Cubans finished in first place in the second half of the league's two-part schedule that year, and only lost a championship playoff to Gus Greenlee's Crawfords by a single game. More important to the long-term health of the team was Pompez's extremely successful proprietorship of his own ballpark, that same element which made Greenlee strong. Pompez had the rights to a stadium named Dyckman Oval at 204th Street and Nagle Avenue in Manhattan, which he turned into a playground for Harlem sports fans. The park had lights for night activities and was the scene of professional boxing, wrestling, and motorcycle racing, in addition to baseball games. Posey stated in one of his columns that the development of the park "showed to what extent a man who loves baseball will go, as Pompez spent more cash money on this venture than any individual had ever put into Negro baseball."[8]

If Pompez could have kept control of his own numbers bank, he would have had few problems, for he later said under oath in court that his operation was grossing $7,000 to $8,000 per day at its height in 1931. However, being taken over by Schultz not only cost him his financial independence—he went from entrepreneur to an employee of the gangster—it involved him in District Attorney Thomas E. Dewey's campaign against the Tammany Hall political corruption that worked hand in hand with Schultz's crime organization.

Pompez eventually settled his own criminal case by turning state's evidence in Dewey's case against James J. Hines, a Tammany politician convicted in 1938 of furnishing protection from the police and courts to the numbers syndicate that Schultz had put together through coercion and threats in 1931. Dewey described Pompez as "one of the large bankers" of that time, although Alex was still at risk of suffering a serious financial setback if a particular number was hit hard. Pompez testified at the trial that he had lost about $70,000 in a single day shortly before Thanksgiving in 1931, when the number 527 had gotten heavy play and turned out to be the winner. "I paid everything I had in the world to the people that hit me," Pompez said.[9]

Schultz, whose real name was Arthur Fleigenheimer, had gotten rich off bootlegging during Prohibition, but was casting about for other income sources when he noticed the American and Latin American blacks banking numbers in Harlem. Schultz had organizational skills and no compunctions about the use of violence as a business method. In addition, some of the groundwork for a takeover was already laid—the numbers bankers already used Schultz's lawyer, J. Richard "Dixie" Davis, and the Tammany Hall politicians to get their underlings out of the trouble periodically brought upon them by the New York City Police Department's vice investigators.

As Pompez described it to the Hines jury, Schultz's methods were direct. In the fall of 1931, Alex was summoned to a meeting at a Tammany Democratic office, where a stranger told him that "he was sent by Dutch Schultz and he wanted me to pay protection." Pompez, who was still heavily in debt from the "527" hit a few weeks before, cooly put Schultz's operative off, saying "Well, you have got the wrong man, . . . because I haven't got the money to pay protection, and furthermore we don't need no protection in this business."

Schultz, of course, was not to be put off, although Pompez stalled his henchmen for several weeks until there was no way out of accepting an "invitation" to meet with the boss himself. Schultz made a specific offer of a $250 weekly salary and 40 percent of the winnings, with promises to back Pompez up if a big hit caused him major losses. Pompez testified he agreed to the deal because it made financial sense, but also for another reason:

> Well, when he walks in, I was natural looking at the man because he was a man with a big, bad name, so when he got in front of this table he pull up a gun from his front like this and put it on top of the table, and I sat right across where he was sitting, . . . and I just wanted to leave the place . . . because I see the things there weren't so good to me.

Incredibly, Pompez, using his remaining debts from the previous fall's big loss as an excuse, stalled Schultz some more. He incurred the Dutchman's further wrath, but apparently no retribution, before officially coming into the fold the following March because "I can't fight a mob that big."

Pompez's outward imperturbability was remarkable. Around Christmastime, Schultz had Pompez brought before him again, complained about Pompez's failure to join his syndicate, put his gun on the table in front of Pompez, and said, "You are going to be the first nigger I am going to make an example (of) in Harlem."

Pompez testified that his reply was, "I am sorry that you should talk that way. You are the first man ever insult me for any reason whatever. I was promised to come here to do business with you and you go and insult me. If you feel that way, we don't do any business." [10]

The New York *Times* reporter covering the Hines trial was also convinced of Pompez's aplomb, describing the witness, "dressed in a perfectly tailored, newly pressed light gray flannel suit," as a "compelling" personality. "When he came through the door he seemed to fill it (and) seemed a tailor-made Goliath as he sat with folded hands in the witness chair. He answered questions quickly and willingly, and his soft words were uttered with a broken, melodious articulation."

In the mid-1930s, Schultz's gambling empire started to fall apart under pressure from federal authorities and Dewey's investigators. He dropped out of sight for awhile, and when he returned to circulation, it was only to be murdered in a gangland slaying in 1935. Dewey's pressure continued, however. Pompez took a trip to Europe in the summer of 1936, turning the Cubans over to an assistant, Roy Sparrow, and putting himself out of Dewey's reach.

But when he returned to New York, he narrowly avoided being arrested in a series of raids on January 14, 1937. Apparently tipped off by an elevator operator on the way up to his office, he eluded the police waiting for him there and fled New York, not to return for nearly a year. Pompez had been good to black baseball, and now it returned the favor. Dick Seay, about to start his first season with the Newark Eagles, but living in Philadelphia for the winter, hid Alex out for several weeks, and Pompez made his way to Mexico. [11]

U. S. authorities reportedly discovered him there through tapping Sparrow's telephone in New York, but Mexican federal lawmen had trouble apprehending him. He beat them to the airport and escaped in an airplane in the port city of Tampico, and shots were exchanged between the police and Pompez's guard the evening before he was finally caught, getting into his car in downtown Mexico City.

"I got lots of friends in New York," Pompez shouted to waiting reporters from the window of his jail cell. He apparently had a few in Mexico, too, because he successfully fought extradition until October. Then, the persistence of the law wore him down, just as lawless Dutch Schultz had done in 1932. Alex always seemed to know when the opposition was too big to be fought.

Hines was convicted and, for his cooperation, Pompez was allowed to plead guilty to misdemeanor charges, and was put on two years' probation. He set about rebuilding his baseball business, but in the interim he had lost most of his assets, including the lease to Dyckman Oval, the team bus, and most of his players, who had moved on to other teams. The reconstituted Cubans re-entered the National League in 1939, but finished dead last their first year. They got progressively stronger, though, winning the pennant and the Negro World Series from the American League's Cleveland Buckeyes in 1947.

The loss of Dyckman Oval put Pompez at a more serious disadvantage than other teams that did not own their own ballparks. In New York City in the late 1930s, there was essentially no one but Gottleib and Leuschner to turn to for a decent place to play. They were more interested in booking a series of clubs into parks such as Yankee Stadium and the Polo Grounds and using the games as profitable showcases for the entire league than turning a park over to a single club.

Until he could forge his own agreement in the late 1940s with the New York Giants to use the Polo Grounds, the Cubans were essentially a team without a home park, suffering a consequent decline in revenue and competitiveness. Pompez' s arrangement with the Giants worked well for him, however. After the Negro National League went out of business in 1948, he went to work for the major league club. He scouted Latin America for the team, signing the region's best players to New York contracts. The successful Giant teams of the 1960s owed a lot to his pursuits of Orlando Cepeda, Juan Marichal, Jose and Felipe Alou, and Jose Pagan.

Pompez lived long enough (until 1974, when he was 83 years old), and was successful enough in his second baseball career with the Giants to shed the stigma organized baseball had attached to the black owners who had been numbers bankers. In 1971, he was named to the ten-man committee that eventually picked the first nine Negro league notables for induction into the Hall of Fame, the very bastion of baseball respectability. So successful was his transition from the dying world of the Negro leagues to organized baseball that one wonders what he could have accomplished if he had not run afoul of Schultz and Dewey.

Given the mix of characters who ran the Negro National League teams, and their frequently divergent personal agendas, it would have taken a strong league president with no axe of his own to grind to keep them all in line. Unfortunately, the league had no such person in charge. Although Greenlee, the league founder, was strong willed enough, he had a team in the league himself, with the conflicts of interest inherent in such a situation. Anyway, he had left the league by 1939 because of his financial troubles. In the 1930s, the league sometimes also had a part-time commissioner—first sportswriter W. Rollo Wilson, and then Ferdinand Q. Morton, who had been civil service commissioner of the City of New York. Morton's excellent credentials for the job did him no good, of course, without the cooperation of the league owners. They paid him little mind and abolished his position in 1938, while he was still holding it.

Leadership of the league thus devolved to Thomas T. Wilson of Nashville, who had an independent team, the Standard Giants, as early as 1918. In 1921 he changed the team's name to the Elite (often pronounced E-light) Giants. The name stuck to the squad for 31 years, although the team moved three times while Wilson owned it, finally settling for its best years in Baltimore. Then, five years after Wilson's death in 1947, the team returned to Nashville, to die itself, as the Negro leagues went into a final period of decline.

Tom Wilson was the son of two doctors, but made his money in the entertainment business. He owned the Paradise Club, a famous black nightclub in Nashville, and built a baseball stadium, Wilson Park, for the Elite Giants. Wilson's obituary in the *Courier* noted he was "highly regarded and admired by baseball owners, players, officials and fans for his good humor, generosity and good sportsmanship," and this apparently was true. Few people had a bad word to say about Tom Wilson, as a person or as a baseball man. These traits, however, made him less than effective as a league president.

Pompez probably got it just right in 1940 when, complaining about Wilson's inability to stop contract jumping by players, the lack of good relations between the league and the black press, and the continual flow of profits to white booking agents, he said that Wilson was "a man with so many friends that he can't do his job."[12]

Notes

1. Rob Ruck, *Sandlot Seasons* (Urbana, IL: University of Illinois Press, 1987), p. 157.
2. Ibid., pp. 138-45; Brashler, *Josh Gibson,* p. 58.
3. Brashler, *Josh Gibson,* p. 59.
4. *Courier,* Oct. 11, 1941.
5. Ibid., Jan. 26, 1935.
6. New York *Amsterdam News,* Jan. 23, 1929.
7. Holway, *Voices,* p. 339.

8. *Courier*, April 20, 1940.
9. New York *Times,* Aug. 20, 1938.
10. Ibid.
11. Rogosin, *Black Baseball,* p. 115.
12. *Courier*,April 27, 1940.

Bibliography

After Effa Manley was "rediscovered" along with Negro league baseball in the 1970s, she gave four long interviews to writers Donn Rogosin and John Holway; to archivist William Marshall, collecting oral histories for the University of Kentucky, and to Allen Richardson, who was working on a master's thesis at San Jose State University in California.

In that same decade she co-wrote her book, *Negro Baseball...Before Integration.* The five sources together form a comprehensive and consistent account of both her life and the history of the Negro National League.

But the ever-organized Effa left two other major contributions to Negro league history, one on purpose and one by accident. Shortly before her death in 1981, she donated a voluminous scrapbook that she had been keeping since the mid 1930s to the Negro Baseball Hall of History, which had been founded in Ashland, Kentucky. The hall closed its doors a few years later, and the scrapbook went with other of its memorabilia to the National Baseball Hall of Fame in Cooperstown, N. Y., where it now resides in the research library.

When Effa left Newark in the mid-1950s, she sold the house in which she and her husband, Abe, had lived. Finished with baseball ownership, she apparently never gave a second thought to the team's business files she had left behind.

Luckily, subsequent owners left the two filing cabinets of papers and photographs undisturbed in the building's basement until 1989. Then a new owner, Eric Adams, found them, and through the intercession of Dr. Lawrence Hogan of nearby Union County College, donated them to the Newark Public Library. The files span the years between 1936 and 1946 and represent an unequalled source of primary material on the Negro leagues.

As the following list of sources shows, many people who knew Effa Manley and her Eagles were happy to talk about them, both to me and to Professor Hogan and Thomas Guy, Jr., who made transcripts available of interviews they conducted for their black baseball film, *Before You Can Say Jackie Robinson.*

The day-to-day happenings in the Negro leagues were chronicled almost exclusively by the black weekly newspapers of the 1930s and 1940s—the white papers rarely took much interest in the black leagues. My main sources were the Pittsburgh *Courier,* the leading black weekly on the East Coast, and the *Afro-American* papers, the New Jersey edition of which covered the Eagles extensively. Some issues of the Newark *Herald,* which later became the New Jersey *Herald-News,* are also available, and were also important references.

A word on the Negro league batting and pitching averages cited: contemporary statistics were notoriously incomplete and were often not even regularly published by the black leagues. To remedy this, a group of researchers, most of them members of the Negro Leagues Committee of the Society for American Baseball Research, have pored through old newspapers to compile the best set of Negro league averages yet assembled for *The Baseball Encyclopedia.* The figures used here, unless otherwise noted, are from that book's eighth edition, published in 1990.

Interviews

Amiri Baraka, by Dr. Lawrence D. Hogan and Thomas C. Guy, Jr.
Charles Biot, by author.
John T. Cunningham, by author.

John M. Dabney, Jr., by Dr. Lawrence D. Hogan and Thomas C. Guy, Jr.
Leon Day, by author.
Harriette Everett, by author.
Bart Giblin, by Dr. Lawrence D. Hogan and Thomas C. Guy, Jr.
Robert Harvey, by author.
Benjamin Hawkins, Jr., by Dr. Lawrence D. Hogan and Thomas C. Guy, Jr.
Eric Illidge, by author
Monte Irvin at Union County (NJ) College, by Dr. Lawrence D. Hogan and Thomas C. Guy, Jr.
Monte Irvin at Cooperstown, NY, by Dr. Lawrence D. Hogan and Thomas C. Guy, Jr.
Monte Irvin, by author.
Jerry Izenberg, by author.
Effa Manley, by William Marshall, A. B. Chandler Oral History Project, University of Kentucky.
Effa Manley, by William Donn Rogosin.
Maxwell Manning, by author.
Francis Matthews, by author.
Jocko Maxwell, by author.
James "Red" Moore, by author.
John "Buck" O'Neil, by Dr. Lawrence D. Hogan and Thomas C. Guy, Jr.
Richard Powell, by author.
Othello "Chico" Renfroe, by author.
Melvin Sanders, by author.
Quincy Trouppe, by author.
James Walker, by author.
Eddie Wilkerson, by Dr. Lawrence D. Hogan and Thomas C. Guy, Jr.
Connie Woodruff, by author.

Books and Dissertations

Baraka, Amiri. *The Autobiography of Leroi Jones.* New York: Freundlich Books, 1984.
Brashler, William. *Josh Gibson: A Life in the Negro Leagues.* New York: Harper & Row, 1978.
Cunningham, John T. *Newark.* Newark: New Jersey Historical Society, 1966.

DiClerico, James M., and Barry J. Pavelec. *The Jersey Game.* New Brunswick, NJ: Rutgers University Press, 1991.

Dixon, Phil, with Patrick J. Hannigan. *The Negro Baseball Leagues, a Photographic History*. Mattituck, NY: Amereon House, 1992.

Dorwart, Jeffery M., and Philip English Mackey. *Camden County, New Jersey, 1616-1976: A Narrative History,* Camden County, New Jersey: Camden County Cultural and Heritage Commission, 1976.

Frazier, E. Franklin. *The Negro in the United States.* New York: Macmillan, 1949.

Gregory, Paul M. *The Baseball Player.* Washington, DC: Public Affairs Press, 1956.

Hagan, Lee, with Larry A. Greene, Leonard Harris, and Clement A. Price. "New Jersey Afro-Americans: From Colonial Times to the Present," *The New Jersey Ethnic Experience,* ed. Barbara Cunningham. Union City, NJ: William H. Wise & Co., 1977.

Hardy, Charles Ashley III. "Race and Opportunity: Black Philadelphia During the Era of the Great Migration, 1916-1930." Ph.D. dissertation, Temple University, August 1989.

Harris, Abram L. *The Negro as Capitalist.* Philadelphia: The American Academy of Political and Social Science, 1936.

Holway, John. *Blackball Stars: Negro League Pioneers.* Westport, CT: Meckler Publishing Co., 1988.

__________. *Black Diamonds: Life in the Negro Leagues from the Men Who Lived It.* Westport, CT: Meckler Publishing Co., 1989.

__________. *Voices from the Great Black Baseball Leagues* (Revised Edition). New York: Da Capo Press, 1992.

Hughes, Langston. "My Early Days in Harlem," *The Negro Since Emancipation,* ed. Harvey Wish. Englewood Cliffs, NJ: Prentice-Hall, 1964.

Ianni, Francis A. J. *Black Mafia: Ethnic Succession in Organized Crime.* New York: Simon and Schuster, 1974.

Interracial Committee of the New Jersey Conference of Social Work in cooperation with the State Department of Institutions and Agencies, *The Negro in New Jersey.* New York: Negro Universities Press, 1969.

Jackson, Kenneth T. and Barbara B. "The Black Experience in Newark, the Growth of the Ghetto, 1870-1970," New Jersey Since 1860: New Findings and Interpretations, ed. William C. Wright. Trenton: New Jersey Historical Commission, 1972.

Johnson, James Weldon. *Black Manhattan.* New York: Alfred A. Knopf, 1930.
Kukla, Barbara J. *Swing City: Newark Nightlife, 1925-50.* Philadelphia: Temple University Press, 1991.
Linthurst, Randolph. *The Newark Bears, the Final Years.* Self-published, 1981.
Manley, Effa, and Leon Herbert Hardwick. *Negro Baseball. . . Before Integration.* Chicago: Adams Press, 1976.
Mayer, Ronald A. *The 1937 Newark Bears, a Baseball Legend.* East Hanover, NJ: Vintage Press, 1980.
Moore, Joseph Thomas. *Pride Against Prejudice.* New York: Praeger, 1988.
Paige, Leroy "Satchel," with Hal Lebovitz. *Pitchin' Man.* Cleveland, 1948.
Peterson, Robert. *Only the Ball Was White.* New York: McGraw-Hill, 1984.
Polner, Murray. *Branch Rickey, a Biography.* New York: Atheneaum, 1982.
Price, Clement A. "The Beleaguered City As Promised Land: Blacks in Newark, 1917-1947," *Urban New Jersey Since 1870,* ed. William C. Wright. Trenton: New Jersey Historical Commission, 1975.
Richardson, Allen. "A Retrospective Look at the Negro Leagues and Professional Negro Baseball Players." Master's thesis, San Jose State University, May 1980.
Rogosin, William Donn. "Black Baseball: The Life in the Negro Leagues." Ph.D. dissertation, University of Texas at Austin, May 1981.
__________. *Invisible Men: Life in the Negro Baseball Leagues.* New York: Athenaeum, 1987.
Ruck, Rob. Sandlot Seasons. Urbana, IL: University of Illinois Press, 1987.
Rust, Arthur G., Jr. *Recollections of a Baseball Junkie.* New York: William Morrow, 1985.
__________. *Get That Nigger Off the Field.* New York: Delacorte Press, 1976.
Seymour, Harold. *Baseball, the People's Game.* New York: Oxford University Press, 1990.
The Baseball Encyclopedia. Eighth Edition. New York: Macmillan, 1990.
Trouppe, Quincy. *20 Years Too Soon.* Los Angeles: S and S Enterprises, 1977.
Tygiel, Jules. *Baseball's Great Experiment: Jackie Robinson and His Legacy.* New York: Oxford University Press, 1983.

Veeck, Bill, with Ed Linn. *Veeck—As in Wreck, the Autobiography of Bill Veeck.* New York: G.P. Putnam's Sons, 1962.
Voigt, David Quentin. *American Baseball.* Volume 2. Norman, OK: University of Oklahoma Press, 1970.
White, Sol. *Sol. White's Official Base Ball Guide.* Columbia, SC: Camden House, 1984.

Articles

Anderson, Jervis. "That was New York: Harlem, Part III, What a City!" *The New Yorker,* July 13, 1981.
Dodson, Dan W. "The Integration of Negroes in Baseball." *The Journal of Educational Sociology,* October, 1954.
Haller, Mark H. "The Changing Structure of American Gambling in the Twentieth Century." *Journal of Social Issues,* Volume 35, Number 3, 1979.
Light, Ivan. "Numbers Gambling Among Blacks: A Financial Institution." *American Sociological Review,* Volume 42 (December 1977), pp. 892-904.
Manley, Effa. "Negro Baseball Isn't Dead." *Our World,* August 1948.
Monroe, Al. "The Big League." *Abbott's Monthly,* April 1933.
"Newark Eagles." Unsigned article. *Our World,* 1947.
Roberts, Ric. "Negro Big League Baseball a Two-Million Dollar Business." *Negro Baseball Pictorial Year Book,* 1945.
__________. "The Game Goes On . . . " *Negro Baseball 1946 Year Book,* 1946.
Robinson, Jackie. "What's Wrong with Negro Baseball." *Ebony,* June 1948.
Wilson, W. Rollo. "They Could Make the Big Leagues." *Crisis,* September 1934.
Young, Frank A. "Rube Foster—The Master Mind of Base ball." *Abbott's Monthly,* November 1930.

Newspapers

Afro-American newspapers, Baltimore and Newark, NJ
Asbury Park, NJ, *Press*
Detroit *News*
Newark *Evening News*
Newark *Herald*
New Jersey *Herald News*

New York *Age*
New York *Amsterdam News*
New York *Daily Worker*
New York *Herald-Tribune*
New York *Post*
New York *Times*
Pittsburgh *Courier*
St. Louis *The Sporting News*

Video

There Was Always Sun Shining Someplace: Life in the Negro Baseball Leagues. Refocus Films, Westport, CT, 1984.

Public Records and Archives

Albert B. "Happy" Chandler papers. University of Kentucky Library, Lexington, KY. "Report for Submission to National and American Leagues on 27 August, 1946."

City of New York Municipal Archives. New York, NY. Abraham Manley and Effa Bush marriage certificate.

National Baseball Library. Baseball Hall of Fame. Cooperstown, NY. Effa Manley Scrapbook.

Newark Public Library. New Jersey Collection. Newark, NJ. Newark Eagle Files.

Pennsylvania Department of Health. Division of Vital Records. New Castle, PA. Abraham Manley death certificate.

Sixteenth Census of the United States. Characteristics of the Population. 2nd Series. New Jersey (1942).

Temple University Urban Archives Center. Philadelphia, PA. File of newspaper clippings on Negro league baseball.

Index

-D-

-E-

-F-

-G-